THE ANSWER WRITING MANUAL

For UPSC Civil Services Examination & State PSC Examinations

SRUSHTI DESHMUKH GOWDA, IAS
DR. NAGARJUN B GOWDA, IAS

WILEY

The Answer Writing Manual

For UPSC Civil Services Examination & State PSC Examinations

Authors: Srushti Deshmukh Gowda, and Dr. Nagarjun B Gowda

Published by Wiley India Pvt. Ltd.,
4436/7, Ansari Road, Daryaganj, New Delhi-110002.

Printed at: Xpress Grafics Pvt. Ltd.

First Edition: 2025

ISBN: 978-93-6386-960-8

Other Wiley Editorial Offices:
John Wiley & Sons, Inc. 111 River Street, Hoboken, NJ 07030, USA
Wiley-VCH Verlag GmbH, Pappellaee 3, D-69469 Weinheim, Germany
John Wiley & Sons Australia Ltd, 42 McDougall Street, Milton, Queensland 4064, Australia
John Wiley & Sons (Asia) Pte Ltd, 1 Fusionpolis Walk #07-01 Solaris, South Tower Singapore 138628
John Wiley & Sons Canada Ltd, 22 Worcester Road, Etobicoke, Ontario, Canada, M9W ILI

Edition: 2025

www.wileyindia.com

Dedicated to all those who Dare to Dream
Remember, the Harder you work, the Luckier you get!
May the Force Be with You!

Acknowledgements

For the idea of this book, we would like to thank the numerous civil service aspirants who got in touch with us regarding their queries about answer writing and UPSC preparation right after the result. The book is a sincere effort to address most of those doubts which an aspirant encounters while writing answers.

We are grateful to our friends Nivedita B (IRTS), Vivek Reddy (IRS), Rahul Sankanur (IAS), Vikram Grewal (IFS), Girish K (IRTS), and Gunjita Agrawal who have contributed to this book and reviewed it.

We take this opportunity to thank our publishers Wiley, especially Vinod Shakya, the editorial team as well as other team members including Deepak Saxena and others. If not for the team, the book wouldn't have seen the light of the day.

Our acknowledgement would be incomplete without thanking each and every person who has been a part of our UPSC preparation journey, right from our teachers, mentors, fellow aspirants, friends, and family. We have tried to put together the best of all that we have learnt in this book.

We thank our parents and family for being the source of constant encouragement in our lives. Special thanks to sweet Charlie, our beagle, and Chiku, our poodle, who have been our constant companions at home while working on this book.

***

Preface

It was during my college days that I started UPSC preparation. During the beginning, I took guidance from online videos, toppers' blogs, and articles of some magazines. After taking a basic foundation course coaching, I had completely dived into the UPSC-CSE preparation at home. Then I realized that though there is ample amount of guidance on what to read and what not to read for civil services examination but only very limited, good quality information regarding answer writing techniques for the UPSC Main Examination.

A middle-class tier 2 city girl like me couldn't dream of going to Delhi for preparation and had no immediate guidance from any seniors. For Nagarjun, he prepared on his own and along with a job with the help of seniors and friends. The absence of a single point guidance for answer writing made it essential to prepare our own strategy and understanding of answer writing to score good marks in the Main examination. We realised that it is the Main's marks alone which can help us get a good rank and achieve the dream of becoming an IAS officer.

I can recall that I spent quite a lot of time on preparing notes on each topic, reading all important articles and writing many practice tests to improve my answer writing skills for the Main examination. In this process, guidance from coaching class, feedback from test series evaluation, toppers, guidance videos, and articles on answer writing helped me further sharpen my ability to present the available content in a better manner on the answer sheets. Eventually by God's grace I ended up getting selected for my dream service in my very first attempt with the highest marks—470 in General Studies Main written examination for that year (CSE 2018).

Over the years right from the day of our selection till today, we have received 'n' number of doubts from aspirants regarding answer writing and we have tried to clear them personally as well. But we always wanted to provide the aspirants with a single comprehensive material on answer writing to rely upon for their preparation for the Civil Services and also for other state services examinations. That is when we decided to come up with a book on Answer Writing Strategy which is finally now in your hands.

In this book, we have tried to use simple language and kept the text in a conversational style. We have added our personal notes, answers, and materials for a more clear explanation of thoughts. We have also taken help from our batchmates for a few sections in which they are good at. The approach of preparation and answer writing has been dealt with separately for each GS Paper. Some chapters of the book like Decoding the Question and Decoding the Answer might require multiple readings to clearly understand the framework. For Essay Writing, we have included a chapter which holistically explains all parts of the essay. Optional selection and Compulsory papers have been discussed as well. This way, all papers for the Main Examination and their multiple angles have been discussed in the book.

Nonetheless, this book is just a specimen guidance tool. And none of the strategies written in the book can claim to be ideal or perfect. The aim of the book is to provide guidance required for better answer writing and better marks. We believe that the strategies should be developed individually based on your own learning during the process of preparation. We sincerely hope that this book will be a helpful tool for all aspirants in that process.

***

Contents

1

UPSC CSE Exam Pattern

UPSC Civil Services Examination is a three-stage examination consisting of Prelims, Mains, and Interview. It is conducted by the Union Public Service Commission (UPSC) to recruit suitable candidates for IAS, IPS, IFS, and other allied services.

Often only known for IAS, this exam gives opportunity in other all India services like Indian Police Service, Indian Foriegn Service, Indian Revenue Service, Railways, Audits, Accounts, Information etc.

These services provide diverse opportunities to work for the government and the people. Though the degree of direct interaction with citizens may differ, these services provide great career options.

UPSC also conducts examinations for other central govt jobs like CRPF, CAFF etc and the general studies syllabus is on similar lines. The good part about the routine of the exam is that it's conducted every year, and the schedule is issued a year earlier. This is in contrast to the few state PSC Exams where exam cycles are often irregular and uncertain.

The UPSC exam pattern for the Preliminary stage consists of two papers, conducted on one day. Both the papers comprise objective type questions with multiple choice of answers. The prelims examination is a qualifying stage to filter candidates for the mains exam. The UPSC exam pattern for the Mains stage consists of 9 papers. All of the mains papers except for the language papers A and B are of a merit ranking nature. Paper A and B are of qualifying nature and candidates must score at least 25% in each for the marks from their Paper I - Paper VII to be given weightage.

Phases	Nature of Exam	Subjects	Marks	Duration
Prelims	MCQ	GS CSAT	200 200	2 Hrs 2 Hrs
Mains	Written/ descriptive	Compulsory Indian Language English Essay GS 1,2,3,4 Optional Paper-1 & 2	300 300 250 250 Each 250 Each	3 Hrs 3 Hrs 3 Hrs 3 Hrs (Each) 3 Hrs (Each)
Personality Test/ Interview	Oral		275	

In the Prelims Exam, CSAT (Paper- 2) is a Qualifying Paper (Students have to score at least 67 marks) and based on GS Marks, a cut off list is declared. In the Mains Exam, Language Papers are qualifying in nature. In Final Merit, only Mains & Interview marks are counted. Merit list is based out of 2025 marks.

***

2

Importance of Answer Writing

The Final merit list includes Mains and Interview marks. 1750 Marks out of 2025 are allocated to Mains and hence answer writing practice plays a vital role in not only getting into the list but also securing a good rank. Learning to write good answers in the UPSC Mains exam is as important as preparing the subject itself. This is because at the end of the day, no matter what you have read, studied or practised, what you have written in the answer booklet is the only thing that matters.

We all tend to read from the exact same sources. For Example, Newspapers such as Indian Express & The Hindu for Current Affairs, Book by M Laxmikanth for Polity, Spectrum Publication for History etc. What makes us different is how we understand and reproduce the available information by properly framing and presenting our answers.

For instance our dear friend Rahul Sankanur scored around 130+ marks in his previous 4 prelims attempts. However, he could not make it to the final list. In his fifth attempt at the Mains examination he worked majorly on Answer writing and its presentation and secured an AIR 17 in UPSC CSE 2018.

If you see the Mains Answer Writing pattern, the candidate has to write 20 questions with a total of 4000 words. That comes to writing 50 pages in the given 3 hours and that is not an easy task. Thus, Practising writing answers becomes extremely important to be able to complete the paper. Initially, one may focus on the quality of answers rather than the speed of writing, but in the later stages of preparation it is advisable to match the time required to answer all questions. One must remember that the examiner will never know how many books you have read or how many hours you have spent on preparation or how much you know. The only thing they can use to judge you is the quality and way of Writing answers. And hence, Answer writing becomes a matter of utmost importance for getting selected.

It is said that Answer writing is an Art. And any form of art can be learnt over a period of time. All it takes is a strong will, intense effort, proper guidance and regular practice. Not just for exams per se, writing helps to comprehend and consolidate whatever one reads. It also makes understanding and retention better. This is why both note making and answer writing complement each other. The more your notes are organised and properly compiled, the better will be your answer writing also.

***

3

Prerequisites Of Answer Writing

In this chapter, we *try* to list out certain things that you need to do before you start answer writing. Trying to frame answers for UPSC questions is not possible from Day -1 and is not recommended. There are a few Prerequisites that you can start with:

1. Know the Syllabus:

   Syllabus is the guiding path on your journey of preparation. UPSC exam syllabus is crisp and indicative but vast in scope. One must read each topic, understand the scope of examination and then make a Mind Map for the subject. Each sub topic has both a 'Static side' which are established facts and a 'Current side' which makes the issue Contextual. One must *try* to look up both sides while studying.

   It's better if you *try* to memorise what's there in the syllabus so that you have the pointers on the top of your head.

2. Read through previous year question papers:

   Question papers are the key to knowing the standard and scope of UPSC examination.

   Initially give some time everyday to read the questions asked in past year mains tests. It is essential to analyse the <u>Type, Language and Framing of questions</u>. The more questions you read, the more you'll be able to categorise them and simplify them in your head.Consequently, you will also see how the topic may remain the same but there are variations in the way the question is asked. This will be helpful when you actually start writing answers.

3. Build your Knowledge base:

   The basic matter of your answer is the topic asked about. This is where NCERTs, Standard and Reference Books come into play. Studying the current happenings in those topics makes your understanding better. One must plan effectively on completing one reading of the topic before attempting any question related to it.

We might be done with all of the above, but most of us keep delaying answer writing for one reason or the other. Some of us feel it's only after completing the entire syllabus that we can start writing.

Honestly, even at the time of entering the examination hall, there are many topics which we haven't revised well or forgot about. There will never be a time when you've mastered all topics. And hence we must start writing answers as soon as we attain a basic knowledge of relevant subjects.

After reading all NCERTs along with browsing through newspapers, one can try writing answers. Remember, your initial 20-30 answers will not be good. But with proper strategy and regular practice, you will go on improving day by day. Practice is what will make you better and there is no other way out.

***

4

General Strategy For Mains Examination

PREPARATION

As far as the syllabus is concerned, the Mains General Studies Syllabus comprises most of that you read for Prelims. In addition, you need to prepare topics like Ethics, World History, Post Independence History, Indian Society, Internal Security and others.

One may sometimes feel that "Everything Under The Sun" can be asked. But that is not true. You may have one or two strange questions here and there but overall the question paper follows the syllabus. If you look closely in the previous year papers you will find certain themes and topics repeating every year. The only difference is the framing of question and context. This is especially true for optional papers.

For these specific themes, one can prepare notes covering various dimensions. Ready frameworks can help you write to the point and save time in the exam hall. The entire syllabus can be divided into two portions - Static and Current Part.

Static information can be found in NCERTs and Standard books of different subjects. With regard to NCERTs, you may feel why do you need to read something you've read in Class 6th after your graduation? But, when it comes to brushing up the knowledge and specially for students from technical background, these NCERTs act like the starting point to UPSC prep. They are very crucial and can help prepare a firm base for all topics.

As for Standard books, you can choose any book which you feel comfortable to read. My Booklist is attached in the annexure. The list can be found online as well. Mostly, we all refer to the same books. Having one Standard book for one subject is sufficient. If required, it can be supported by some Reference Books. But once, you've zeroed in on the resource, you should not run behind new materials and books. Multiple revisions of the same book must be done religiously.

Current affairs portion can be found in Newspaper, E media articles, Magazines, News Channel and Parliamentary debates, Yearly government and International publications etc.

While preparing these, keep going back to the questions, so that you know the extent and depth of learning required in a particular topic.

Current Affairs plays a huge role in the overall scheme of GS. Many questions asked in the exam are directly or indirectly rooted in the current happenings. For instance while you're preparing you may come across an article on Left Wing Extremism or Naxalism and how it has been changing. With this information for your reference, you can back track the movement, its development, affected areas, nature of operation etc. Connecting these aspects with economics of arms, sociological impact, geographical influence etc can help you prepare the topic in a multi dimensional manner. This interconnection of arguments shows a complete understanding of the topic and hence will fetch you more marks.

NOTE MAKING

To make notes or not, is a common question. Sometimes the Book itself is *very* crisp and to the point. In that case, one need not make separate notes. You can underline, highlight, flag mark in the book itself and revise it whenever required. For Example Books like

Spectrum Publication on Modern History, Book by M. Lakshmikanth on Polity.

But there are other Books which are vast and dense where revision is not possible in a short time. These books are often used for reference and hence their notes can be helpful. For Example Book by Ramesh Singh on Economy, By DD Basu on Constitution.

Some samples of my Static notes have been presented below. Remember, there is no ideal or model way to prepare. They should only be crisp and do some value addition to already available information.

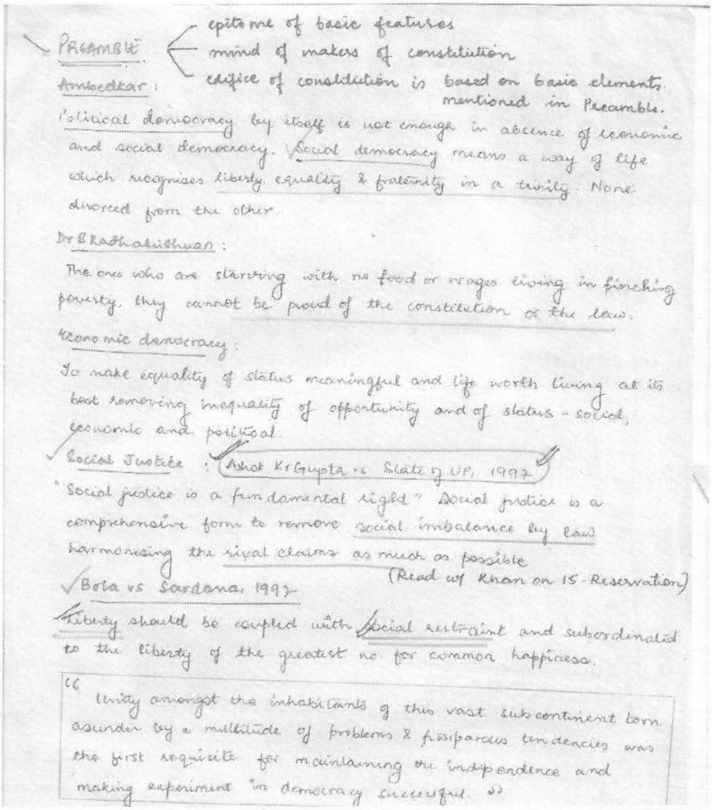
PREAMBLE – epitome of basic features
– mind of makers of constitution
Ambedkar: – edifice of constitution is based on basic elements mentioned in Preamble.
Political democracy by itself is not enough in absence of economic and social democracy. Social democracy means a way of life which recognises liberty, equality & fraternity in a trinity. None divorced from the other.
Dr S Radhakrishnan:
The ones who are starving with no food or wages living in pinching poverty, they cannot be proud of the constitution or the law.
Economic democracy:
To make equality of status meaningful and life worth living at its best removing inequality of opportunity and of status - social, economic and political.
Social Justice: Ashok Kr Gupta vs State of UP, 1997
"Social justice is a fundamental right" Social justice is a comprehensive form to remove social imbalance by law harmonising the rival claims as much as possible
(Read w/ Khan on 15-Reservation)
Bola vs Sardana, 1997
Liberty should be coupled with social restraint and subordinated to the liberty of the greatest no. for common happiness.
"Unity amongst the inhabitants of this vast subcontinent torn asunder by a multitude of problems & fissiparous tendencies was the first requisite for maintaining the independence and making experiment in democracy successful."

By amendments:

42nd : 1976 : 39A (Legal Aid) & 43A (Mgmnt in Workers)

44th 1978 : 38 B

86th (2002) : RTE 45 | ECCE 69th Delhi

97th : 2011 : 43 B (Cooperative Societies)

CONFLICT B/W FUNDAMENTAL RIGHTS & DPSPs.

1951 : Champakam vs SOMadras: While FR are enforceable by 32, 226(1), Courts are bound to declare laws void which are inconsistent with FRs (13) but DPSPs are not enforceable (37) and any law cannot be declared void on grounds that it violates DPSP.

1971 : 25th CAA : Inserted 31 C.

A1 Laws giving effect to 39 (b) & (c) cannot be questioned on grounds that contravene someones' 14 & 19.

A2 It cannot be called into questioned, whether giving effect to 39 b&c in any court

1973 : Kesharananda Bharati Case vs State of Kerala

Held 25th CAA Part 1 as valid as establishes eqm b/w FR & DPSPs

Invalidated Part 2 as contravenes basic structure judicial review

1976 : extended protection of 31C to all DPSPs (not only 39 b&c) 42nd CAA

1980 : Minerva Mills Case vs UOI.

- Struck down expansion of 31C by 42nd CAA, restored to position of 25th CAA as it violated basic structure
- Fine balance b/w FR & DPSP established by Constitution must be adhered to by "Harmonious Reading" of the two w/o giving preference to one. (Principle of Harmonious Construction)

2002 86CAA Outside 14 & 19, the 1951 position persists such that DPSP cannot be held over an FR other than 14 & 19 being violated. Eg. by Implementing 45, 30 (1) of Minority Inst is upheld

SEPARATION OF POWERS. → Horizontal separation

Montesquieu and Madison have propounded Sep. of Powers to preserve human liberty, avoid conc. of power, absolutism & tyranny.

Article 50: Separate Judiciary from Executive (SOP)

* State of TN vs State of KL 2014 : Separation of Powers b/w 3 organs are nothing but consequences of principles of Equality enshrined in Article 14.

Hence Breach of SOP is negation of Equality.

* KBC, 1973 : Amendment cannot be such that it violates Basic structure. Separation of powers is basic structure part, hence no dilution

* Indira Gandhi Nehru vs Raj Narain, 1975 : Adjudication of a specific dispute is a judicial fn', which Parliament, even under Constitution Amending power cannot exercise. Hence ultra vire.

Separation: E | L → collectively responsible

1. Art 105 : Judiciary cannot call in quest^n anything said/vote given protection in Legislature (J & L)
2. Art 121, 211 : Conduct of judge of HC/SC cannot be ~~questioned~~ discussed by SC/HC Legislature discussion (J & L)
3. Art 122 : Courts cannot call in quest^n proceedings of Parliament (J & L)
4. Art 74, 78 : COM Advice and Cabinet discussions cannot be questioned in court. (J & E)
5. Art 361 : President and Governor enjoy Immunity from court proceedings (J & E)
6) Art 50 : J & E

Lord Acton : Power corrupts & Absolute Power tends to Corrupt Absolutely. Modern State has evolved from (non interventionist,) minimal to Welfare State, Protector, Arbiter, Controller. Distinction b/w (Essential & Incidental) Powers

Checks & Balances:

Legislative Control
On Judiciary | On Executive

1. LEGISLATIVE CONTROL

On Executive - Power to determine the law - Lokpal/Lokayukta
- Budgetary Provisions - Question Hour
- Adjournment / No Confidence / Calling Attention
- Committee System - CAG, RBI Gov

On Judiciary - Impeachment of judges
- NJAC Appt Envisaged - Final approval

2. EXECUTIVE CONTROL

On Legislative - If Majority, laws be passed
- Bills / Timing

On Judiciary - NJAC Appt Envisaged - final approval
- Quasi judicial bodies appt.

3. JUDICIAL CONTROL

On Legislative - Defection proceedings; Cash 4 Query disqual Raja Ram Pal vs Hon'ble Speaker Judiciary final arbiter
- Shiv Menon Case 1971 - Office of Profit criteria
- Amendment Proceedings - KBC 1973 Basic Structure
- 13 Article Judicial Review - ~~due process of law~~ Maneka 1978
IR Coelho Case IX Schedule 1973 post - Basic Structure amendment

On Executive - DDA 2004, grounds of reviewing administrative action are illegality, irrationality, procedural impropriety
- Public Interest Litigation
- SR Bommai - President's rule

(AA)

Ordinance A

Press, Enlightened Citizenry, CSO, NGO

Vertical SOP
- decentralisation
- devolution
- subsidiarity principle

Making notes of Current Affairs is also a common dilemma. Whether to put in efforts to separately make notes? Or simply refer to the swarm of notes available on the internet and coaching classes?

As all our learning levels and styles are different, this is a question you need to answer for yourself. There is no one magic way out. For most of us, writing down any topic enhances its retention. Hence it's preferable to jot down important points of editorials or other articles and categorise them based on subjects.

It is advisable, that if you are giving the exam next year, you read the current affairs from this year's January. Over a period of 1 year, you will find many topics repeatedly in the news. Everytime, you will get some new piece of relevant information or a statement which you feel is authentic and can be quoted in the answer. It is good if you can jot down some of these under that topic heading and keep updating it whenever required. Digital notes are easy to update, erase and edit. Whereas hard copy notes (which I preferred) are old school style but require greater time, energy and are not easy to erase and update.

Some samples of current notes are given here.

1

GST & TOBACCO ISSUE

1. Tobacco will be subjected to 28% highest rate + cess
(But not so) This should ideally mean all products - bidis & chewing tobacco.
2. As a measure of good governance & anti-corruption, bidis must be classed as demerit goods.
3. Its exempted as considered - a poor man's puff
But; govt has responsibility to protect the health & it becomes discriminatory against the poor because its the poor who suffer the greatest burden in terms of disiases caused by smoking as they are least able to afford healthcare.
Tobacco Use ∝ Poverty (Medical expend↑ Earnings↓)
4. ∴ Tobacco Control - pro-poor policy
5. Tobacco Control policies: reached the urban middle class
 - Access to TV and radio advt/ info.
 - Smoke free public zones
but not in rural areas.
6. Taxation: most effective measure of reduce tobacco use specly bidis, but its underutilised.
Its a win-win situation: inc revenue & red. consumpt espclly for young and poor.
7. The only realistic barrier - potential impact on bidi workers. - few livelihood alternatives.
(sustainable business alternative) Dedicated funds financed by tobacco taxes can be used to transition out of tobacco industry or gain better welfare services; home based alternatives for women to bidi rolling.
8. Sustainable dvpt across all sectors and expanded GST to support the most vulnerable - poor.

WHO : Global Adult Tobacco Survey -
India's distinct pattern of tobacco consumption.
Diverse forms - bidi, khaini (smokeless tobacco), (chewing tobacco) cigarettes

Middle/Higher [→ Cigarettes 14%,
LIG. - [→ Bidis, Khaini, Chewing Tobacco Pan Masala - 89%.

* Competitive dynamics & pricing
unit level pricing of tobacco products
→ only Cigarettes kept under GST, so no effective rate inc. in other forms of tobacco.

— Removal of excise & tax exemptions irrespective of the size of the unit, removal of all excise, other tax exemptions irrespective of size,

3

SECURITIES MARKET

- Its not enough if they are considered successful only by international investors or financial experts. Wealth Creation is good but not the main motive.
- Real value lies in contribution:
  - Dvpt of Nation • Improvement of all sectors • welfare of all

1. Primary aim of our stock market - help in raising capital for productive purposes. How well its functioning in providing capital for infrastructure (rare)
   - Need for liquid long term bond market.
   - Need for municipal bond market - Smart cities

2. Must provide benefit to largest section of society - farmers
   - True measure is impact on villages.
   - Innovative ways for projects in agriculture.
   - Commodity markets must be useful to farmers not just avenues for speculation. [eNam - SEBI]
   - Derivatives can be used by farmers to reduce risks.

3. Those who generate profits, must make fair contribution to nation building by paying taxes.
   - illegal activities / fraud / structure of tax laws.
   - Simple and transparent; fair and progressive

Courtesy PM's Speech

6

25/01/17

LABOUR ECOSYSTEM – GOVT INITIATIVES

Indian labour market is becoming vibrant and sought after globally.

- Employment Generation – Upgrade status of workforce
- More dignified, valued & financially sound – Safety

Tech Based: Shram Suvidha Portal
NCS
VAN

Labour Reforms: Simplification and Amalgamation of 43 laws into 4 labour codes:
Code of Wages; Code of Industrial Relations
Code of Social Security; Code on Safety & working condition
: Simplification of Registers from 56 to 5.

Initiatives: PM Rozgar Protsahan Yojana – Govt pays 8.33% EPS
Apparel Sector: 12% employment concentrat-

Ease difficulty: to cope w/ demonetisation – financial inclusion of workers 44.53 lakh a/cs

Legislations: Amended Bonus Act, Child labour Act, Maturity Benefit Act, Model shops & Establishment ~~Act~~ bill.
1IP – 2 dispensaries

Amnesty Scheme: by EPFO and ESIC to promote enrollment of workers
Wages ceiling for coverage – 15000 to 21000/-
per insured 1250/- to 3000/-

Commitment: Job Security, Wage Security, Social Security

7

01/01/17

INDIA's CYBER SECURITY ESTABLISHMENTS

IT ACT - 2000

Section 70A: National Nodal Agency with respect to critical Information Infrastructure Protection (CIIP)

Section 70B: Indian Computer Emergency Response Team serve as national agency for cyber security.

National Cyber Security Policy, 2013
- protecting public & private infra from cyber attacks

National Cyber Security Coordinator, 2014.

But → No National Security Infra/ Architecture, that can assess the nature of cyber threats and respond to them.

→ Need to put in place permanent/ semi permanent staff which is technically proficient in cyber operations both defensive and offensive.

- National Cyber Security Agency — need for Secretariat.

07/02/17

CHENNAI OIL SPILL

Risk: Petroleum oils are complex mixtures of chemicals that are toxic, bioaccumulative and persistent in the environment. Benzene is carcinogenic. They enter body through inhalation, ingestion and skin.

INCOIS: Spill estimate that 20 tonne of spill at this time, more than 60% would be beached by the 9th day

CLEANING: Oil spill clean up is a hazardous waste remediatⁿ exercise. Chennai youth rolled up sleeves and scooped emulsion bare handed using buckets + handling toxic oil with inadequate protective gear

Dangers to marine habitat are imminent.
Rocks remain covered w/ oil and sludge from the nearby shore/gaps b/w rocks filled with toxic oily residues

Other:
- dumping dredged sand into Ennore wetlands
- Discharging tonnes of chemical effluents.
- Power plants discharging coal ash
- Hot waste water into wetlands.

Jotting down some trivia like the rank of India in International reports, facts like % of population affected etc. can be very helpful. This trivia can be used to support the argument proposed in the answer. This way you create your own DATA BANK which you can refer to anytime.

(*) "Eliminating child marriage in India" (2017, Report by Action Aid India. (Census 2011)
" Every 3rd child bride in ~~the~~ World is an Indian "
→ 75% in Rural Areas.
→ UP 1st ; AP, WB, RJ, BH, MP, MH. = 70% of all

(*) Red Brigade, Lucknow: (Eg)
Sexual abuse survivors/victims - girls + boys
group - defence / equality / consent.

→ National family health Survey -
1 in 4 women 20-24 yrs - married as minor
RJ - 65% rate JH - 63%.
→ NCRB Data - poor case registration 1/yr

→ Law Commission - consent age - 16 yrs. (reduce)
→ Marriage - 18-18 yrs of m/F Patriarchal not'n
→ 16-18 yrs - Voidable
→ below 16 - Void ab initio.
(KT : below 18/21 void abinitio)

* Promotive, Preventive, Curative, Geriatric, Palliative, Dental, Mental Healthcare

पृष्ठ सं.:
दि.: / /
www.ashram.org

HEALTH

1) Rapid Survey on Children 2015.
only 45% infants are being breastfeed w/in an hour of birth
only 9.6% children receive adequate diet in 6-8 months.
38% stunted & 35.7% are underweight

2) India contributes to 21% of global disease burden but lowest health spending. (1.3%) ▼BRICS least.

3) "Public Health System Paralysis."
Chronic Systemic problems

4) Rural Sanitation Coverage - 39% (was)
Now : 70%
250 million (Indonesian pop) stopped defecating in open.

5) State of food security & Nutritⁿ in World 2017
(FAO, IFAD, UNICEF, WHO, WFP.)

2005 - 2014-15

① Obesity	② Anaemia at Reproductive
2.1% ⟶ 3.6% (2014)	53.2% (2005) ⟶ 51% (2016)

Hunger ↑

(5) Malnutrition & Stunting

(6% reduct^n 9% reduction)

6. LANCET JOURNAL- INDIA's MILLION DEATH STUDY

→ 1 million ~~studies~~ deaths averted

→ Pneumonia & Diarrhea Mortality – reduced by 60%

→ Mortality from birth related breathing & trauma by 66%.

→ Measles & tetanus – by 90% mortality.

7. Paediatric Obesity Survey- by 2025. 17 million obese children

8. UNICEF 'Every child Alive' 25% Global burden

India – 600000 children die/yr. 25.4/1000 :

Political will rather than economic standing matters

Eg. SL: 5/1000, US: 3.7/1000

GLOBAL NUTRITION REPORT, NOV'17

Dept Intn Poverty Research Ltd IFPRI

* 51% Indian women anaemic
* 38% <5y children stunted
* 22% women obese & 16% adult men obese

Diabetic Capital 2030

✓ Global Nutrition Summit: Milan, Italy

✓ Nutrition for Growth N4G

* The no. of children born in India each year is greater than those born in any country at any point in history

can be a huge loss of potential

HEALTHY STATES PROGRESSIVE INDIA

* – All Sex Ratio @ Birth (all states declined)

No one >1000 females/1000 males.

NEWSPAPER ARTICLE ANALYSIS

Sometimes you may find an article or editorial in the newspaper which appears to be relevant to the syllabus and consists of some good data points or statements that can be used in the answer. In that case, you can note it along with the subject head. Many people ask about how to go about it. So, for your reference, I have quoted 2 articles here from reputed newspapers and explained what all can be important and Why.

The article was published in THE HINDU on 23 Dec. 2021

THE HINDU

Looking beyond the Forest Rights Act

Schemes and programmes already drafted for the tribal people need to be implemented everywhere

MADHUSUDAN BANDI

The Forest Rights Act (FRA) has been in existence for 15 years. As on April 30, 2020, the Ministry of Tribal Affairs had received 42,50,602 claims (individual and community), of which titles were distributed to 46% of the applicants. If the Forest Department's views are considered, the implementation process is more or less over. But the supporters of tribal rights allege that the Department is overlooking the genuine claims of the tribal people. Despite the Ministry being the implementing agency, the role of the Forest Department in granting titles is crucial because the lands claimed are under its jurisdiction. While both sides hold extreme positions, the situation on the ground presents a mixed picture.

Issues in implementation

The journey of the FRA's implementation has never been smooth. The Act provides for democratic tenets in the implementation process. In the first stage, it requires the constitution of a Forest Rights Committee comprising members from within the village by conducting a Gram Sabha with two-thirds of the members present at the meeting. The process was not followed in many places. These committees were mostly constituted by the Panchayat Secretaries upon the directives received from District Magistrates at short notice. The nominations for members for the taluk-level and district-level committees were also not transparent. The contribution of women to the forest economy is well known. The FRA provides for equal rights in titles issued under the Act for women. They have the equitable role at every stage of decision-making. However, on the ground, the women were hardly visible in this regard.

It was disappointing that in the initial stages of implementation, there was insistence on satellite images as evidence while other admissible proofs were ignored, as happened in Gujarat. This resulted in mass rejections of claims by the authorities. It is a different matter that a writ petition filed by the civil society groups in 2011 forced the authorities to look into the matter afresh in the State.

In some villages around Bastar, Chhattisgarh, the plots claimed and the documents confirming the award did not match. Besides, the extent of land that was awarded was far smaller than what was claimed within the ceiling. The claimants did not protest anticipating that whatever little they had received could be taken back by the authorities. Further, various welfare and developmental schemes of the Rural Department were not extended everywhere to the tribal people who received documents of land possession under the FRA despite the directives issued by the Ministry to treat them on a par with others.

Overall, poor awareness levels among the tribal people proved to be a handicap, especially in the scheduled areas which are remotely located. To effectively present claims, a fair understanding of the Act and its implementation process is necessary. Some NGOs, like in Dang district of Gujarat, made a difference by hand-holding the beneficiaries at every step. However, the involvement of NGOs was missing in some interior areas in States like Chhattisgarh where insurgency was affecting the lives of the people. Evidence suggests that implementation was better in areas which were fairly close to urban settings or where accessibility was easy. In these places, most Central and State government schemes and programmes such as Deendayal Upadhyaya Gram Jyoti Yojana, Janani Shishu Suraksha Karyakram, Mahatma Gandhi National Rural Employment Guarantee Scheme, National Food Security Act, National Health Mission; Pradhan Mantri Awas Yojana; and Pradhan Mantri Gram Sadak Yojana were implemented, empowering the people to assert their positions.

Declining produce, livelihoods

Many tribal areas are witnessing a decline in the quality of forest produce in their vicinity, thus forcing them to look for other sources of livelihood. In Chhattisgarh, in many villages, earnings from activities such as collection of tendu leaves for rolling local cigars were affected when there was an influx of labourers from Bihar who were willing to work for low wages. Poor market and exploitation by local traders/middlemen were no less demoralising.

The recognition given to their lands under the FRA gave the tribal people a psychological boost. However, they possess lands (including the lands recognised under the FRA) that are small, of poor quality (particularly lands located on hill slopes) and are not very fertile. The lack of irrigation facilities forces them to depend only on rainfall. To enhance their income, they migrate to work as construction or road-laying labourers. In their opinion, this will continue until the wages earned through any source in the villages matches with the wages in urban areas.

NGO representatives working in the tribal areas believe that the livelihoods of the locals would improve if horticulture practices are promoted in addition to bamboo and aloe vera plantations with an assured market. A popular recommendation is medical and ecotourism along the lines of the Kerala model. On the other hand, given the quality of education received by the youth in the remote districts, the possibility of acquiring meaningful jobs remains thin. Those accustomed to urban culture do not feel like going back to their villages. Civil society groups, therefore, believe that providing skill-based education with assured jobs on a large scale in proportion to the demand would do wonders in these areas.

A majority of the tribal communities in India are poor and landless. They practise small-scale farming, pastoralism, and nomadic herding. On the Human Development Index, the tribal-populated States always rank lower than the national average. Not long ago, a tragic news article was published about a tribal man walking 12 km in Odisha carrying his dead wife on his shoulder all night. A Chhattisgarh tribesman who had led the members of his village in a march to Delhi in 2004 to demand forest rights told this researcher that the lives of the tribal people are insignificant for our leaders. He said the Central government in the 1970s generously welcomed refugees from Bangladesh into forests and provided them a house and a land to farm, whereas natives were still being denied the same.

The way forward

The FRA was never going to be a panacea to address all the issues of the tribal people, but it is important. To improve the condition of the tribal people, especially those living in remote areas, there needs to be a push on every possible aspect of their socioeconomic life. This can be attained if schemes and programmes already drafted for the tribal people are implemented in letter and spirit across the country. With protective laws like the Panchayats (Extension to Scheduled Areas) Act, 1996, in place, it is only a matter of will. One way forward could be to induct people who are sensitive to the cause of tribal people in the decision-making process at every stage.

Madhusudan Bandi is a faculty member with the Gujarat Institute of Development Research, Ahmedabad. Email: madhusudan_bandi@gidr.ac.in

This article is about the Forest Rights Act passed in 2006. This is an important Act for the Scheduled Tribes who live in Forest areas. Its legal aspects, practical difficulties and way forward have been suggested in this article. From a good editorial, you can not only learn about the topic but also understand how an answer needs to be structured.

Opening paragraph brings out 2 facts :

1. 46%of claims have been approved for title.
2. Ministry of Tribal Affairs is the implementing authority (and not Forest Ministry) - THIS WAS ASKED IN PRELIMS 2021

Issues are listed out in next para:

1. Procedure of calling Gram Sabha not followed well.
2. Women were hardly given say on ground despite having high contribution
3. Insistence on Satellite images initially in Gujarat
4. Extent of land awarded is far smaller than claims
5. Various welfare schemes are not extended to tribal people who get rights.
6. Poor awareness levels among tribes in scheduled areas.
7. Inter state Migration of labourers affecting livelihoods.
8. Poor market and exploitation by Middlemen
9. Land parcels are small, not fertile and lack irrigation facilities.

Way Forward provides for some solutions and good practises:

1. Livelihoods will improve with aloe Vera plantations and bamboo
2. Medical and Eco-Tourism in Kerala
3. Skilled Based Education with assured jobs.

Note closely that the closing paragraph (aka Conclusion) is not repetition but comprises of 2 new ideas- (THIS CAN BE DONE IN OUR ANSWERS AS WELL)

1. Protective laws like Panchayat Extension to Scheduled Areas 1996 are applicable.
2. Inducting people who are sensitive to the cause of tribals in decision making at all stages.

Even if you don't get a separate question on the forest rights act, this article was helpful in explaining the issues faced by tribals and provided some way out along with examples.

There are certain keywords or parts in an article which can be researched further or recorded for the exam. In this article they were following:

1. List or Example of Schemes in Rural Areas- DDUGJY, JSSK, MGNREGA, NFSA, PMAY, NHM, PMGSY.
2. Human Development Index

The article was published in THE INDIAN EXPRESS on 22 Dec. 2021

A larger circle of diplomacy

R-Day invitation to leaders of five Central Asian republics is recognition of region's new geopolitical significance

The third meeting of the India-Central Asia Dialogue in Delhi on Sunday served a purpose to sensitise the Central Asian interlocutors that it attaches primacy to geoeconomics. But India will have a challenge on its hands to flesh out the '4Cs' concept that External Affairs Minister S Jaishankar presented at the event — commerce, capacity enhancement, connectivity, and contact being the four pillars of a new geoeconomic partnership. There is hardly a month left to flesh out this concept before the five Central Asian leaders arrive to attend the Republic Day parade on January 26 as chief guests.

MK Bhadrakumar

THE GOVERNMENTS inviting the leaders of the five Central Asian countries — Tajikistan, Uzbekistan, Turkmenistan, Kazakhstan and Kyrgyzstan — as guests for Republic Day on January 26. This is a timely move. The Taliban takeover in Afghanistan has catapulted the Central Asian region as a geopolitical arena where great contestations for influence are unfolding.

Gladiators from faraway lands are appearing in the region with increased frequency, raising anxieties and causing disquiet. It is exciting and worrying when the Great Game, lingering in the shade for long, begins to creep up to the centre stage. There is a growing awareness that for leveraging influence in Kabul and harvesting that influence in the form of material gains, a firm footing in Central Asia is a prerequisite. Given the vast untapped mineral wealth of the region encompassing the five Central Asian countries and Afghanistan — estimated to be worth a few trillion dollars — there is a significant economic dimension to the unfolding saga.

There is geopolitical rivalry too, as the locus of global power is inexorably shifting to Asia. For centuries, prosperity was to be found in the West, but that is no longer so. That lures nefarious elements to the Silk Route from the killing fields of Syria and Iraq to Afghanistan, with eyes cast on the steppes and the Pamirs, and deep into China and the Indian Subcontinent. And, all this when things are at an inflection point in Eurasia with confrontation brewing between Russia and NATO. Washington hopes to create in Central Asia a vector of its Indo-Pacific strategy to contain China and Russia. At the same time, governments in Moscow and Beijing are circling the wagons.

India needs to work on an intricate network of relationships with the regional states while remaining mindful of the "big picture". Delhi's moribund non-aligned mindset needs to be turned into a strategic asset to navigate its long-term interests. India's membership of the BRICS and SCO will help. So indeed will the prospect of the resumption of India-China strategic communication at the highest level, with Moscow's helping hand.

Delhi's decision to invite the Central Asian leaders into the first circle of Indian diplomacy cannot be a "stand-alone" event. There were fleeting glimpses of a new line of thinking during President Vladimir Putin's recent visit to Delhi. Putin's one-on-one talks with Prime Minister Narendra Modi in the ambience of their warm personal equations and the presence of Nikolai Patrushev, Russia's "security tsar", at the dialogue of national security advisers in Delhi on November 10, hosted by NSA Ajit Doval, have breathed life into the new thinking on regional security.

The deepening of the traditional Indo-Russian mutual understanding has injected dynamism into Delhi's regional strategy on the whole. It is bound to have a calming effect on India's tensions with China. Central Asia and Afghanistan form a vast landlocked region where Russia and China are big-time players for whom the region's stability falls within the First Circle of their respective national security agenda.

India has no direct access to the region but has vital stakes. Delhi cannot have an effective Central Asia strategy without the cooperation of these two big powers. India can use the card of regional connectivity to stimulate partnerships. The time may have come to reopen the files on the TAPI and IPI gas pipeline projects. Both involve Pakistan.

Russia is well-placed to act as guarantor and help build both these pipelines, while China too will see advantages in the normalisation of India-Pakistan ties. Similarly, it will be a "win-win" for India if it chooses to undertake the completion of the 600-km railway line from Ghurian (near Herat) eastward across northern Afghanistan. Apart from job creation in Afghanistan, the rail link will facilitate cargo being carried from the Chabahar Port to the Central Asian region and well beyond, including Russia and China.

Recent reports suggest that the new leadership in Bishkek is all set to approve the construction of the railroad segment across Kyrgyz territory that can connect China with the Uzbek rail grid to the Afghan border town. The point is, Delhi must do everything possible to convince the Central Asian states that its new found interest in that region is anything but a by-product of geopolitical considerations or a mere offshoot of tensions with Pakistan.

From such a perspective, the third meeting of the India-Central Asia Dialogue in Delhi on Sunday served a purpose to sensitise the Central Asian interlocutors that it attaches primacy to geoeconomics. But India will have a challenge on its hands to flesh out the "4Cs" concept that External Affairs Minister S Jaishankar presented at the event — commerce, capacity enhancement, connectivity, and contact being the four pillars of a new geoeconomic partnership. There is hardly a month left to flesh out this concept before the five Central Asian leaders arrive to attend the Republic Day parade on January 26 as chief guests.

The signal from the December 19 conclave is that Jaishankar has kindled hopes. Now, ITEC (Indian Technical and Economic Cooperation Programme) is a hackneyed tool — Central Asians are learning English even without India's tutoring. The key areas are transit and transport, logistics network, regional and international transport corridors, free trade agreements, manufacturing industry and job creation. They ought to be front-loaded into India's Central Asian strategy. Certainly, the EAEU integration processes must be speeded up.

A host of new possibilities open up if India's initiative on Central Asia runs on a parallel track with an improvement in relations with China. India kept away from the recent G7 ministerial in Liverpool that berated China and Russia — and was the only Quad member to do so. Jaishankar's call for coordination between Russia, India and China over Afghan issues is a call to energise the RIC format. India's regional strategies must be anchored on a non-aligned, independent foreign policy.

The writer is a former diplomat who worked on the Iran-Pakistan-Afghanistan desk in the Ministry of External Affairs

This article is relevant as it talks about the Indian relationship with its Extended Neighbourhood which is Central Asia. This focus on Central Asia has come as India invited heads of the Central Asian countries for its Republic Day function in 2022.

The article opens up with the importance of Central Asian Countries amongst all the jargon used :

1. For Leveraging influence in Kabul (in context of changing circumstances in Afghanistan)
2. Vast untapped mineral wealth of the region as the economic dimension.

India - Russia outlook

1. Recent one-on-one meeting between heads of state and National Security advisors.
2. Central Asian Stability falls in the first circle of national security agenda for both

Bottom line of the article is that India cannot have an effective Central Asian strategy without cooperation from Russia and China. BRICS, SCO Membership can help.

Examples of Projects:

India- PakProjects -TAPI and IPI pipelines

India - Afghanistan Project - 600 Railway line from Ghurian to North; Chahabar to central Asia.

China - Uzbekistan - Uzbek Rail grid from China to Afghan border.

4 C's at India- Central Asia Dialogue by Foreign Minister:

1. Commerce

2. Capacity Enhancement
3. Connectivity
4. Contact

Important events andOrganization:

1. ITEC - Indian technical and Economic Cooperation Programme for transit, transport, free trade agreements, Logistics network, manufacturing industry, trade corridors.
2. EAEU integration process
3. India's non attendance at G7 ministerial in Liverpool that berated Russia and China (all other Quad members attended)

If you notice, the author has used many jargons to show the relations between different countries. This terminology can be used to represent your deeper knowledge about International Relations.

> Geopolitical rivalry

> Non-aligned Mindset as a Strategic Asset

> RIC Format - Russia, India, China

Note that in the conclusion, an event is mentioned that is an example of how India is trying to balance it out when it comes to the West and Beijing-Moscow. 'Non-aligned Independent foreign policy' is also mentioned

The article provided a lot of examples which can be used to support your argument in whichever question is asked around Russia, China, Pakistan, Central Asia etc.

Whether it is making notes on paper or digitally. Whether it's about highlighting the book or underlining. At the end of the day, it's all about understanding the arguments and memorising the information. It's only after building a decent knowledge base, that your answer can come out as relevant and complete.

REVISION AND PRACTISE

No matter how much one reads or makes notes of, only that much is useful which you can remember in the exam hall. Many times, it may happen that you have read a lot, but you still can't remember it at all. It may happen you know the topic well, but you are unable to structure your answer properly.

For all of this, Revision and practice are very essential. When it comes to revision, The 'Spaced Repetition Strategy' comes to help. Whatever you read now, First revision Interval should be in a short period like a week or so. That same topic, if revised in a short interval will be fresh in your head and you will require less time to recall. Rather, you should try to take half the time required of the first reading for Revision.

After a week, you may keep fortnight or a month as the Second Revision Interval. In this, you may miss out on some facts or points. Re read and concretise the idea by connecting it to some example or cue in your head. Other Active recall strategies like quiz or test can be used as well.

Answer writing can be a good way of revision. Once you have completed some chapter or topic, you may try to write it down in the form of an answer. This way you can consolidate your learning of the topic and also see how the examiner asks that topic.

Many sample questions or previous year questions can be found in books and online websites can be referred for it.

Practising answer writing is very crucial. Do not get disheartened by your initial answers as they are bound to be below average. The more answers you attempt, the more you will get confident in facing questions in the exam. Every question has a different expectation and twist. It is crucial to face questions of different flavours to be exam ready.

Online websites provide free question content for answer writing and there are multiple test series available which you can take help from. Comparing your answers to your friends' will also help you out to see how a question can be answered in different ways.

In the following chapters, I will walk you through some important themes and topics in each GS paper and share common preparation knacks for it. Notes and Answer Formats are also shared at the end.

BRIEF NOTE ON THE MAINS EXAMINATION

Mains examination is conducted for 5 days where one has to write 9 papers. Apart from Day 1 i.e. Essay paper, rest all 4 days will have 2 sessions of examination (morning and afternoon session). With so many facts to revise and remember, management of your schedule and health during these days becomes very important.

1. **Pressure** – With so much at stake it is natural that any aspirant will be under tremendous pressure of performance. It is important to realise that the mains examination tests one's overall preparation and understanding of issues and concepts from the day 1 of the preparation. Confident attitude, calm mind and healthy body are the key to perform better in this situation. I suggest one should meditate for at least 10 minutes on the day of each paper for a relaxed mind. Or you can also take a brisk walk, listen to soothing music etc for a short while, whichever calms your racing mind.

2. **Food and Health** – It is very important to stay physically fit during and before mains examination. It is important to watch out what you eat so that you remain energetic and also to not fall ill at the same time. Strictly consuming naturally cooked hygienic food is recommended during the last one month of the preparation. Also one must make sure that they don't suffer from any kind of injury or ill health due to any reasons. It is also important that you have adequate food before entering the examination hall even though it is natural that during an anxious period one wouldn't feel like having food. Also be sufficiently hydrated on the examination day.

3. **Revision-** The day before any paper it is important to revise the whole syllabus. But it is also impossible to go through each and every line. So one should stick on to only the self prepared brief notes, highlighted points, Data points and other such important materials. And it is important to TRUST that you will recollect the things you have prepared.

4. **Examination campus-** Do not involve in any last minute discussions and conversations with other aspirants. Focus on your revisions or mind maps or just be calm. Avoid listening to songs on the morning of the examination as it tends to reverberate later. Carry enough energy bars and also energy drinks if needed into the examination hall.

5. **Between Papers** – You will have a two hour gap between the papers as lunch break. During this break have optimal lunch and stay away from groups discussing the morning paper and showing off revising for the upcoming papers. If your stay is nearby you can also take a quick 20 – 30 minutes nap to refresh your mind. You can also do a quick revision for the upcoming paper but try to do it alone or in the company of your loved ones.

***

5

Strategy For General Studies Paper I

Paper I comprises mainly of

1. **History + Art and Culture**
2. **Geography**
3. **Society**

Both 1 and 2 are vast subjects which require wide reading. One can start from NCERT Books (New ones should suffice) and go into reference books like GC Leong, Tamil Nadu textbooks etc.

While preparing you can stress on certain themes which are repeatedly asked in the exam in one form or the other. Preparing ready frameworks for these themes will help in easy recall and reduce time wastage in exams.

You can prepare mind maps or gather data points to be used in the answer around these themes. Let us deep dive into few important topics from Paper 1:

1. **Revolt of 1857:**

   This was the starting point of the Freedom struggle in India and hence questions regarding participants of the Revolt, their role and impact are frequently asked. Several events, kingdoms and leaders involved must be thoroughly studied.

   Examples of questions asked in previous years :

   1. The 1857 uprising was the culmination of the recurrent, big and small local rebellions that had occurred in the preceding hundred years of British rule. Elucidate. (Answer in 150 words) 10 Marks (2019)

2. Explain how the uprising of 1857 constitutes an important watershed in the evolution of British policies towards colonial India. (Answer in 150 words) 10 Marks (2016)

2. Role of Gandhiji:

It is crucial to understand the life and works of Gandhiji in detail as in UPSC, related questions are asked in GS Paper I and GS Paper IV and Essay also. While studying the Indian National Movement, special focus should be on Gandhiji's role. His ideology and ideas like Truth, Non-Violence, Satyagraha, Sarvodaya, Swaraj, Trusteeship and others must be understood well.

Examples of questions asked in previous years :

1. Bring out the constructive programmes of Mahatma Gandhi during Non-Cooperation Movement and Civil Disobedience Movement. (Answer in 250 words) 15 Marks (2021)
2. Many voices had strengthened and enriched the nationalist movement during the Gandhian phase. Elaborate. (Answer in 250 words) 15 Marks (2019)
3. Throw light on the significance of the thoughts of Mahatma Gandhi in the present times. {Answer in 150words) Marks 10 (2018)

3. Regionalism:

Given the Cultural diversity of our country, this theme is asked every year. It needs to be understood well along with Causes, Impact, idea of State formation etc. How regionalism impacts the behaviour of people and how it can be connected to the economy of a place. All these ideas must be explored well in advance.

Examples of questions asked in previous years :

1. Do you agree that regionalism in India appears to be a consequence of rising cultural assertiveness? Argue. (Answer in 150 words) 10 Marks (2020)

2. Do we have cultural pockets of small India all over the nation? Elaborate with examples. (Answer in 250words) 15Marks (2019)

4. Globalisation:

Equally Important theme is Globalisation. It needs to be studied in all dimensions namely Cultural, Social, Economic and Political aspects. How Globalisation started, how it is being driven because of the economy and how it has deep driving impacts on our social fabric. These questions are worth pondering.

Examples of questions asked in previous years :

1. Is diversity and pluralism in India under threat due to globalisation? Justify your answer. (Answer in 250 words) 15 Marks (2020)

2. Are we losing our local identity for the global identity? Discuss. (Answer in 250 words) 15 Marks (2019)

5. Caste:

Every year a 15 marker is asked in context of Caste and hence a sociological understanding is a must. Since it's a basic system of stratification found in Indian Society, it is also linked with a lot of markers like health, education, standard of living, opportunity etc. Similarly, Caste has been harnessed for political mileage and is used as an identity to organise and voice opinions. These aspects need to be read in detail.

Examples of questions asked in previous years :

1. Has caste lost its relevance in understanding the multi- cultural Indian Society? Elaborate your answer with illustrations. (Answer in 150 words) 10 Marks (2020)

2. Caste system is assuming new identities and associational forms. Hence, caste system cannot be eradicated in India." Comment. (Answer in 150 words) Marks 10 (2018)

5.1 Scheduled tribes and Scheduled Castes: Specially in the context of SCs and STs, the Constitutional provisions, Government schemes and welfare aspects need to be seen closely.

Example:

1. What are the two major legal initiatives by the State since Independence addressing discrimination against Scheduled Tribes (STs)? (150words) 10Marks (2017)

2. Why are the tribals in India referred to as 'the Scheduled Tribes'? Indicate the major provisions enshrined in the Constitution of India for their upliftment. (2016)

6. Poverty:

In recent times, poverty is not just seen as an economic concept of having less or no income, but multiple pointers like having food, house, roof, health, education service etc. This muti- dimensionality of poverty is often questioned on trends and linkages. Poverty Alleviation measures are asked and examples needed to be read well. No matter how much capitalist growth our country exhibits, without the Socialist undercurrents of equality, poverty is still existent. In this backdrop, poverty as a subject must be prepared well and once done, this topic is asked in all GS I, II and III papers. Hence a very High yield topic.

Examples of questions asked in previous years :

1. Despite implementation of various programmes for eradication of poverty by the government in India, poverty is still existing'. Explain by giving reasons. (Answer in 150words) 10Marks (2018)
2. An essential condition to eradicate poverty is to liberate the poor from the process of deprivation. "Substantiate this statement with suitable examples. (2016)

7. Women, their conditions, organisation etc:

The Gender perspective on each topic is a must to understand. Any theme you study you should try to see how it differently affects women. Bringing out their perspective will show Gender sensitivity which is essential for any person to have.

Examples of questions asked in previous years :

1. What are the continued challenges for women in India against time and space? (Answer in 250 words)15Marks (2019)

2. Women's movement in India has not addressed the issues of women of lower social strata.' Substantiate your view. (Answer in 250 words) Marks 15 (2018)

8. Negative Fallouts of Urbanisation:

India is a developing country and rate of urbanisation is high. Many questions are asked on how it creates population pressure on the land, water and other resources. How inadequate service provisions for drainage, fire control, judicious water use etc can wreak havoc are also highlighted.

Examples of questions asked in previous years :

1. what are the environmental implications of the reclamation of the water bodies into urban land use? Explain with examples. (Answer in 150 words) 10 Marks (2021)

2. Account for the huge flooding of million cities in India including the smart ones like Hyderabad and Pune. Suggest lasting remedial measures. (Answerin 250 words)15 Marks (2020)

9. INDIAN GEOGRAPHY:

The Geography Part in Paper 1 seems to be a vast and difficult subject to cover in toto. So, Breaking down the syllabus into different topics and then preparing on those pointers can be helpful.

a. Monsoon:

Origin, Formation, Importance for India, Regions, Monitoring, Duration theories, Changed Patterns, Factors, Global Climate effect, EI Nino, La Nina, Indian Ocean Dipole, Oscillation.

b. Earthquakes :

Formation, effects, Regions, Incidents, Disasters, Steps required, Best practices

c. Volcanism:

Origin, Theory, forms, effect on landforms, regions, incidents theories, disasters.

d. Cyclones:

Formation, effects, factors, Regions- specific monitors, naming, tackling disaster

e. Himalayas:

Formation, the role they play, effects, changes, ranges, vegetation, civilization, scope of development around

f. Climate Change:

Global warming, melting glaciers, ice caps, treaties, Himalayas, effects - Regional, Local.

g. Rivers:

Major drainage, India and world, effects, landforms, economic waterways development, watershed development, conservation efforts.

h. Mountains:

Important formations, significance, change, effect, habitat, region, world.

i. Forests:

Origin, Importance --Biological, Economical, Environmental, Forest Reports, World Climate change effects, deforestation.

j. Ocean and Lakes :

Origin, role, effects, uses, economic transport, ramsar sites, treaties, resources, different oceans, currents

k. Biodiversity Conservation:

National Parks, Wildlife sanctuary, Initiatives, effects, Need, Relation with Climate Change

l. Population Distribution:

Density, Effects on environment, effect on geography

m. Other Disasters:

Floods, Landslide, Avalanche, Forest Fires

n. Industries in India and World:

Location, Reason , Estimated changed pattern if any, effects.

o. Resources:

Natural distribution - Minerals, Solar ,Winds, Hydro Renewables Management, Land water efficient practices.

p. Agriculture:

Zones, distribution, pattern, crops, trade, geographical aspects, location.

Examples of questions asked in previous years :

1. Differentiate the causes of landslides in the Himalayan region and Western Ghats. (Answerin 150words) 10Marks (2021)

2. How will the melting of Himalayan glaciers have a far- reaching impact on the water resources of India? (Answer in 150 words) 10 Marks (2020)

10. WORLD GEOGRAPHY:

1. The Earth and Universe
2. Landforms
3. Atmosphere
4. Wind System
5. Clouds and Precipitation
6. Hydrosphere
7. Different Climate Types
8. Economic Geography: Location of industries
9. Human Geography Angle
10. Ocean geography and Currents around the World

Examples of questions asked in previous years :

1. Briefly mention the alignment of major mountain ranges of the world and explain their impact on local weather conditions, with examples. (Answer in 250 words) 15 Marks (2021)

2. How do ocean currents and water masses differ in their impacts on marine life and coastal environment? Give suitable examples. (Answerin250words) 15Marks (2019)

3. Account for variations in oceanic salinity and discuss its multi-dimensional effects. (Answer in 250 words) 15 Marks (2017)

   Especially in a subject like Geography. Maps and Diagrams can be used very well for illustration purpose in GS - I.

11. World History and Culture :

With regard to World History, the reading material is vast and Questions asked are uncertain. Similarly, goes for Art and Culture. In Both these aspects, one must refer to basic books or notes. Spending too much time on such topics is not recommended as the yield is not very high. A Recent book by Mudit Jain Sir (IRS 2017) on World History is a good version of all basic facts and information in a simplistic manner to understand and remember well. Answering some sample questions for important topics can be of help as well.

***

6

Strategy For General Studies Paper II

Paper 2 is mainly about Polity, Governance, Social Justice and International Relations. Most of the questions in this paper are derived from Current events and issues. In this paper, it is first required to know the background theory, and then build on it with the current news, only then one will be able to answer the questions in UPSC appropriately.

Important themes for Preparation of GS-2:

1. **Recent development in Constitutional Bodies and their processes** like the Speaker, CAG, Election Commission of India, National Commission of Scheduled Castes, Lieutenant Governor and issues arising out of them. Appointments to the Constitutional and Statutory bodies and their terms are very confusing and hence such short notes can help. Constitutional articles for reference can be directly quoted in an answer.

Name	Article	Mem-bers	Chair who appoints	Removal	Mode of Salary	Tenure	Misc.
CAG	148-151		President (seat) Govt. appoints	Like SC Judge misbeh-avior incapacity	Charged upon II schedule	6 yrs. - 65 yrs. [not in constit-ution]	Not eligible for appointment. Takes oath CAG Act 1991 Service bond by Parliament.
EC	324-329	1 +2	President Govt. appoints	Like SC Judge misbeh-avior incapacity		6 yrs. - 65 yrs. [not in constit-ution]	Eligible for reappointment President determines service conditions. Governor

Name	Article	Mem-bers	Chair who appoints	Removal	Mode of Salary	Tenure	Misc.
SEC	Like HC Judge removal						
UPSC/ SPSC	315-323	9 to 11 1 / 2 Offic-ers	President resign Governor resign	Only by President Insolvent, OOP infirmilg Misbeh aviour SC Enquiry	Charged upon II schedule	6 yrs. - 65 yrs. /62 yrs.	Negligible but notaflex UPSC of Chairman ½ m- GO! officers 10 yrs service and by President
NCST/ SC 38th (2003)	t338/ 338A	1+1+3 = 5 eve	President' (Seat)	-	Made Upon	3 yrs [Not in Consti-tution Report to President (NESC) OBCS/ Anglo Indians]	Condition by President
FC	280	C + 4 =5 Public	President Govt appoint-ment	Term Indicated By President	Made Upon	Service cond by Parlia-ment	Eligible for reappt Finance commission act 1951 Every Sycs Report to Incident
AG	78		President Govt appt		Made President	Pleasure of President	
Officer of Lin-guis-ticmim	350(B) 7th CM		President			President	
JPSC	By Act of (Statutory) Parliament [State Legislative]		President	President	Charged	6-62 yrs	Repot to Governors

Name	Members	Appt Committee	Tenure	Misc	Removal	
NHRC 1993 Act	C+4 = 5 CJ! Retd-C SC Judge + HC Judge + 2 HR	6 Member PM+LS+RS L00+L00 +MHA (Judge & CJ!)	5 yrs- 70 yrs	1993 Act -Ex Officers NCST/SCJ NCBC/NEW Reappt allowed	Only by President -uniformity OOP-insolvent SC Enquiry/ Misbehaviour	
SHRC	C+2=3	By Governor CM+L+As+ CCs	5 yrs- 70 yrs	1993 Act Ex Officers NCST/SCJ NCBC/NEW Reappt allowed	Only by President	
CBI	Director + 1	Govt CVC+VCs+ Home Sc	2 yrs eve, 2003	Santhanam DSPE 1946 MoP, DopT, Allocated Officers		
CVC	C +2 =3	President (Seal) DM+MHA+ LOO	4 yrs- 65 yrs		Only by President Informity- OOP Insolvent SC Enquiry/ Misbehaviour	
CIC	C+10=ll	President PM+LOO+ Cab Member	5 yrs- 65 yrs	Executive Resolution under RT! 2005	Only by President Informity- OOP Insolvent SC Enquiry/ Misbehaviour	
SIC	C+10=ll	CM+ LOO+ Cab Governor	5 yrs- 65 yrs		By Governor	Report to Gove- rnment - SL
Lokpal	C+8=9	5 Member PM+ LSs + LOQs +CJ! +Jurisdr- iction	5 yrs- 65 yrs	No SUO MOTTO Civil Court Own agency to investigate		

FC : Finance Commission, EC : Election Commission,

AG : Advocate General, CIC : Central Information Commission,

SIC : State Information Commission,

Examples of questions asked in previous years :

1. Once a speaker, Always a speaker'! Do you think the practice should be adopted to impart objectivity to the office of the Speaker of Lok Sabha? What could be its implications for the robust functioning of parliamentary business in India. (Answer in 150words) 10 Marks (2020)

2. The Attorney-General is the chief legal adviser and lawyer of the Government of India." Discuss. (Answer in 250 words) 15 Marks (2019)

2. **Major Supreme Court judgements** and understanding of constitutional questions around them. One can quote the statements by Honorable Chief Justice of India and other honorable SC / HC judges to substantiate / refute any argument. The judgements are written after a lot of research and debates, thereby their authenticity is very high. Many judgments themselves become the Law before any law is drafted. Example: The Guidelines by the Supreme court in 1997 Vishakha vs State of Rajasthan in Judgement against Sexual Harassment at Workplace were the source of law later passed in 2013. Until then, it was the basis of action and procedure elsewhere.

Important judgments of 2017, I had noted down for ready reference and a question was asked in CSE 2018 about the Data privacy with regard to the Judgement in KS Puttaswamyvs Govt of India.

2017 : Rocky Year for SC & Constitution

1) ABHIRAM SINGH vs CD COMMACHEN : RPA prohibited any kind of appeal to caste, community, language, religion.
- these markers of identity are inherently divisive, impeded the format^n of universal citizenhood.

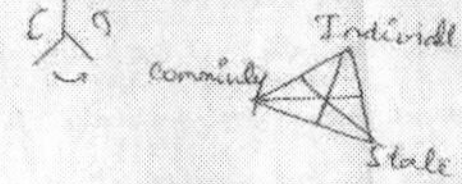

2) SHAYARA BANO vs UOI : triple talaq arbitrary illegal

3) K S PUTTASWAMY vs UOI : fundamental right to privacy, a relationship in which individual & state, indi. rights to dignity, autonomy, liberty were paramount, whether privacy of home, personal info, decision making - protected, promoted & fulfilled individual autonomy & dignity.

4) HADIYA CASE : Vindication of individual rights & primacy of individual under the constitut^n will remain a struggle

(5) KRISHNA KUMAR vs STATE OF BIHAR

(6) NCT Delhi vs UOI

OTHER COURT ORDERS

1) National Anthem being mandatorily played in cinema halls
2) Jolly LLB be vetted by lawyer panel
3) Book ban upheld (KT)

2018 OPPORTUNITIES

1) GOOLROKH GUPTA CASE : ques of Parsi women's status upon marrying outside religion
2) Constitutional challenge to Aadhar
3) NCT Delhi - Case reopens.
4) Female Genital Mutilation - Bohra Muslim community

Examples of questions asked in previous years :

1. The jurisdiction of the Cental Bureau of Investigation(CBI) regarding lodging an FIR and conducting probe within a particular state is being questioned by various States. However,

the power of States to withhold consent to the CBI is not absolute. Explain with special reference to the federal character of India. (Answer in 250 words) 15 Marks (2021)

2. Whether the Supreme Court Judgement (July 2018) can settle the political tussle between the Lt. Governor and elected government of Delhi? Examine. (Answerin250words) 15 Marks (2018)

3. **Bills proposed in the house and Important laws** like representation of people's act 1951, Prevention of Corruption Act, Anti Defection Law.

- Any bill having implications on multiple sectors will be debated and will become important for the exam.
- RSTV Big picture, Spotlight Analysis by All India Radio are good forums to listen to debates and important issues.
- PRS Legislative research is a good web source for the same.

4. **Important Articles of Indian constitution and debates around it.**

Example:

Preamble	Amendment to constitution
Fundamental Rights	Local Self Government
Directive Principles of State Policy	Annual Financial Statement
Centre State Relations	
Separation of Power	
Judiciary	

Examples of questions asked in previous years :

1. Parliament's power to amend the Constitution is a limited power and it cannot be enlarged into absolute power." In the light of this statement explain whether Parliament under Article 368 of the Constitution can destroy the Basic Structure of the Constitution by expanding its amending power? (Answer in 250 words) 15 Marks (2019)

2. Explain the constitutional provisions under which Legislative Councils are established. Review the working and current status of Legislative Councils with suitable illustrations. (Answer in 250 words) 15 Marks (2021)

5. Local Self Government:

One question is asked every year from this theme and it should be prepared well on the aspects given below. Data from across the country must be gathered and examples can be kept ready.

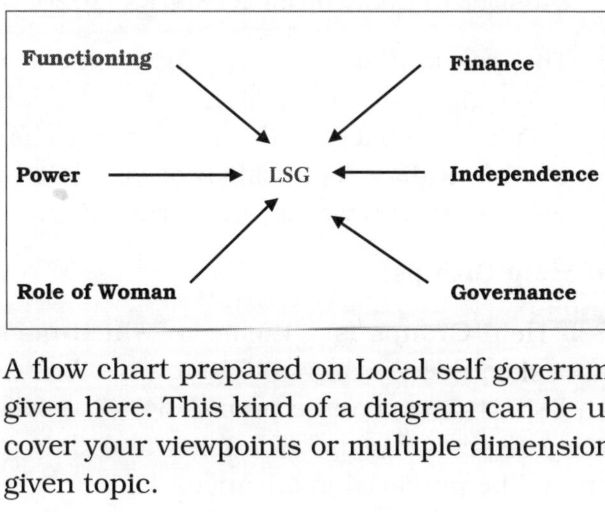

A flow chart prepared on Local self government is given here. This kind of a diagram can be used to cover your viewpoints or multiple dimensions in a given topic.

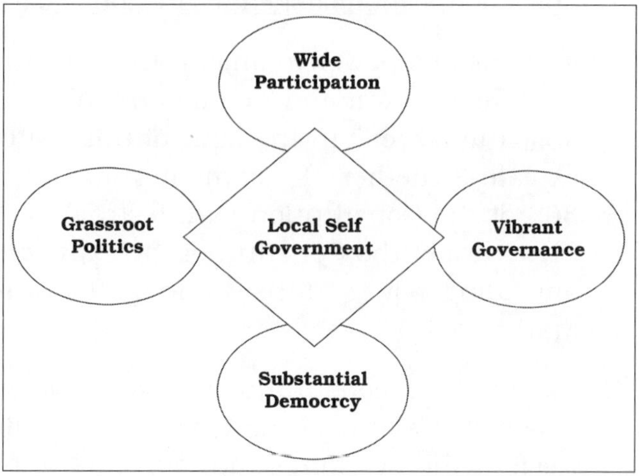

Examples of questions asked in previous years :

1. The strength sustenance of local institutions in India has shifted from their formative phase of 'Functions, Functionaries and Funds' to the contemporary stage of 'Functionality'. Highlight the critical challenges faced by local institutions in terms of their functionality in recent times. (Answer in 250 words) 15 Marks (2020)

2. The reservation of seats for women in the institutions of local self- government has had a limited impact on the patriarchal character of the Indian Political Process." Comment. (Answer in 250 words) 15 Marks (2019)

6. Self Help Groups:

Self Help Groups is a theme in which questions are asked Every year in different ways. Framework and short notes can be prepared on the following given aspects. Again, examples and data points should be prepared in advance.

Examples of questions asked in previous years :

1. Can the vicious cycle of gender inequality, poverty and malnutrition be broken through microfinancing of women SHGs? Explain with examples. (Answer in 150words) 10 Marks (2021)

2. Micro-Finance as an anti-poverty vaccine, is aimed at asset creation and income security of the rural poor in India". Evaluate the role of Self-Help Groups in achieving the twin objectives along with empowering women in rural India. (Answer in 250 words) 15 Marks (2020)

3. The emergence of Self Help Groups(SHGs) in contemporary times points to the slow but steady withdrawal of the state from developmental activities'. Examine the role of the SH Gs in developmental activities and the measures taken by the Government of India to promote the SHGs. (Answer in 250 words) 15 Marks (2017)

7. POVERTY And HUNGER:

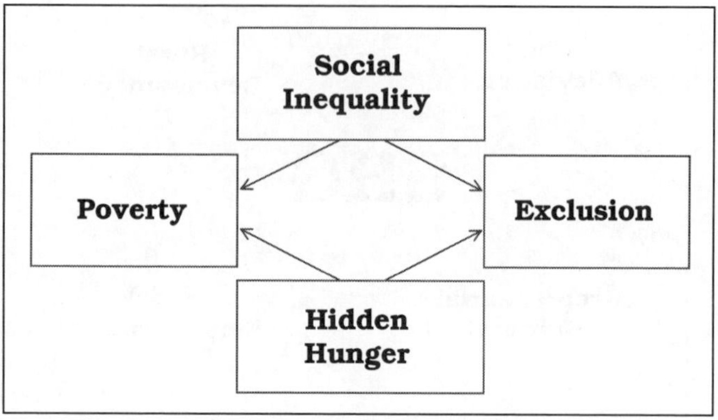

Frameworks around both Poverty and Hunger must be prepared well with data points, keywords etc. Once you have the basic resources and arguments, With practice you can write decent answers to questions asked in Any form in the exam.

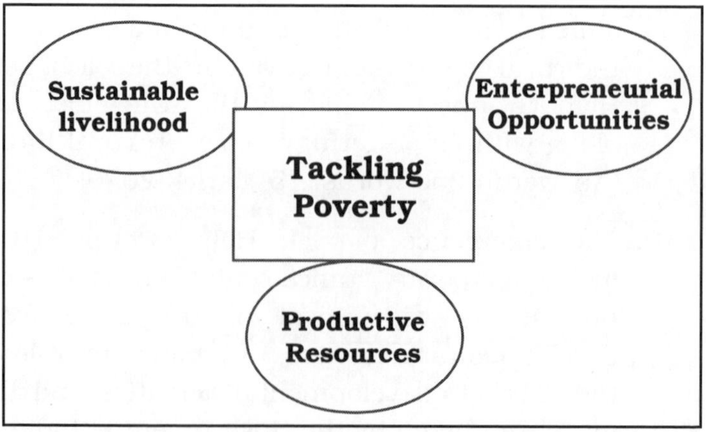

Residential Vulnerability	Social Vulnerability	Occupational Vulnerability
- Access to land	-Deprivations in SC, ST, Minority Community	- Poor working conditions
- Basic Service	- Lack of Social Protection	- Lack of job Security
	- Governance hurdles	- Informal sector

Examples of questions asked in previous years :

1. The incidence and intensity of poverty are more important in determining poverty based on income alone". In this context analyze the latest United Nations Multidimensional Poverty Index Report. (Answer in 250 words) 15 Marks (2020)

2. There is a growing divergence in the relationship between poverty and hunger in India. The shrinking of social expenditure by the government is forcing the poor to spend more on Non- Food essential items squeezing their food - budget. Elucidate. (Answer in 150 words) 10 Marks (2019)

8. INTERNATIONAL RELATIONS:

The dynamics of India's relations must be analysed deeply on three fronts for UPSC Examination

1. India's neighbourhood: China, Pakistan, Bangladesh etc and Indian Subcontinent .

2. Major Countries and Regions - US , UK, Japan, France, UAE , Africa, Central Asia etc.

3. International Organisation: Quad, International Solar Alliance, Shanghai Cooperation Organization and our role as well as issues around it.

Study of basic historical background is necessary to understand what events have helped shape the current diplomatic relations. Herein your world history study will also help you in understanding. TV debates and newspaper articles can be the source for judging the important issues and preparing around them.

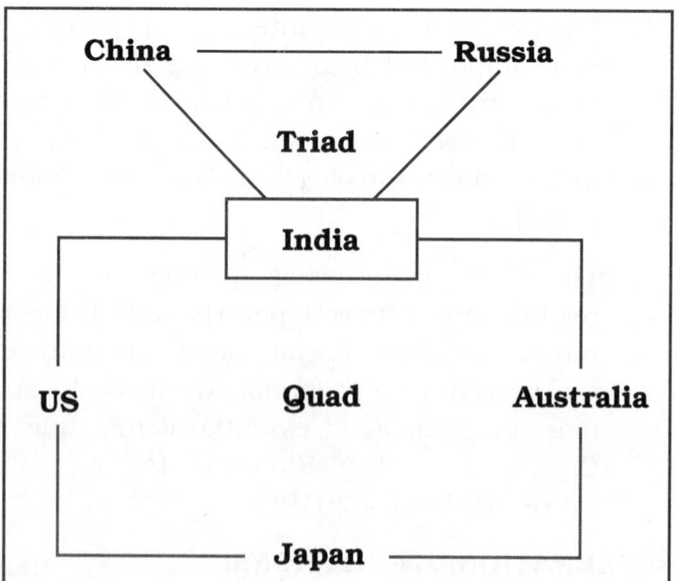

Some other excerpts from notes for International Relations are:

INDIAN DIASPORA

3Cs
- **Connect**
- **Contribute**
- **Celebrate**

— **Know India Prog.**

— **Scholarships**

— **Bharat Ko Jano Quiz**

4Ts
- **Talent**
- **Technology**
- **Training**
- **Team Work**

Cheque Book Diplomacy

Examples of questions asked in previous years :

1. The newly formed tri-nation partnership AUKUS is aimed at countering China's ambitions in the Indo-Pacific region. Is it going to supersede the existing partnerships in the region? Discuss the strength and impact of AUKUS in the present scenario. (Answer in 250words) 15 Marks (2021)

2. What is the significance of Indo-US defence deals over Indo-Russian defence deals? Discuss with reference to stability in the Indo-Pacific region. (Answer in 250 words) 15 Marks (2020)

3. What introduces friction into the ties between India and the United States is that Washington is still unable to find for India a position in its global strategy, which would satisfy India's National self esteem and ambitions" Explain with suitable examples. (Answer in 250 words) 15 Marks (2019)

***

7

Strategy For General Studies Paper III

General Studies paper 3 comprises of Economy, Technology, Internal Security and Agriculture etc which are very dynamic in nature. The striking nature of GS3 is that the questions asked in exams are more often in line order of the topics listed in the syllabus. If you perhaps prepare notes on all the topics carefully, answering will be easy.

Preparation Strategy and Themes:

1. Budget,Economic Survey and Niti Aayog Reports:

They are very crucial documents wherein information about economy, trade, agriculture, investments can be found. Hence, after reading basic economics one can go through these to understand contemporary issues of national importance. Many tables, pie charts and data points can be directly quoted from these documents and reproduced in the answers as they are authentic government sources.

Examples of questions asked in previous years

1. Explain the difference between computing methodology of India's Gross Domestic Product (GDP) before the year 2015 and after the year 2015. (Answer in 150words) 10 Marks (2021)

2. Do you agree with the view that steady GDP growth and low inflation have left the Indian economy in good shape? Give reasons in support of your arguments. (Answer in 150 words) 10 Marks (2019)

2. Inclusive Growth:

It is a repetitive theme asked every year in one form or the other. How, Why and What needs to be understood well specially given the rising level of inequality in the Indian Scenario. International reports often write about the need of inclusive

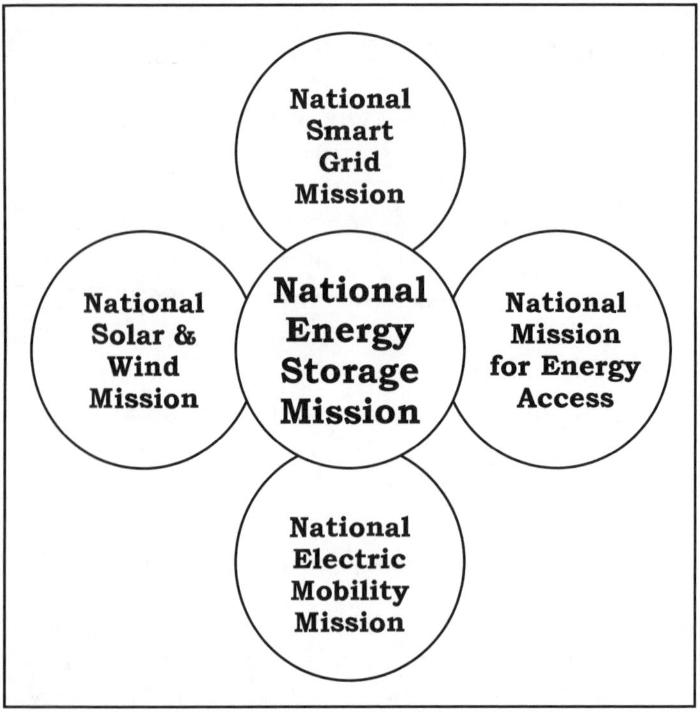

growth and these can be quoted.

Examples of questions asked in previous years

1. Explain intra-generational and inter-generational issues of equity from the perspective of inclusive growth and sustainable development. (Answer in 150 words) 10 Marks (2020)

2. It is argued that the strategy of inclusive growth is intended to meet the objectives of inclusiveness and sustainability together. Comment on this statement. (Answer in 250 words) 15 Marks (2019)

3. AGRICULTURE:

Agriculture as a topic can be prepared on the following pointers.

3.1 Agricultural Revolutions like Green, White, Golden revolution etc. the origin, spread, benefits of these revolutions are often asked.

Examples of questions asked in previous years

1. Explain various types of revolutions, took place in Agriculture after Independence in India. How these revolutions have helped in poverty alleviation and food security in India? (Answer in 150 words) 10 Marks (2017)

3.2 Cropping patterns in different regions of the country based on seasons and soil type and quality needs to be understood well so that the economic side of it can also be connected.

Examples of questions asked in previous years

1. What are the present challenges before crop diversification? How do emerging technologies provide an opportunity for crop diversification? (Answer in 250 words) 15 Marks (2021)

2. How far is Integrated Farming System (IFS) helpful in sustaining agricultural production (Answer in 150 words) 10 Marks (2019)

3.3 Public Distribution System : This is a crucial system in our country and a big reason why India has been able to keep away hunger for such a huge population. The system had some loopholes which were bridged by the JAM trinity of Jan Dhan Account, Aadhar and Mobile. Many states like Chhattisgarh have come out with several good initiatives to bridge these gaps and make their system more effective. Committees like the Shanta Kumar Committee have given recommendations that can be studied and quoted. WTO often questions these policies so the international perspective also needs to be studied in this.

Examples of questions asked in previous years

1. What are the salient features of the National Food Security Act, 2013 ? How has the Food Security Bill helped in eliminating hunger and malnutrition in India? (Answer in 250 words) 15 Marks (2021)

2. What are the reformative steps taken by the Government to make food grain distribution system more effective? (Answer in 250 words)15Marks (2019)

3.4 Food Processing Industries : This is a common question over the years because the Agricultural sector is prominent in the *country* and one way of promoting the Industrial Sector is by first pushing ahead the Food Processing Industries. Several aspects like Opportunities, Government Schemes, Bottlenecks, Supply Chain Management, Upstream and Downstream Linkages can be studied. Some examples from across the world and successful initiatives in some states can be noted.

Examples of questions asked in previous years

1. What are the challenges and opportunities of food processing sector in the country? How can income of the farmers be substantially increased by encouraging food processing? (Answerin 150words) 10Marks (2020)

2. Elaborate the policy taken by the Government of India to meet the challenges of the food processing sector. (Answer in 250 words) 15 Marks (2019)

3.5 Land Reforms: This topic has various aspects like Economic for better production and efficiency, Social for welfare of Landless Farmers, Political for how different parties have adopted these laws and Regional aspects of how differently these reforms have been implemented. One must prepare well along all these lines.

Examples of questions asked in previous years

1. How did land reforms in some parts of the country help to improve the socio-economic conditions of marginal and small farmers ? (Answerin 150words) 10Marks (2021)

2. Discuss the role of land reforms in agricultural development. Identify the factors that were responsible for the success of land reforms in India. (2016)

3.6 5 'I' Pointers:

a) Irrigation

b) Infrastructure

c) Investment

d) Insurance

e) Incentification

These factors are important with regard to Agriculture and can help you cover all major issues.

Examples of questions asked in previous years

1. How and to what extent would micro-irrigation help in solving India's water crisis? (Answer in 150words) 10Marks (2021)

2. What are the main constraints in transport and marketing of agricultural produce in India? (Answer in 150 words) 10 Marks

4. Energy and Other Sources:

How Energy matters for India's growth and development, the sources available with us, how efficiently they can be utilised are some important points to ponder on. Renewable energy like Solar, Wind, Hydro, Nuclear and Geothermal energy can be studied along with their technical feasibility and economics angle. Several Projects and Schemes of the Government of India and States can be studied. International perspective also is important in this aspect.

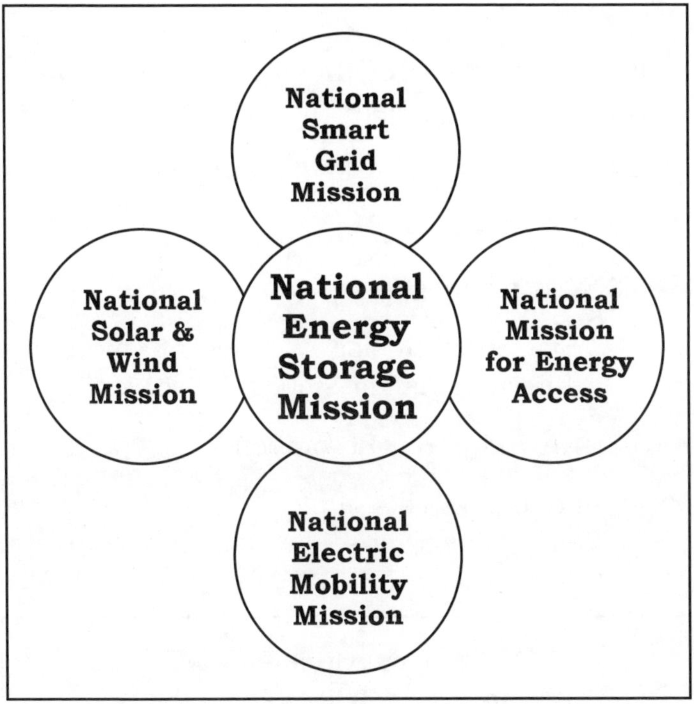

Examples of questions asked in previous years

1. Describe the benefits of deriving electric energy from sunlight in contrast to the conventional energy generation. What are the initiatives offered by our Government for this purpose? (Answer in 250 words) 15 Marks (2020)

2. With growing energy needs should India keep on expanding its nuclear energy programme? Discuss the facts and fears associated with nuclear energy.

(250 Words) 15 Marks (2018)

5. Technology :

It's a wide topic of the syllabus that concerns with technology related to:

5.1 Biotechnology- GM crops to Cloning

5.2 Robotics

5.3 Nanotechnology

5.4 Space Technology - Recent Indian and International mission and discoveries

5.5 4th Industrial Revolution

And others.This topic is very dynamic and hence, cues must be taken from Current Affairs.

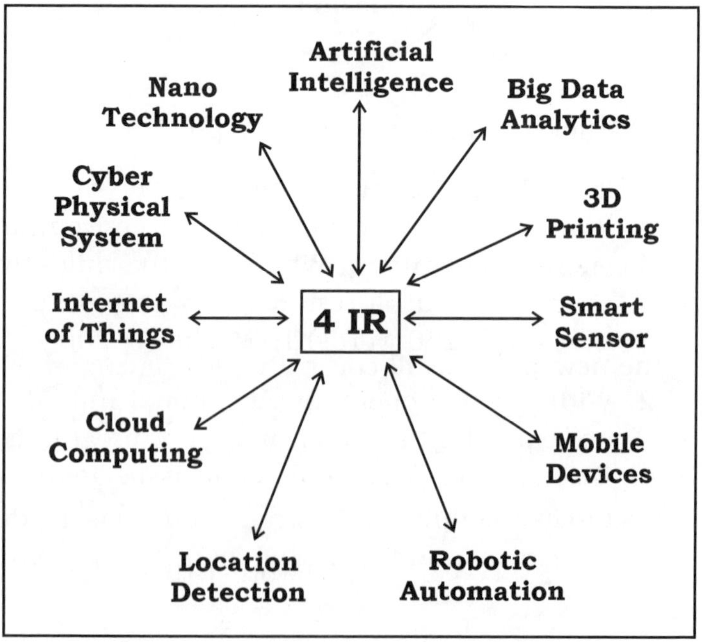

I had prepared a Mindmap on 4th Industrial Revolution using online search and then prepared on different pointers separately. This way all the concepts related to one other could be understood well.

Examples of questions asked in previous years

1. What are the research and developmental achievements in applied biotechnology ? How will these achievements help to uplift the poorer sections of the society? (Answer in 250 words) 15 Marks (2021)

2. COVID-19 pandemic has caused unprecedented devastation worldwide. However, technological advancements are being availed readily to win over the crisis. Give an account of how technology was sought to aid management of the pandemic. (Answer in 250 words) 15 Marks (2020)

6. Disaster Management:

This is an important theme as a question is asked every year in this section. India's vulnerability mapping must be studied to understand the looming disasters for various reasons. If at all there is any cyclone or an earthquake or floods, the newspapers will cover it well by giving articles of analysis. They come in handy to connect the geographical aspect of disaster with the reality of impact in terms of loss of life, property and resources. As an administrator, one has to deal with disasters and hence, the management aspect becomes crucial.

6.1 ARC Report : The 3rd Report of the 2nd Administrative Reforms Commission (ARC) report on 'Crisis Management' is a good source to understand these aspects.

6.2 NDMA Rules, Committees - The National Disaster Management Authority, its laws, byelaws, rules and other points.

6.3 International Reports - Sendai and Hyogo framework and other Mutual International Agreements can be studied to give examples in answers.

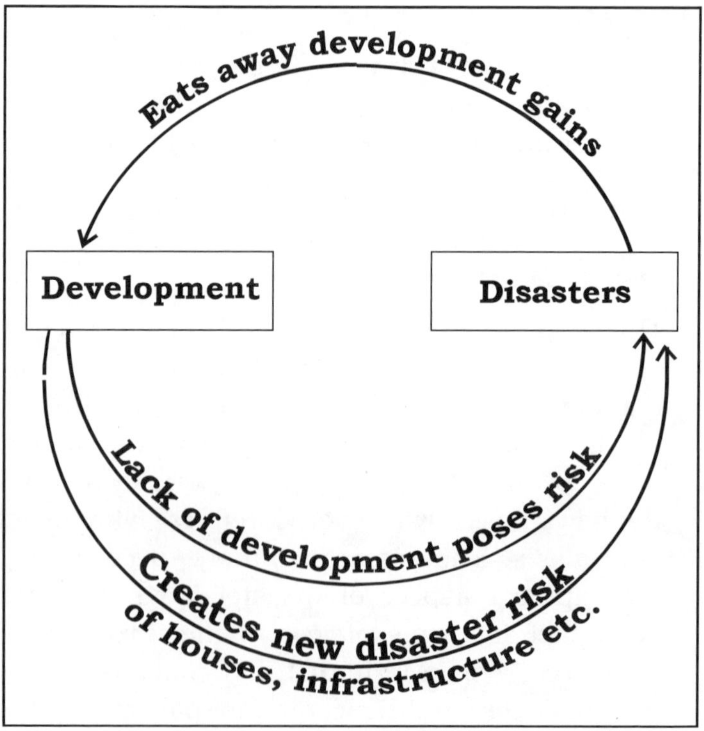

Examples of questions asked in previous years

1. Discuss the recent measures initiated in disaster management by the Government of India departing from the earlier reactive approach. (Answer in 250 words) 15 Marks (2020)

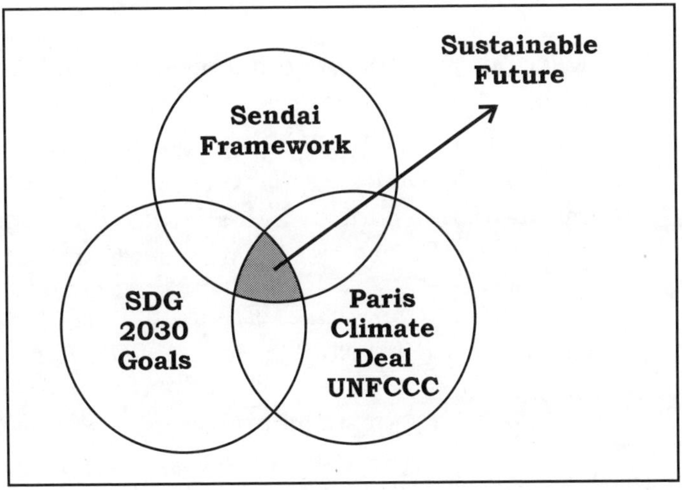

2. Describe the various causes and the effects of landslides. Mention the important components of the National Landslide Risk Management Strategy. (Answer in 250 words) 15 Marks (2021)

3. Disaster preparedness is the first step in any disaster management process. Explain how hazard zonation mapping will help disaster mitigation in the case of landslides. (Answer in 250words)15Mark (2019)

7. Environment, Biodiversity and Climate Change:

You would have studied this aspect of Environment for Prelims exam. In Mains, few questions based on theory in context of the current happenings can be asked.

Examples of questions asked in previous years

1. Describe the major outcomes of the 26th session of the Conference of the Parties (COP) to the United Nations Framework Convention on Climate Change (UNFCCC). What are the commitments made by India in this conference? (Answer in 250 words) 15 Marks (2021)

2. How does the draft Environment Impact Assessment (EIA) Notification, 2020 differ from the existing EIA Notification, 2006? (Answer in 150 words) 10 Marks (2020)

3. Define the concept of carrying capacity of an ecosystem as relevant to an environment. Explain how understanding this concept is vital while planning for sustainable development of a region. (Answer in 250 words) 15 Marks (2019)

8. Internal Security:

This is a topic specific to Mains and surely there is a question asked every year. There are limited topics in this subject but the basic narrative of low / non inclusive development, political ideology, economic benefit to perpetrators, international factors etc remain the same. Holistic Analysis of these issues must be done to be able to write well. Relevant maps, diagrams, illustrations can be prepared.

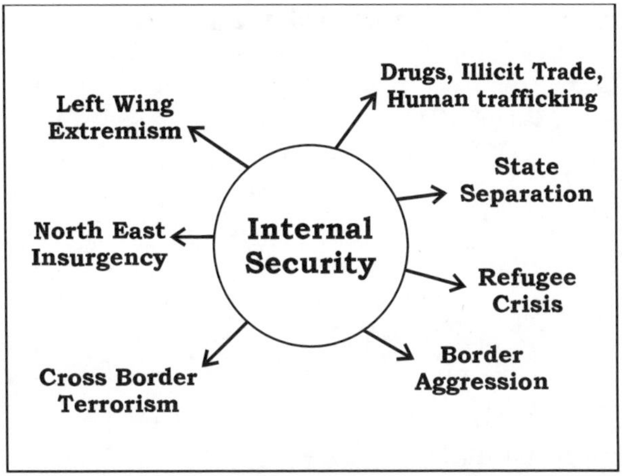

Examples of questions asked in previous years

1. Analyse the multidimensional challenges posed by external state and non-state actors, to the internal security of India. Also discuss measures required to be taken to combat these threats. (Answer in 250words) 15 Marks (2021)

2. Analyse internal security threats and transborder crimes along Myanmar, Bangladesh and Pakistan borders including Line of Control (LoC). Also discuss the role played by various security forces in this regard. (Answer in 250 words) 15 Marks (2020)

3. Indian Government has recently strengthened the anti-terrorism laws by amending the unlawful Activities (Prevention) Act (UAPA), 1967 and the NIA act. Analyze the changes in the context of prevailing security environment while discussing the scope and reasons for opposing the UAPA by human rights organizations. (Answer in 250 words)15Marks (2019)

***

8

Strategy For General Studies Paper IV

The General Studies Paper IV can be mainly divided into 2 Sections.

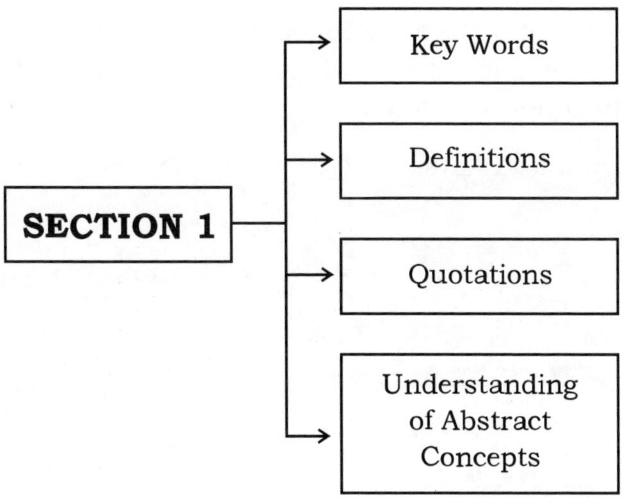

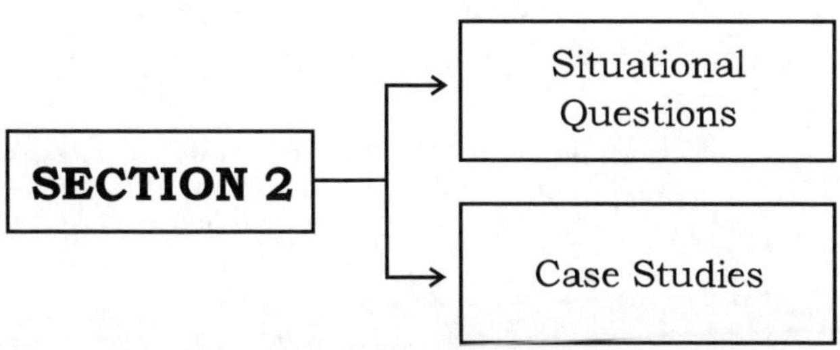

Strategy for Section - I :

1. The keywords mentioned in the syllabus are the crux of this paper. You should understand each concept clearly so that you can write about it in simple words.

   For this, one must take any standard book for basic definitions and also refer to the internet. I had made short notes of what a concept means and an example to show it in real life. Once our concept is clear, one can connect it whichever way it's asked in the exam.

   Example of Notes

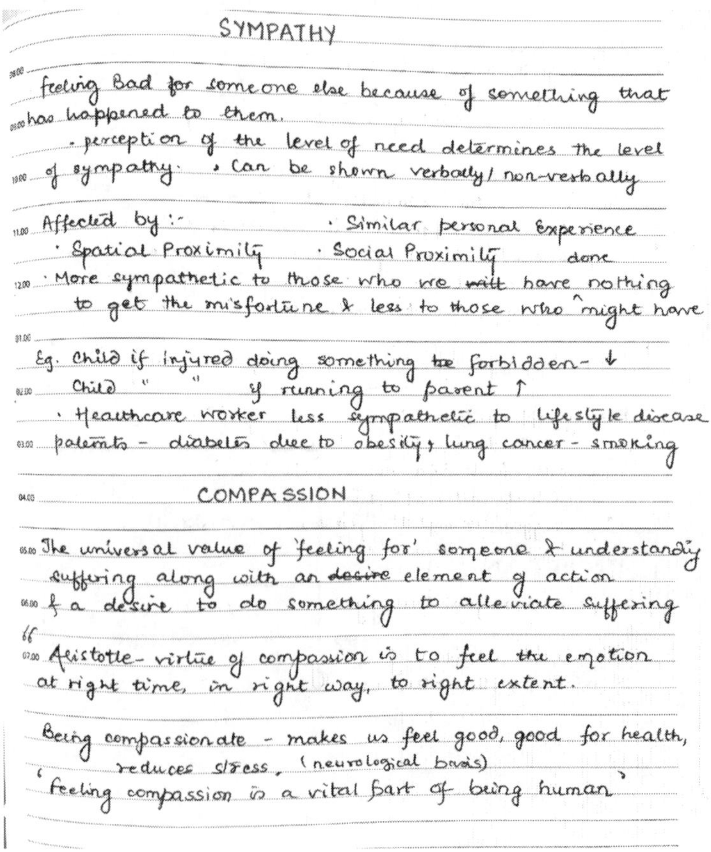

SYMPATHY

feeling Bad for someone else because of something that has happened to them.
- perception of the level of need determines the level of sympathy. • Can be shown verbally / non-verbally

Affected by :- • Similar personal Experience
• Spatial Proximity • Social Proximity done
• More sympathetic to those who ~~will~~ have nothing to get the misfortune & less to those who might have

Eg. Child if injured doing something ~~to~~ forbidden - ↓
Child " " if running to parent ↑
• Healthcare worker less sympathetic to lifestyle disease patients - diabetes due to obesity, lung cancer - smoking

COMPASSION

The universal value of 'feeling for' someone & understanding suffering along with an ~~desire~~ element of action
& a desire to do something to alleviate suffering

Aristotle - virtue of compassion is to feel the emotion at right time, in right way, to right extent.

Being compassionate - makes us feel good, good for health, reduces stress, (neurological basis)
'Feeling compassion is a vital part of being human'

Feeling concern about someone else, wanting to do something to help & then doing it, is good for you, for those around you & for society as a whole

Compassion at work – among workers or by employer can make more them committed to job.

• invokes cooperation from workers, distressed. •

* Compassionate – knack of understanding others & carry service orientation, tendency to attend subtle social signals to indicate what others need/want

"Twin sister of love & its offspring is charity."

! Taking appropriate action is imp. Eg- 'Give a man a fish & you will feed him for a day, teach him how to fish & you will feed him for a lifetime.'

→ immediate alleviatⁿ can even be detrimental
Eg: Beggar (young/ strong/ able)-, expressed in right way can be long term solution.

! Compassion fatigue : putting health care/caregivers at risk.

To vulnerable sections of society, victims of asymmetric access to health, edu, nutritⁿ etc.

EMPATHY

sympathy++
action element

» Capacity to understand other people's feelings by imaginatively stepping in their shoes as if we were feeling it ourselves. - Part of EI.

Barack Obama argues that if we are more empathetic Eg to a child who is hungry, to a family who lost his/her house in a disaster etc. it becomes harder not to act or help whether its a family member or a stranger.

As a civil servant - have to understand & help others in some way,- putting the needs, pain & suffering at centrestage enables us to see the situation differently and perhaps offer more useful support & assistance

5 key elements of Empathy -

1. Understand° others - Sensitivity
2. Developing others
3. Service Orientatⁿ - 'go the extra mile'
4. Leveraging Diversity - acting against stereotypes
5. Political Awareness - sensing group's undercurrents & power relatⁿˢ

At Mercedes poll found 70% employees had never driven a Merc & could not understand customer issues ∴ Striving for customer delight than satisfactⁿ, to empathise.

Never criticise anyone b4 you have a walked a mile in their moccasins

American Proverb.

COURAGE

>> Courage is not the absence of fear but is a virtue of managing & overcoming fear to stand up for our own values and take action in a thoughtful appropriate manner

→ Winston Churchill

"Courage is what it takes to stand up & speak. Courage is also what it takes to sit down & listen"

Ensuring to act courageously, one must not either be overcome by fear or take unnecessary risks because of over confidence

↳ Courage is about finding the right balance b/w Fear & Over confidence by thoughtful action, careful evaluation and then pushing onself to stand for ones values, rationally.

TOLERANCE & INTER CULTURAL AWARENESS

>> Ability or willingness to recognise and respect the beliefs and practices of others & (existence of opinions) or behaviour that one dislikes or disagrees with

Public Service entails interaction w/ diff people from all walks of life, requiring to work extensively with them, sometimes on specific issues.

Acceptance & flexiblity can nurture an open attitude & make copperation with subordinates as well as seniors more fruitful and easy.

Example of Previous Year Questions :

1. What are the main components of emotional intelligence (EI)? Can they be learned? Discuss. (Answer in 150words) 10 Marks (2020)

2. What do you understand by the term 'public servant'? Reflect on the expected role of public servant. (Answer in 150words) 10 Marks (2019).

2. Read through basic philosophical ideas about law, public service, government , happiness, success, leadership, teamwork, peace etc. Concepts given by Philosophers like Immanuel Kant, Aristotle, John Rawls, Confucius, Machiavelli etc can be studied.

   Ideas from National leaders like Swami Vivekananda, Gandhiji, Dr. APJ Abdul Kalam etc and International leaders like Lincoln, Nelson Mandela, Martin Luther King Jr., Dalai Lama etc. as well as Religious philosophy like that of the Gita, Buddhism and instances from epics etc. can be read through to make a sound base for an ethical perspective. It will also provide a plethora of ideas on the basis of which one can make decisions in day to day life.

3. With each keyword/ concept, one must connect day to day examples. Ethical dilemmas, Real life narratives and examples of officers or public figures who have done inspirational works must be added for a more contemporary understanding. For Example, The dashing Kiran Bedi Mam, also a Ramon Magsaysay award winner who was the first woman IPS officer is known for her work of extensive prison reforms in Tihar Jail. Similarly Ms Sanjukta Parashar, IPS who is recognised for her work against militants in Assam.

In the Swachh Bharat Abhiyan, Parmeswaran Iyer, Secretary Government of India, mobilised the revolution in the leadership of the Honourable Prime Minister. In COVID times, Maharashtra IAS officer Dr Rajendra Bharud who planned in advance for oxygen supply in his district Nandurbar and was able to avert shortages in the second wave.

These can be readily used in the answers to elaborate and elucidate any concept.

4. In this section, Quotations from famous personalities or simply Statements are given and the examinee is supposed to elaborate on the same. These questions mainly test our interpretation of that quote or sentence in the light of Ethics and Aptitude. To proceed, Read the statement twice, then try to identify the key idea or concept. Practise these questions in advance by randomly selecting quotations and understanding the context. Finally you can elaborate the idea and then illustrate its relevance by giving examples.

   Example of Previous Years Questions:

   1. "We can never obtain peace in the outer world until and unless we obtain peace within ourselves." - Dalai Lama (Answer in 150 words) 10 Marks (2021)

   2. "In doing a good thing, everything is permitted which is not prohibited expressly or by clear implication". Examine the statement with suitable examples in the context of a public servant discharging his/her duties. (Answer in 150 words) 10 Marks (2018)

5. 4th Report of the II Administrative Reforms Commission (ARC) on Ethics and Governance is a good source to get an overall orientation about Ethics and Probity. Apart from this, Editorials from reputed newspapers, websites and TV debates on current issues like euthanasia, data privacy etc can bring out multiple arguments in several issues that are in news. Knowing more perspectives will help you to reach your own understanding of the topic..

Strategy for Section - II

The second part of Paper- IV is based on Case Study where situations are provided and you are expected to give the due course of action.

1. Identify the Stakeholders:

   Stakeholders are the people involved in the case study who have some stake i.e. they are being impacted by the actions taken or are the decision maker in the case.

2. Practice role Analysis:

   Each case study gives you a particular role to be in. You must answer some questions to think through the situation.

   a. What is the basic role and responsibility of that person?

   b. What are the different expectations from him/her?

   c. What are the different approaches which he/she can take?

   d. What are the ideal solutions to his/her situation?

   e. What are the practical difficulties?

f. What are the values, principles or ethical concepts involved?

3. After doing this analysis, Develop the Different options that a person has in that situation. I always started with the most inappropriate and ethically unsound option which I would reject. The most ethically sound option would be the last which I would eventually justify and choose.

   Whatever course of action you suggest has to be keeping in mind the best interests of the stakeholders which you have identified, without compromising on the ethical standpoint.

4. Recognise the challenges, difficulties, issues and dilemmas. This will show that you are in touch with the contemporary reality and not in some ideal world in your pursuit of the ethical pathway. Being able to illustrate the dilemmas involved and the competing options available will show your practical understanding.

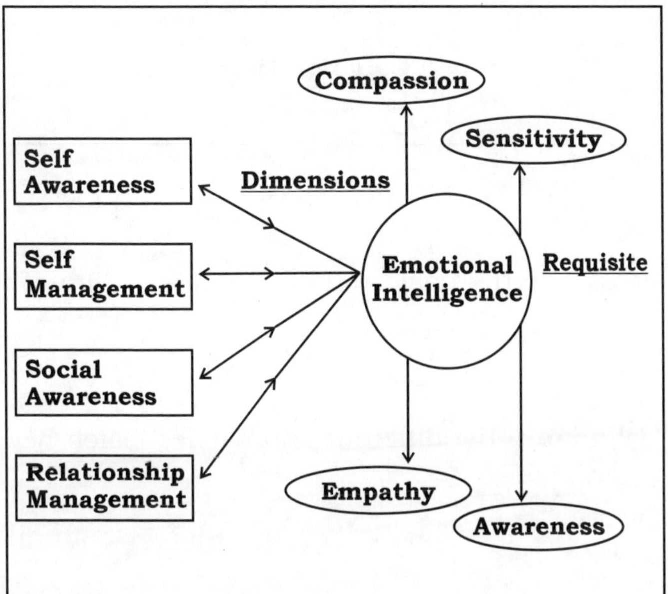

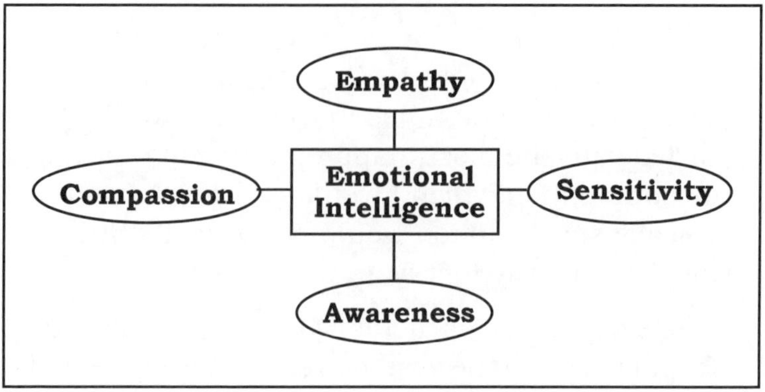
Empathy
Compassion
Emotional Intelligence
Sensitivity
Awareness

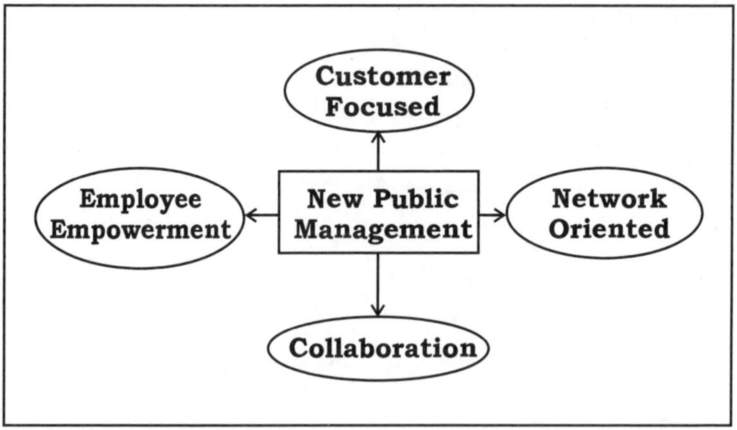
Customer Focused
Employee Empowerment
New Public Management
Network Oriented
Collaboration

***

9

Question Directives

Before we go into decoding the question, we must go through the type of question words that can be asked. There might be minor to major differences in the way the question is answered depending on the keyword. You might know well about a topic, but instead of writing What you Know, you have to write What is Asked. This is very crucial and creates a difference in the amount of marks you are awarded.

To understand a question fully, one must know that a question has a particular directive word. Frequently used directives are, 'Examine', 'Comment', 'Analyse', ''Evaluate', 'Discuss', 'Critically Examine', Critically Comment', 'Critically Analyse' and 'Assess'.

Below is the table of Keywords asked in the Questions of Mains Answer Writing with their explanations:

Question Word	What should you do?
Discuss	In this type of question, the answer should have both the pros and cons or should be a kind of discussion for and against the statement. In general, a debate or argument backed up with facts and finally with a conclusion. Example: Major cities of India are becoming more vulnerable to flood conditions. Discuss.
Describe	Focus should be only on that particular subject matter and a detailed explanation must be provided. Example Describe the benefits of deriving electric energy from sunlight in contrast to conventional energy generation.
Distinguish	Answers should be based on, How the subject of the question differs from other things or topics mentioned in the question.
Differentiate	There should be a detailed comparison and distinguishing (as said above) the subject of question with others. Example : Differentiate the causes of landslides in Himalayan region and Western Ghats.

Examine	The key is to investigate and establish main facts of the issue. The answer should consist of both the advantages/ positive/ For points and the disadvantages/ negative/ against points of the subject of the question. A way forward or conclusion can be given. Example: In The Indian Governance System, the role of non-state actors has been only marginal. Examine the statement.
Enumerate	As the term suggests, one must enlist the reasons, or issues associated with whatever is asked. Answering in point format is recommended specially for this kind of question word. The conclusion can be given to provide a closing statement at the end of listing. Example : How does Indian society maintain continuity in traditional social values? Enumerate the changes taking place in it.
Explain	This keyword demands answering in detail about Why, How and For what, of the subject in question. Any complex concepts should be written in a simple manner in the answer. Example : Explain various types of revolutions that took place in Agriculture after Indcpendence in India. How these revolutions have played in poverty alleviation

Elucidate	In this keyword, one has to Illustrate the argument in the question with some examples. One has to give arguments to substantiate the statement as to how that statement is found to be true or otherwise. Example : The 1857 uprising was the culmination of the recurrent big and small local rebellions that has occured in the preceding hundred years of British Rule. Elucidate.
Evaluate	This keyword demands to give your own reasoning or assessment about any issue or topic. This should not be a personal opinion but a reasoned assessment based on facts and evidence. Performance evaluation of any scheme can be asked and hence negative aspects or shortcomings can be mentioned here. Example : Evaluate the nature of Bhakti Literature and its contribution to Indian culture.
Analyse	The word Analyse is basically a detailed account of all the parts of the question. If the question has a statement then the keywords mentioned need to be explained. Their interrelationships, for and against arguments can be given. Example : Analyse the economic and strategic dimensions of India's Look East Policy in the context of the post-Cold War International Scenario.

Comment/ Express your views	This type of question requires a person's opinion or perspective on a particular subject. The views given must be supported by evidence or facts or some data points. Extreme views based on any specific ideology must be avoided. Example : The South China Sea has assumed great geopolitical significance in the present context. Comment.
'Critically'	This prefix or suffix can be given with any other keyword. The significance of this word is to provide a fair judgement of the topic by weighing both the for and against of the topic. In this one can explain the issue in question and provide constructive criticism in that regard.
Elaborate	This keyword mandates providing detailed information and arguments about the topic mentioned. It also means to expand the given statement using one's own viewpoints and facts. For Example : Elaborate the scope and signicance of the food processing industry in India.

Explore	Under this directive, the nature of arguments should be exploratory giving several possible viewpoints rather than being assertive and focusing on any specic argument. In an objective manner, several composite parts can be explained. For Example : Explore and evaluate the impact of 'work from home' on family relationships.
Justify	This is a directive in which strong arguments and evidence need to be provided in favour of the statement or topic mentioned in a convincing way. In this, it can also be provided why the other side of the argument is unsatisfactory and why your argument is preferable. For Example : Do you agree with the view that increasing dependence on donor agencies for development reduces the importance of community participation in the development process. Justify your answer.
Argue	As simply the name suggests, this keyword demands explicitly to provide arguments in favour and/or against the given statement. Like in 'Debate', appropriate facts, information and examples must be used to support the arguments written. For Example : Public Interest Litigation, a novel tool to democratise access to justice is a double edged sword for the judiciary. Argue with illustrations.

Assess	The keyword demands weighing upto what extent the given argument/ scheme or idea is true by giving relevant arguments. At the same time, there is scope to point out the flaws or shortcomings as an objective assessment is expected. For Example : Assess the role of National Horticulture mission(NHM) in boosting the production, productivity and income of horticultural farms.
Substantiate	This word directs us to provide evidence and logical points for an argument already taken as true. Hence reasons, causes and points must be used to support the claim of the statement. For Example : How has globalisation pushed labour in the informal organisation of work? Substantiate your answer with reference to Indian society.

***

10

Decoding The Question

In order to write a decent answer it's important to be able to understand what exactly an examiner expects in that answer. And that you can do once you closely observe the question. This chapter is a sample analysis of questions so that you can pick up the keys and decode the question. The better you get an understanding of what is expected to be written, the easier it will be to write in the correct direction.

In the current scenario, UPSC Mains General Studies papers (I to IV) comprise 20 questions.

Questions	Marks	Space Provided	Time (Avg allotted)
10	10	2PP	7Min
10	15	3PP	11 Min
20	250	50PP	180 Mins

Based on the marking scheme of the question the scope of answer is decided. A 10 marker is supposed to be a brief account of the topic in question and detailed analysis should be avoided. But a 15 marker can be a detailed account covering multiple dimensions of the question.

Each question can be divided into the following aspects. You must start to identify these parts as these are the keys to writing a relevant answer.

1) BACKGROUND:

The background refers to the broad theme or subject on which the question has been set up. This is the backdrop of the question, but may not be the exact question. It depends on the context and the word limit how much we can elaborate on the background given. If it's a 15 marker, detailed information about the background can be discussed but if it is a 10 marker then a small reference or definition will be enough. Nevertheless, a mention and elaboration of the background can be done in either the 'introduction' or in the 'conclusion' part to show that we are aware about the backdrop or the theme talked about.

2) FOCUS POINT:

It is the point or the topic on which the actual argument or information is expected to be written in the answer. The focus point is based on the 'background theme' but it refers to a specific phenomena, incident or issue which is the target of the question. One must not confuse between the two and should and one must properly identify the actual focus point and then answer succinctly.

3) HINTED FLOW :

The direction in which the examiner wants to know your perspective is the hinted flow. You may add other dimensions apart from the flow mentioned but the major arguments should be given around this hinted flow.

4) QUESTION WORD:

Explain, Discuss, Describe, Critically Analyse which decide the structure and content of the answer.

Many times we beat around the bush and end up writing irrelevant things. Once you are able to decode the question, you know what is required to be written and you can effectively 'Structure' your answer. By going from one question to another, we will try to break it into different parts and give a rough draft of what can be included in the answer. These are just frameworks for your reference and should not be considered as ideal answers. Some highlighted sentences are meant to give you additional pointers to be used elsewhere. The different parts of the question should also be identified at the outset so that you can decide the weightage to be given for each part.

Examples on decoding the question:

Example 1 : QS in GS 02 UPSC CSE 2020

'Once a Speaker, Always a Speaker,! Do you think this practice should be adopted to impart objectivity to the office of the speaker of Lok Sabha? What could be its implications for the robust functioning of Parliamentary business in India?

(150 words)

1. Parts - 02 parts
   i. Do you think. ?
   ii. What could be ?
2. Background- Parliamentary Businesses
3. Focus Point - Speaker of Lok Sabha and its Appointment and Removal.
4. Hinted Flow-

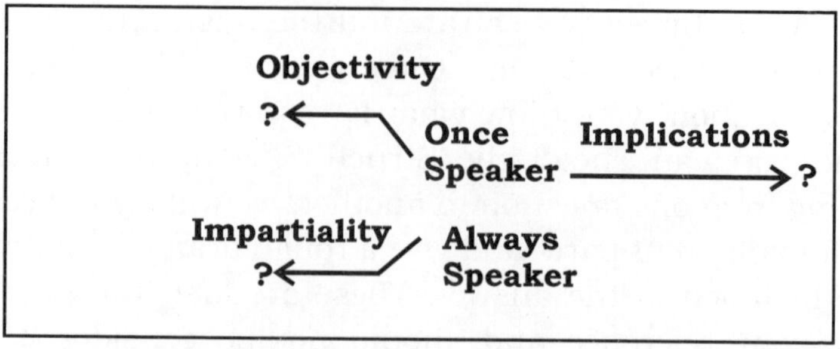

5. Question Word- Do you think? What?

In most scenarios, Background theme can be used to give an introduction or write a conclusion. In this case, one could start by introducing the Parliamentary business in the country in the first para. But the focus point is Speaker Appointment. And hence, the current practice must be explained in brief.

What is expected is an imagined scenario or how it works in other countries. You must know objectivity and impartiality is being harmed in the current scenario in order to support your argument. One or two examples can be quoted as well. Implications can be given in the later part of the answer.

<u>Example 02: GS 3 UPSC CSE 2020</u>

<u>Suggest measures</u> to improve water storage and irrigation system to make its judicious use under depleting scenario

1. Parts - 2 Parts - Water storage -- Irrigation
2. Background - Depleting water scenario
3. Focus points - Water Storage
   --- Irrigation Systems
4. Hinted Flow

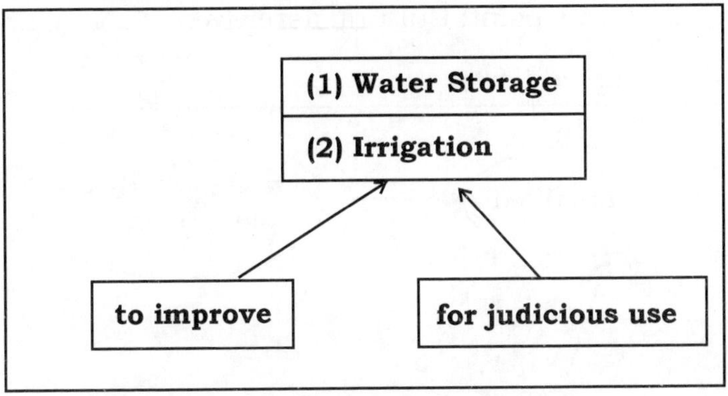

5. Question word - Suggest Measures

Since its a 250 word answer, you can start by giving the background of water scenario in the country and around the world. (Since India is not mentioned in the question, one can give a global perspective if possible.) The depleting scenarios mentioned can be substantiated by some facts, reports, findings and issues caused due to depleting water. Water use analysis can be done in line of household use, industrial or agricultural use etc.

Then measures to improve can be listed. Some examples from around the world can be given of how judicious use of water can be done. Some government schemes or social sector initiatives can be listed. **Quoting Government Scheme in the question gives an impression that the examinee is aware about the contemporary relevance of the question.**

<u>Example 03: GS 01- Q16 UPSC CSE 2020</u>

<u>Do you agree that regionalism in India</u> appears to be a consequence of rising cultural assertiveness? Argue. (Answer in 150 Words)

1. Parts - 2

2. Background theme : Regionalism

3. Focus point: Cultural assertiveness.

4. Hinted flow:

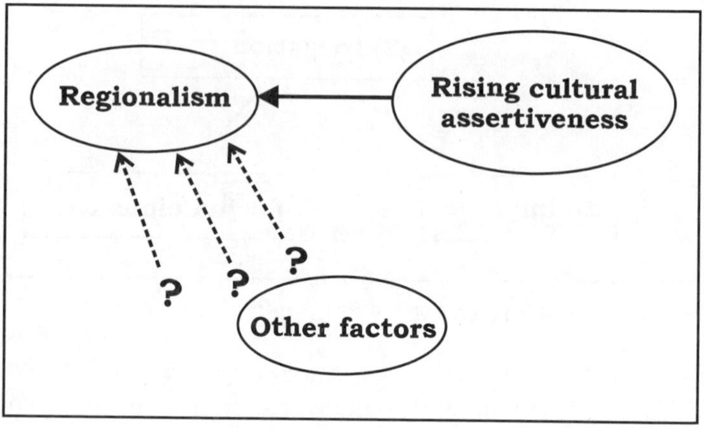

5. Question Word-Argue

Regionalism is a repetitive theme in the UPSC Paper 1 and hence 1-2 sentences on what exactly it is can be prepared in advance. In this question, Cultural Assertiveness needs to be explained briefly too. Thereafter one can go on to either support that Regionalism is a result of this in recent times or one can refuse saying that the cultural diversity differences are anyway high in the country which create a natural regional tendency. Besides this hinted flow, one can talk about how other factors like Politics, Media, Employment and Migration can aggravate or affect Regionalism.

<u>Example 04: GS IV- Q 3 b UPSC CSE 2020</u>

'The will to power exists, but it can be tamed and be <u>guided</u> <u>by rationality</u> and <u>principles of moral duty.'</u> <u>Examine</u> this statement in the context of international relations. (150Words)

1. Parts - 1
2. Background theme: International Relations

3. Focus Points: Will to power, Rationality, Moral duty

4. Hinted flow:

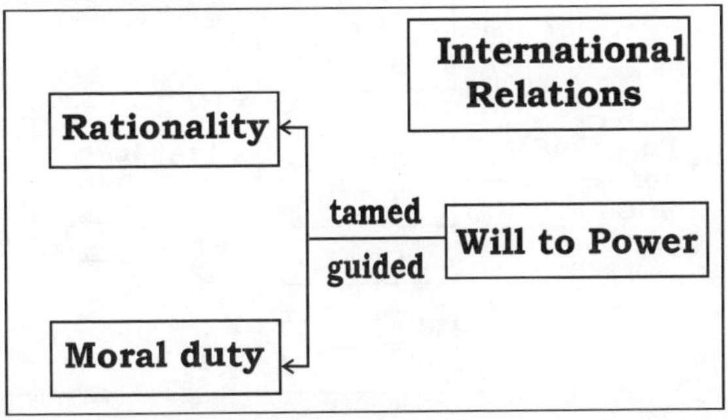

5. Question word: Examine

Since, the International context is specifically given and it's a 10 marker, one must avoid giving general or other perspectives. The keyword is Examine and hence both sides should be explained in equal ratio. You can think about 2-3 examples of how it can be tamed by rationality and moral duty and few examples of tyrants, terrorists or of recent leaders like in North Korea where Will to power is not tamed.

The language of the question appears to be generalistic and hence, there is scope to use specific examples whatever you can think of.

Example 05: GS 2 CSE 2020

"Micro-Finance as an anti-poverty vaccine, is aimed at asset creation and income security of the rural poor in India". Evaluate the role of the Self Help Groups in achieving the twin objectives along with empowering women in rural India.

1. Parts: a) Statement
   b) Question

2. Background theme: Poverty in Rural India

3. Focus point: Self Help Groups
4. Hinted Flow:

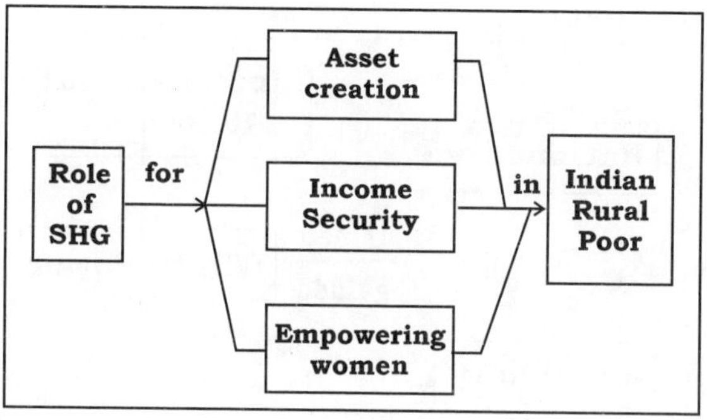

5. Question word: Evaluate

Just like Regionalism, Self - Help Group is a repetitive theme in Paper 2 and hence, framework must be prepared for it. Generally it is asked in the context of poverty alleviation and women empowerment itself. Hence, some data points and examples must be kept handy in these questions.

Note that the Statement is only used to provide you a background theme, it is not the Question Exactly. Your answer should focus on evaluating whether the SHGs were able to do this or not. Both success points, challenges and shortcomings can be mentioned. **Since it's a 250 word answer, there is scope to write in detail. Conclusion or a way Forward must be given for a 15 marker to give your answer a sense of completion.**

Example 06: GS 2 Question: CSE 2019 UPSC

There is a growing divergence in the relationship between poverty and hunger in India. The Shrinking of social expenditure by the government is forcing the poor to spend more on non-food essential items squeezing their food budget. Elucidate

This Question is wrapped up in different **Keywords** like Poverty, Hunger, Social expenditure, Food budget, Non food essential items etc. These types of questions might appear to be complicated on first reading but are not so. You just need to simplify the language in your head and then think about arguments. If you look closely, non-food essential items are Health and Education which is what social expenditure is. This question is about increased Spending on social head by the people.

1. Parts: 2 Statements
2. Background theme: Poverty and Household; Multiple dimensions of Poverty; Spending
3. Focus points: The spend on health and education of poor Indian Households
4. Hinted Flow:

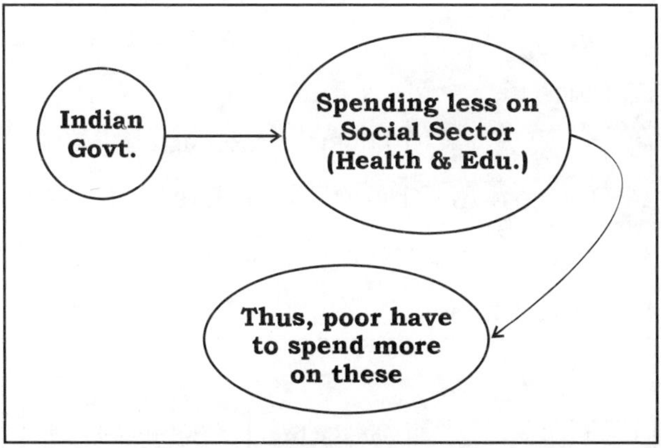

5. Question Keyword: Elucidate

The question word Elucidate, indicates that one needs to give examples in the question and substantiate the statement. The falling social expenditure by the Government is in the news for quite some time. Here is where analytical articles on Budget come to your help.

In such questions where issues or problems are asked, two things must be kept in mind.

Firstly, Constructive Criticism of the government is acceptable. But remember, you are writing from the perspective of a bureaucrat and not a journalist. **Secondly, some suggestions to improve the situation can also be given keeping in mind the time and space constraints.** This provides an optimistic perspective to your answer.

Example 07: GS3: Que09 UPSC CSE 2019

The banning of 'Jammat-e-Islami' in Jammu and Kashmir brought into focus the role of over-ground workers (OGWs) in assisting terrorist organizations. Examine the role played by OGWs in assisting terrorist organizations in insurgency affected areas. Discuss measures to neutralize influence of OGWs.

(150words - 10marks)

1. Parts- 2 a) Examine the role
   b) Discuss Measures
2. Background theme: Terrorism
3. Focus Point: Over ground workers (OGWs)
4. Hinted Flow:

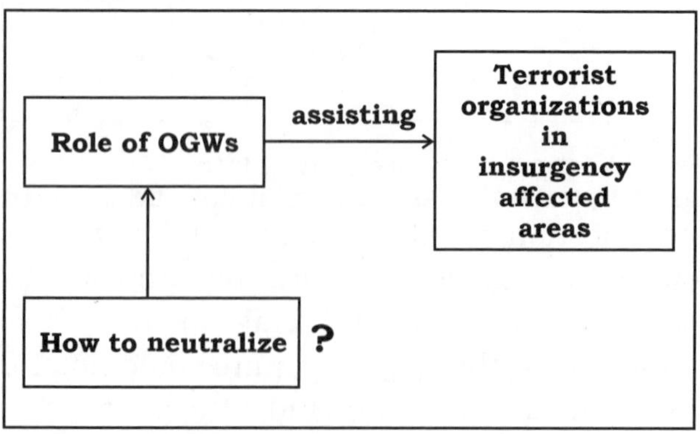

5. Question words: Examine, Discuss

Terrorism or Insurgency are important security issues. Since, the question is 10 marker and is itself divided into 2 parts both can be given equal weightage. Firstly, start by simplifying exactly what Over Ground Workers are in the context of insurgency. While examining their role, few examples can be given from recent news where their role was highlighted or some official govt statement can be used.

This question explicitly asks for measures and hence both long and short term measures can be provided. **Note carefully that while the Statement has a reference of J&K, the Question sentence is not limited to that region and hence, one can quote examples from other areas like North- East and Naxal areas also.** This way you may be tricked to be only writing about one thing, while question is general.

Example 08: Question 17: UPSC CSE GS-2 2019

The need for cooperation among various service sectors has been an inherent component of development discourse. Partnership bridges the gap among the sectors. It also sets in motion a culture of 'collaboration' and 'team spirit'. In the light of statements above examine India's development process.

(250 Words/15 Marks)

Vague/ Generalistic question language > Can give Pointed examples and can be imaginative

1. Parts: a) Statements - 2
   b) Examine
2. Background theme: Partnership and cooperation in service sectors and Development discourse.

3. Focus Points: India's Development Process.

4. Hinted Flow:

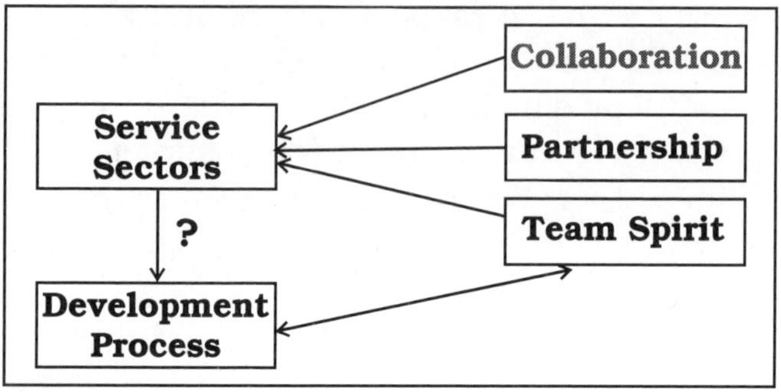

5. Question word: Examine

Sometimes, it becomes difficult to make sense of what exactly an examiner expects from you. One or the other 15 markers in a paper will turn out to be like this. This leaves scope for you to give examples and connect whatever you can think of. In this particular case, service sectors like Health, Education, IT, Tourism, Financial Services etc can be shown how their collaboration can help India's development process. Some recent examples can be quoted where you feel that an integration is illustrated.

Example 09: Question 8- GS 04 - UPSC CSE 2019

Honesty and Uprightness are the hallmarks of a civil servant. Civil servants possessing these qualities are considered as the backbone of any strong organization. In line of duty, they take various decisions, at times some become bonafide mistakes. As long as such decisions are not taken intentionally and do not benefit personally the officer cannot be said to be guilty. Though such decisions may, at times, lead to unforeseen adverse consequences in the long-term. (10 marks) 150words

In the recent past, a few instances have surfaced wherein civil servants have been implicated for bonafide mistakes. They have often been prosecuted and even imprisoned. These instances have greatly rattled the moral fibre of the civil servants.

How does this trend affect the functioning of the civil services? What measures can be taken to ensure that honest civil servants are not implicated for bonafide mistakes on their part? Justify your answer. (250 words)

1. Parts - a) Base Para - Incidents
   b) How does it affect?
   c) What measures?
2. Background theme: Civil Servants
3. Focus Points: Implicating Civil Servants for bonafide mistakes?
4. Hinted flow:

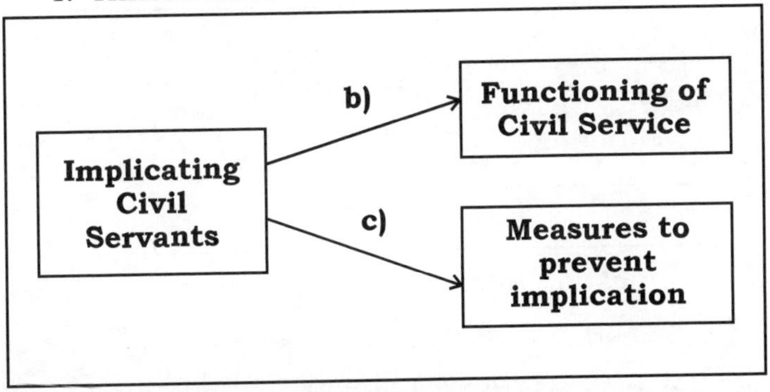

The paragraph talks about a particular scam in which a Civil servant had to go to jail because of an Audit Report. The decisions taken at a time, was post-facto found to be causing huge losses to the public exchequer. This particular idea of being punished years after the decision was taken, will only promote indecision and laxity. The promptness and initiative will naturally be affected. Such points can be included. As far as measures are concerned, Administrative, legal and informal measures can be suggested. Some examples from other countries can be given as well.

Example 10:Question 18:GS03 UPSC CSE 2019

Disaster preparedness is the first step in any disaster management process. Explain how hazard zonation mapping will help disaster mitigation in the case of landslides. 250words -(15marks)

1. Part: a) Statement
   b) Question sentence
2. Background Theme: Disaster Mitigation and Preparedness.
3. Focus point: Landslide
4. Hinted Flow:

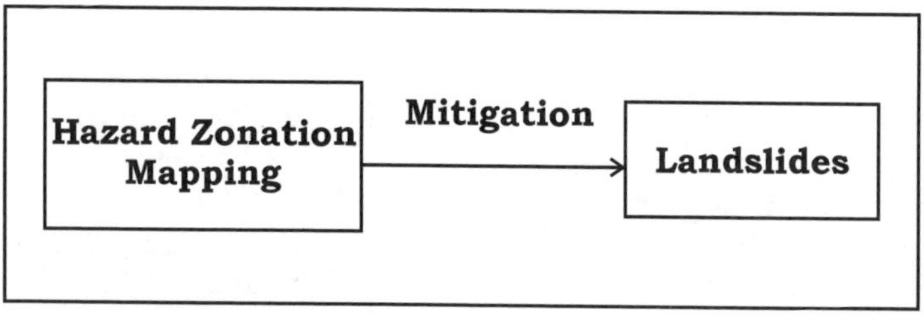

5. Question Keyword: Explain how

The question includes all Disaster Management key terms like preparedness, mitigation, mapping, zonation etc. But the specific point of answer is Landslides. The given question is a 15 marker and hence, there is scope to explain in detail the terms mentioned in the question. Here one can start with the broad theme of Disaster Management, define Hazard Zonation Mapping in simpler terms and then move to specifics of Landslides. Other forms of Disaster Preparedness can be explained as well. **Some flowchart or data point or location both India and Globally can be quoted.** International frameworks, agreements {like Sendai, Hyogo} can be given.

Example 11 - Q8- GS1 UPSC CSE 2022

Explore and evaluate the impact of 'Work From Home' on family relationships.

(Answer in 150 words) 10

1. Parts : 2
2. Background Theme : Changing nature of work
3. Focus Point : Work from Home
4. Hinted Flow :

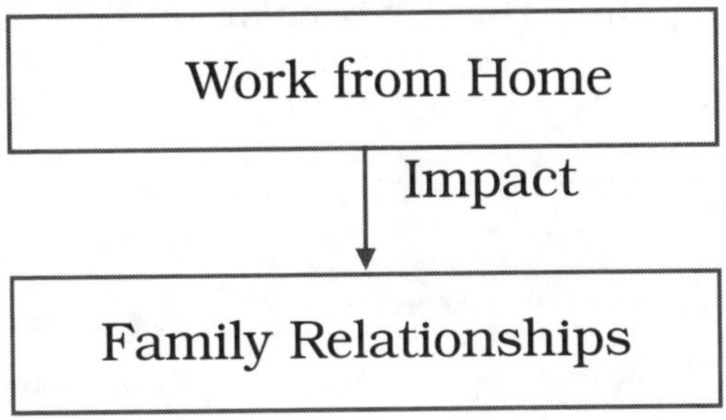

5. Question word : Explore and Evaluate

Note that this Question has two question words before a single sentence. This means that the following statement needs to be interpreted in both the contexts of - Explore and Evaluate. So while exploring the impact of work from home, the different aspects of the changing nature of work can be written. The tone has to be exploratory which means an overview of the topic can be given.

In the second part of 'Evaluate', one's own assessment can be given of how much impact has occurred, as people started spending more time at home. Example - a working mother will be able to spend more quality time with her young children with this arrangement. Another impact can be extended working hours and no cut-off time for work causing more stress at home and with family. One must carefully align arguments along both the question words. Since no specific Indian context is mentioned, global reference can be given in this regard.

Example 12 - Q19- GS1 UPSC CSE 2022

Are tolerance, assimilation and pluralism the key elements in the making of an Indian form of secularism? Justify your answer. (Answer in 250 words) 15

1. Parts : 1
2. Background Theme : Secularism
3. Focus Point : Key elements of secularism
4. Hinted Flow :

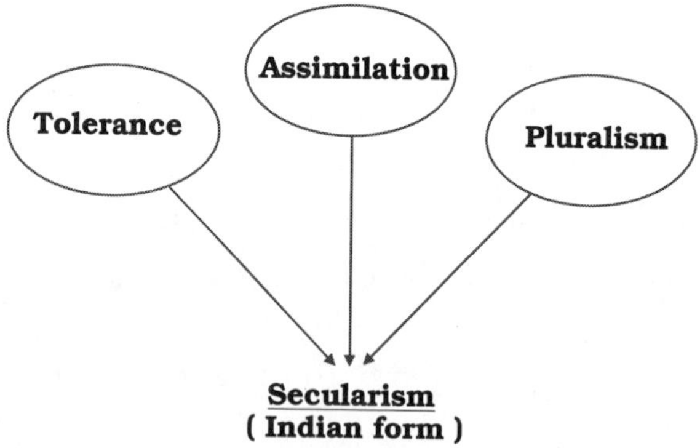

5. Question word : Justify

Secularism is an important theme to prepare in GS 1. Since its a 15 marker, background explanation to the Indian concept of secularism must be given. Here, the unique aspects of diversity of religion, culture, ethnicity in India can be given and also, the role of the State can be explained. But the major question is to justify the importance of the three terms given.

Preferably, one should be able to define all these keywords of assimilation,pluralism and tolerance independently. In order to justify, examples can be provided with each as to why they are a key element in the concept of secularism. They can range from historical events, cultural elements to day to day life practises. The constitutional references, rules in IPC and laws related to religious tolerance, prevention of discrimination etc can be quoted as well. There is also scope to define what other factors are there in Indian secularism and how absence of these factors can create mutual tensions and harm the peace of the society.

Example 13 - Q4b- GS4 UPSC CSE 2022

Online methodology is being used for day-to-day meetings, institutional approvals in the administration and for teaching and learning in the education sector to the extent telemedicine in the health sector is getting popular with the approvals of the competent authority. No doubt it has advantages and disadvantages for both the beneficiaries and the system at large. Describe and discuss the ethical issues involved in the use of online methods particularly to vulnerable sections of society.

(Answer in 150 words) 10

Parts : 2

Background Theme : Online methodology in all sectors

Focus Point : Ethical issues involved in general and for vulnerable sections

Note how the question is content heavy in the first two sentences giving the background of how online methodology has impacted the different sectors around us including administration, education, private work, health etc. It also recognises that the above process has both positives and negatives for all the stakeholders involved. But the demand of question is only to recognise the ethical issues involved and specially in the context of vulnerable sections - women, poor, elderly, children, persons with disability, marginalised, rural, less educated, minority, tribal etc.

Question word : Describe and discuss

Since it's a 10 marker, background can be only addressed in Introduction and main body should only be divided to address the 'describe' and 'discuss' part. The 3 A framework of Accessibility, Availability and Affordability can be discussed with reference to vulnerable sections to bring out the ethical issues. If not properly handled, the digital transformation can become another factor for exclusion.

Conversely, it should also be stated that with the advent of the digital world this is only going to increase in coming times. Hence strong data privacy laws, cyber security investments, training and awareness become crucial for the system.

<u>Example 14 - Q6 b- GS4 UPSC CSE 2022</u>

In the contemporary world, the corporate sector's contribution in generating wealth and employment is increasing. In doing so, they are bringing in unprecedented onslaught on the climate, environmental sustainability and living conditions of human beings. In this background, do you find that Corporate Social Responsibility (CSR) is efficient and sufficient enough to fulfil the social roles and responsibilities needed in the corporate world for which the CSR is mandated? Critically examine. (Answer in 150 words)

1. Parts : 1
2. Background Theme : Onslaught on human life, climate and sustainability.
3. Focus Point : Sufficiency of CSR according to its mandate.
4. Question word : Critically Examine

This question is very intriguing since it has levelled up the discussion on CSR from the usual role / importance of CSR to whether it is sufficient to compensate for the negative impact the corporate expansion is having on nature and human life. It is crucial to first lineate the social roles and responsibilities of CSR. After this, a critical examination of the impact of corporate expansion is required.

One can portray how an industry might be consuming gallons of water and polluting soil, but in the name of CSR, might be only doing activities like community constructions, marathons, local volunteering or cleanliness drives etc. These are not sufficient enough for the mandated role. Another example can be dependence on NGOs who only work for visibility and name. Conversely examples can be given about the upcoming local brands of clothing, food etc in which the whole supply chain is concerned with sustainability. These brands are marketed as 'conscious labels' and are a welcome step as only CSR cannot be efficient to reach the social goals.

***

11

Decoding The Answer

After the structure of the question is well understood, now let's move on to the answer. For understanding, Answers can be divided along the following aspects.

- STRUCTURE
- CONTENT
- PRESENTATION

A healthy balance at all these 3 levels can bring about a decent answer. Let us understand this through an answer I wrote. The answer is only there as a specimen **to explain different parts of an answer** and is not a model answer.

SAMPLE QUESTION :

Child marriage is failure of Indian society in its efforts to women empowerment and inclusiveness. In this contract while highlighting the prevalence of Child marriage in India. Elaborate on the factors responsible for it and measures to prevent it.

DECODING THE QUESTION

1. **Parts:** Highlight the prevalence, Elaborate on the factors, Measures to prevent
2. **Background:** Indian Society, Women Empowerment, Inclusiveness
3. **Focus Point** : Child Marriage
4. **Hinted Flow** :

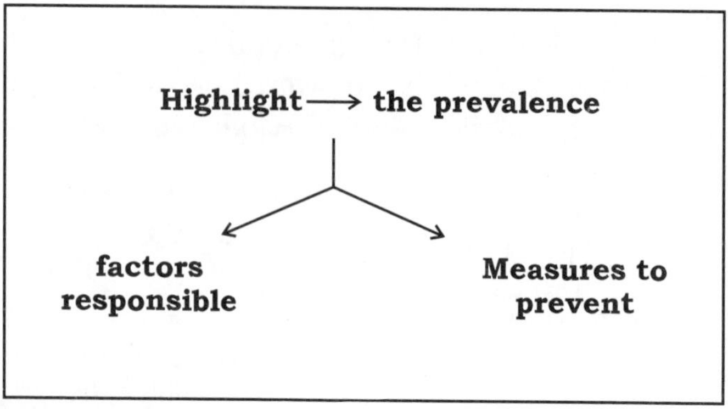

SAMPLE ANSWER:

Child marriage is one of the worst social issue prevalent in India that reflects our inadequate efforts towards' women empowerment, social change and inclusive development.

$^1/_3$ of total child brides in world are Indian (UN Population fund) NFHS survey reflects that aged between 21-24 years, near to 50% women were married as minors. Rajasthan & Jharkhand have a prevalance rate of 65% & 63% respectively suggesting the gravity of issue.

Factors responsible for child marriage:

- Low Education among girls - it has a cyclical relation with marriage, due to which they are married early.
- Conservative patriarchal attitude - of considering girls 'Paraya Dhan' or a burden on family due to dowry expenses.
- Poor self autonomy to women - who are not even taken consent from before being married off.
- Norms to control sexuality of women - early in life and Sanctity / purity of marital norms.

- Need for extra hands to labour at home - due to larger families example in rural areas, prompts bringing daughter in laws early.

- Concern for safety of single young girls - Example in slum areas prompts early marriage too.

Measures to prevent this scourge :

- Education of women and training - who can delay marriage of their daughters/ sons.

- Educating girls and sensitising them.

- Preventing school Dropouts & child labour by constant school monitoring & parent teacher interaction .

- Punishment of religious priests solemnising such marriages and media activation.

- Sensitising about health risks, psychological and physical burden on young girls due to marriage.

- Strict implementation of prevention / prohibition of child marriage Act 2006.

- Child helplines and civil society support to report cases of child marriage.

- Novel approaches Eg: Karnataka declares marriage below 18-21 years for girls and boys as void ab initio.

- CABE Committee recommendation of making girls education free till post graduation.

- Sensitising boys about responsible and late marriage as well as employment / education.

A sustained effort is required to prevent child marriages and allow rights of self determination of healthy living to girls and boys in India.

DECODING THE ANSWER:

STRUCTURE is related to the **Organisation of Answer.** This is the basic skeleton of an answer and remains on the same line for all. It has the following pointers:

- **Introduction** :

  1 or 2 lines which give an idea about the 'Background' of the answer or some hard facts can be the opening.

- **Addressing each part of the question** :

  There might be more than 1 sub part to a question. Don't forget to answer them all as each carries some marks.

  In the above sample, there are 3 parts :

  > Highlighting the prevalence

  > Elaborate on factors

  > Suggest measures

  All these parts need to be answered to make sure you can claim points.

- **Required weightage given to each part of the question:**

  Each sub part might not demand the same weightage. How much to write for each part must be gauged by how the question is framed.

  In the sample,

  > 'Highlighting' is only required to set a context and is not the major focus of the answer.

Hence, 2-3 lines will suffice. Data points used to support the prevalence improve the authenticity of the argument.

> 'Elaborate on factors' and 'Suggest measures' are more likely to be equally weighed and hence they can be given similar space.

This way you must judge for each question how to structure the answer.

- **Way forward:**

This is Not a summary of what you've written in the whole answer. Some additional points, govt scheme, constitutional or other references can be given.

In this answer, there is a very generalistic conclusion. Answers could be concluded in any other way by highlighting some major report, finding, law, judgement, International agreement etc. If none of these come to your head at the moment and you have invested enough in the main part, such a conclusion should suffice.

- **Conclusion** :

This can be given in the later part of the answer whenever there is scope to provide ideas for how things should be. This brings out an optimistic side of any issue and shows that there is scope for better.

In this answer, 'Suggest measures' was a part of the question itself and hence, giving a different 'Way Forward' was avoided.

CONTENT is the crux of the answer. It is the basic matter of what is asked in the question and comprises of:

- **Basic Information:**

  Basic information about the 'Background' and 'focus points' of the answer can be the starting.

- **Definitions** :

  Some Keywords or Technical terms can be defined in simpler words. This can be done at the Introduction level itself. In this sample, Child Marriage could be defined by explaining the legal age of marriage.

- **Facts:**

  Some statistics or data can be quoted in the answer to increase its weight.

  In the sample, these are given to substantiate the prevalence of child marriage in India.

- **Arguments** :

  This is the part in which we present our arguments in favour or against any topic asked.

  In the sample, the major Arguments are supposed to be around the 2 parts of the question.

What you write inside will be determined by how well you know the syllabus and how properly you have prepared that topic. The better read you are about the topic, the better you'll be able to analyse and write accordingly.

PRESENTATION consists of how the answer is presented to break the monotony of long statements

- **Use of flowcharts:**

  It can be done to effectively present the information you have or to present some points in less space. Few flowcharts can be prepared beforehand so that we can use them in the relevant subject. For Example:

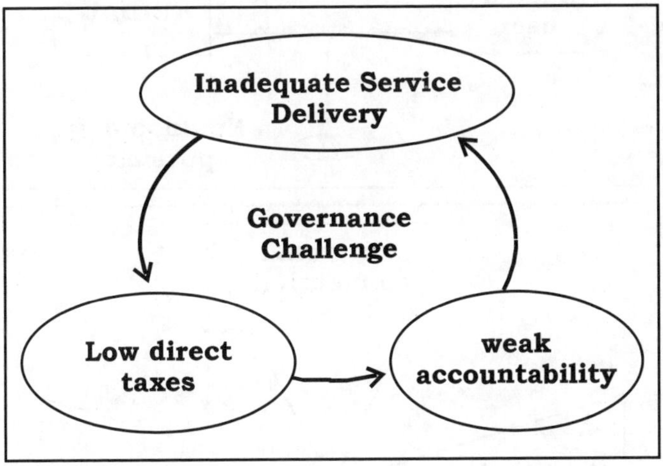

- **Usage of Examples** :

  Indian or International examples for various categories can be given to substantiate.

  In the Labour sector, Govt schemes like **PM** Rozgar Protsahan Yojana, Shram Suvidha Portal and 4 labour laws.

  In Water Conservation, NGT lauded the Jal Samvardhan Yojana of Rajasthan in which the traditional water bodies were rejuvenated and requirement of tankers was reduced.

- **Diagrams:**

  They can be used to illustrate certain aspects in the question in an easy manner. This will enhance the overall presentation of the answer.

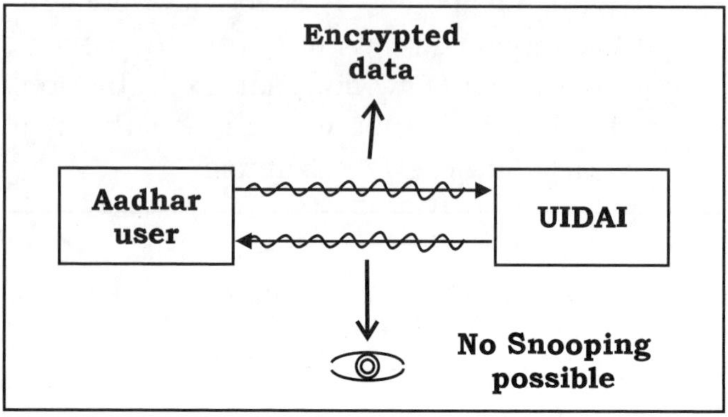

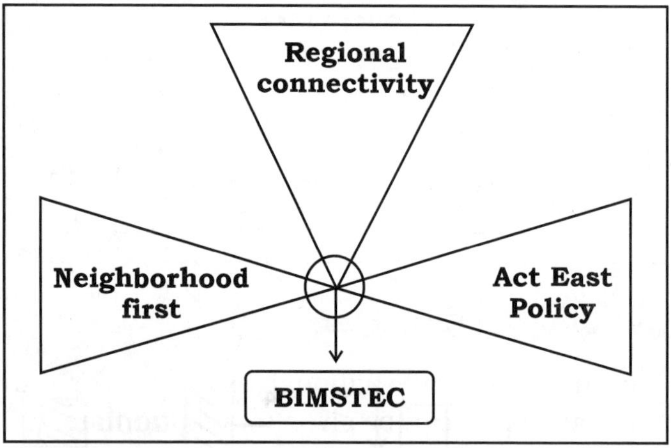

- **Maps:**

  Both India and World Maps Can be drawn in the paper in a simplistic manner so that any location based industries or other such things can be indicated in the map itself. Similarly, in other questions of geography, the wind, waves or other phenomena can be represented through the world map.

- **Innovative ways like bar graph, pie chart** :

  a) For showing issues like Man-Animal Conflict, Tribal Rights etc,

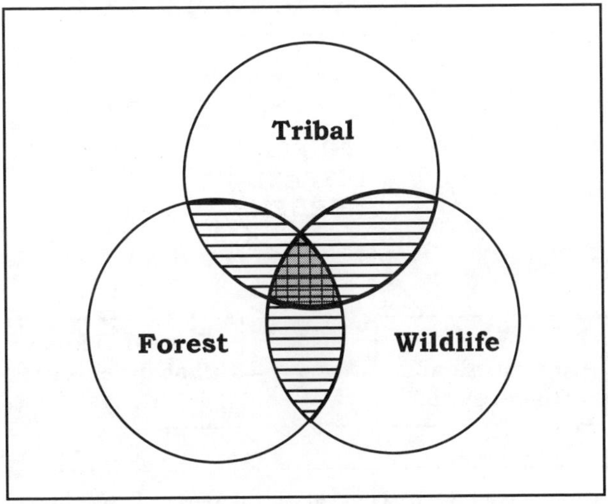

  b) Share of Irrigation Sector based on sources, how it is distributed between Canal and Groundwater

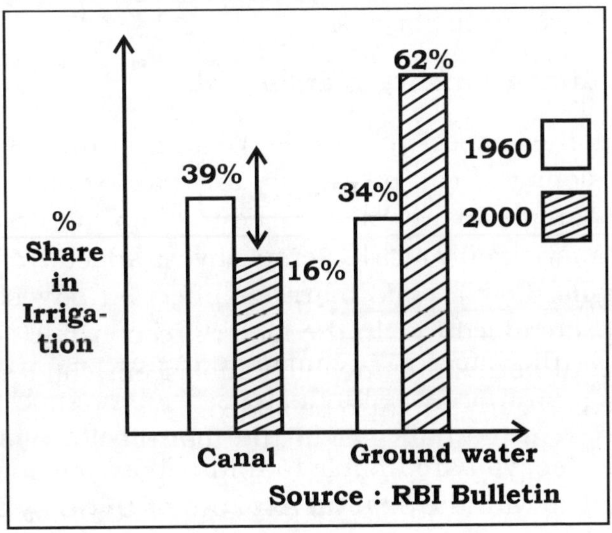

c) For Health related triple burden theory,

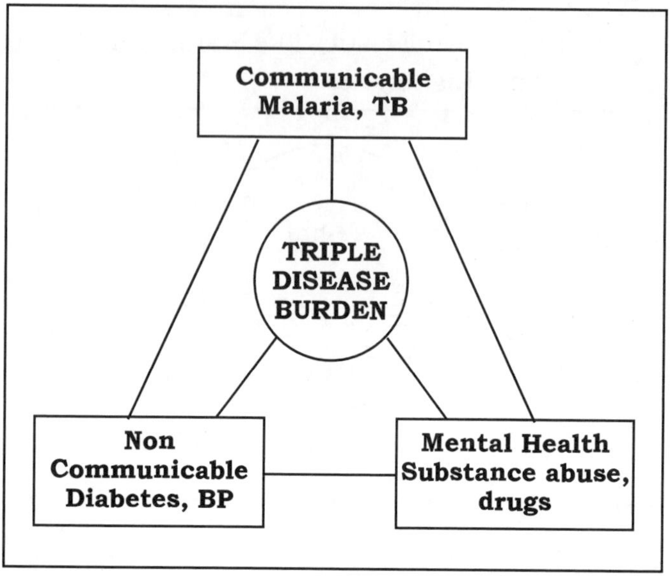

Once your structure and content have come at a decent level, you must start supplementing your answer with some or the other point which enhances the presentation to make your copy slightly different from other copies in the bundle.

Multi dimensionality of arguments

Another aspect in Answer Writing is the different dimensions you can present for any particular subject. In the sample answer above, if you see in the first part of the answer, only a girl's perspective is added. To make it holistic, how a child marriage affects a **boy** should have been added too. In the factors responsible, Tribal - Cultural norms due to which adolescent children are married off early can also be added.

In case, you are unable to think about dimensions, you can go with the **Several Aspects of UPSC syllabus itself.** For example - Factors and Consequences can be elaborated on the following aspects:

Historical	Environmental
Cultural	International
Geographical	Legal
Social	Security
Political	Administrative
Economic	Technological

This can make an answer more comprehensive and organised.

Similarly, Sometimes the points can be elaborated on the **Question Words** :

1. What
2. How
3. When
4. Where and
5. Why

Another aspect is by elucidating on the **Different Stakeholders** and Special sections of the Indian Society.

1. Women
2. Children
3. Specially Abled
4. Scheduled Caste and Scheduled Tribe
5. Senior Citizens
6. Transgenders, LGBTQI community etc.

This **shows the sensitivity of an examinee** with regard to the marginalised sections of the society and the awareness of how things affect them differently.

Interconnection of Points

While elaborating various dimensions in any question, the final important aspect is Interconnection of Points. Whatever dimensions you are mentioning, their relevance will come out well only when they will be interlinked to the question and with respect to each other. This will come with practice when you connect multiple topics with each other.

Given the vastness of the exam syllabus, we are unable to read in detail about everything. And hence the Art of Answer writing is also about capitalising whatever you have read. This means effectively presenting the available information in the best possible manner.

***

12

Salt Of Answer Writing

The major portion of an answer is the 'Content' - the arguments and information which you write to present your view point. But there are certain additions which can be used to enrich the answer. They can also help in substantiating one's statement and enhancing the authenticity of an argument. These additional pointers help Break the monotony of written statements and thus Improve presentation of the answer.

I have called these additions 'Salt' because it is a supplement and needs to be used moderately in an answer. Too much usage will deviate the answer from its core argument.

1. Facts and Statistics:

Some data trends or facts in percentage format can be given. The sources of these data should preferably be quoted along with it.

Example

1) According to the Economic Survey, 4.8% of the workforce was unemployed despite seeking active employment in 2021.

2) Between the First Lok Sabha (1952) and the Seventeenth Lok Sabha (2019) women's representation has increased from 4.4 per cent to 14.4 percent, while the Global average is 22.9 percent.

3) According to the NASSCOM Report, more than 2,250 startups in India were added in the year 2021, over 600 more than what was added in the previous year

2. Government Schemes:

Any relevant scheme of centre or state can beused to explain how the given idea is implemented on ground or what steps have been taken by the government. This will reflect the contemporary knowledge of your preparation.

Example

1) Ministry of Textiles PM Mega Integrated Textile Region and Apparel (PM MITRA) Parks Scheme. PM MITRA aims to develop integrated large-scale and modern industrial infrastructure facilities for the entire value chain of the textile industry.

2) Pradhan Mantri Krishi Sinchayi Yojana (PMKSY) aims to Introduce sustainable water conservation practices, among others.

3) Shunya programme for NZEB and Net Positive Energy Buildings (NPEB) were launched to encourage energy efficient buildings

3. Constitutional References:

Preamble, Fundamental Rights, Directive Principles of State Policy and other relevant articles can be quoted in an answer to connect the principle talked about. The ideas in our constitution are the basic source of government action and intention hence, they can be used accordingly.

Example

1) The article 21 of Indian Constitution, not only envisages right to life and liberty but also, encompasses individual dignity.

2) Some rights are outside Part III as well. E.g., Right to Property (Article 300A) which is a constitutional right and not fundamental.

3) Article 50: Obligation over the State to separate the judiciary from the executive.

4. **Supreme Court Judgements and Laws:**

Many Supreme court judgements are landmark in their decision and judicial interpretation. They can substantiate an argument effectively. Similarly legal sections and provisions can be presented.

Example

1) Mohammad Salimullah vs Union of India : Right not to be deported is concomitant to Article 19 and available only to Indian Citizens.

2) Aparna Bhat vs State of Madhya Pradesh Where judgement of MP High Court which prescribed tying Rakhi as a condition for bail in sexual harassment case was set aside and court directed training of judges in gender sensitisation.

3) The Dam Safety Act 2021 to provide for surveillance, inspection, operation and maintenance of the dam for prevention of dam failure related disasters and to provide for institutional mechanisms to ensure their safe functioning.

5. **International Organisation Reports:**

Many Globally significant organisations release reports that are relevant. Some might present data points after proper research which can be helpful.

Example

1) India ranks 3rd in the 'Renewable Energy Attractive' Index released by Ernst and Young.
2) According to World Inequality Report 2022, in 1990, 63% of the global carbon inequality was due to 'between country' inequality but in 2019, 63%of global carbon inequality was due to 'within country' inequality. (Showing how inequality affects the Climate change parameters.)
3) According to the Annual Global Risks Report published annually by the World Economic Forum, there was a 435% increase in ransomware in 2020.

6. Government Committees and their Reports:

Many government committees are set up to give recommendations about specific sectors. They are presented after an in depth analysis of the topic and their findings are authentic sources for us.

Example

1) BN Srikrishna committee regarding data privacy and issues related to it.
2) Bibek Debroy Committee in 2015 recommended that private entry into running both freight and passenger should be allowed to bring in competition with Indian Railways via liberalisation and not privatisation.
3) Standing Committee chaired by Mr Jadhav on Critical evaluation ofMGNREGA suggested an increase in the number of days job is offered from 100 to 150 days in view of COVID situation.

7. Maps:

Both India and World maps can be used to effectively locate and show a geographical scenario. With Practice one can quickly draw a map and indicate the required information.

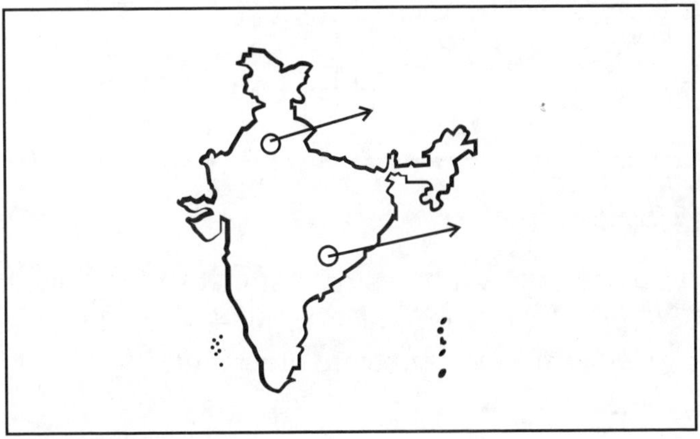

8. Flowcharts:

They are an effective way to present information in an interesting graphical manner. These can be thought of in advance and simply using flowcharts as illustrated previously, can improve the presentation.

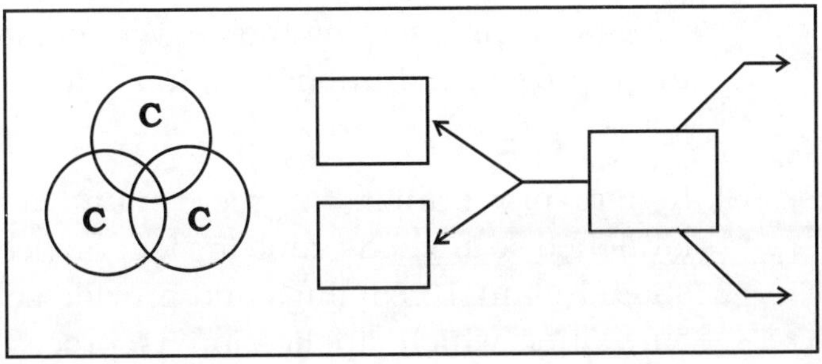

9. Diagrams:

In geography, environment and otherwise, such diagrams help make illustration easier.

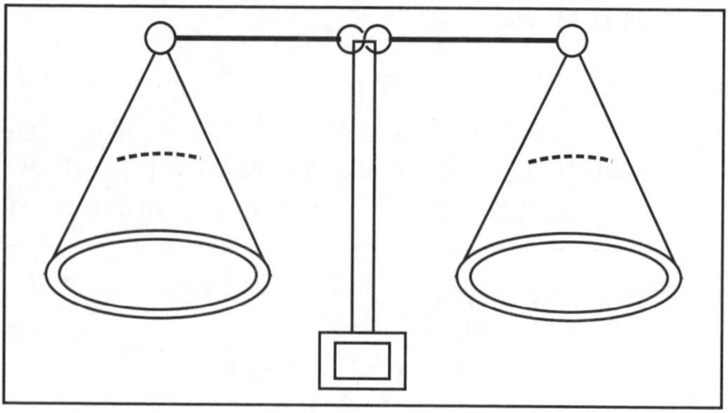

10. Examples:

Real life examples or instances of inspirational people, officers, best practises can be given in the exam to illustrate our point.

Example

1) Rajendra Singh known as the Water Man of India works extensively for water conservation by rejuvenating water through the ancient methods in villages.

2) In the aspirational district of Kandhamal in Odisha, Bike and Auto Ambulances along with Maternity waiting rooms were deployed to improve institutional delivery in tribal pockets.

3) In Firozpur Punjab, a green initiative was launched so anybody applying for gun license should plant 10 saplings and provide selfies only after which application is processed. This has led to 10000 plants being planted already.

11. Definitions:

It is generally an important introductory framework when a question is about a certain technical or abstract concept which needs to be explained before other arguments can be given about it.

Example

1) Climate change - refers to long term changes in temperatures and weather patterns. These maybe natural, but since the 1800s have been primarily due to burning of fossil fuels which produce heat trapping gases.

2) Ethics is a system of moral principles that affect how people make decisions and lead their lives. It concerns the perception of right and wrong and moral principles around it.

3) Hybrid Annuity Model in Infrastructure is a mix of BOT and EPC model wherein the government contributes 40% of project cost in the first five years and remaining is given on the basis of asset creation and performance of the developer.

12. Keywords:

There are certain concepts which are specific to some subjects. These keywords can be used to show your technical understanding of the topic or wide reading. They help to present a concept in a combination of interesting words. Some slogans, acronyms can also be listed in advance for usage.

Example

1) Cooperative and Competitive Federalism - in context of Centre State and Inter State relations for a healthy relationship among all stakeholders and performance in key indicators.

2) Cheque Book Diplomacy - in the context of countries like China, who flush lots of resources in other countries in the form of investment in infrastructure which creates obligations towards them.

3) LIFE - Lifestyle for Environment as a one word movement urging mindful and deliberate utilisation instead of mindless and destructive consumption.

All the above listed items can be sparingly included in our answer to make it more presentable and fetch us 1-2 marks extra.

***

13

Q & A Analysis

GS Paper 1

Special measures taken to empower scheduled castes have come to crossroads and demand a relook. Do you agree? Argue your case.

DECODING THE QUESTION:

- Parts - 1 Statement and 1 question
- Background theme : Scheduled Caste empowerment
- Focus point : Performance of special measures taken for SCs

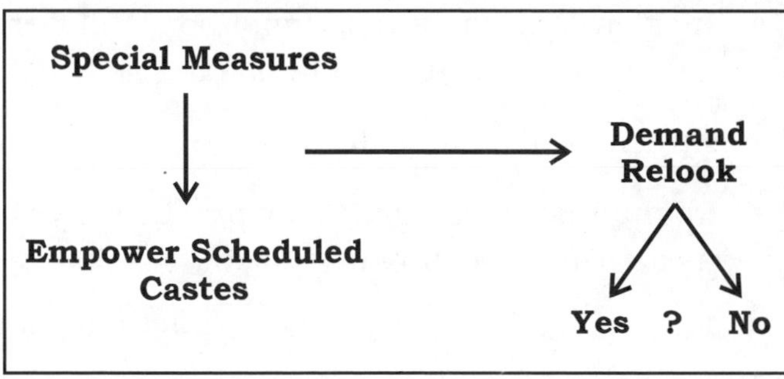

- Hinted Flow:
- Question words : Do you agree, Argue.

DECODING THE ANSWER

{Introduction}

Indian Society from its very origin has a special characteristic of the hierarchical caste system. This system has resulted in historical discrimination of Scheduled Castes. (SCs)

{Before putting forward argument, mentioning the measures taken}

Special measures taken to Empower SCs:

- Reservations in Educational Institutions, government jobs given by the constitutional articles.
- Abolition of Untouchability as in Article 17.
- Laws like Prevention of Atrocities Act 1989.

{Why is relook necessary?: Arguments}

In Spite of all the above measures, there have been several issues.

- Horizontal percolation of benefits of reservation leaving the lower strata of the community.
- Incidents of caste discrimination still persist, Untouchability in rural India etc.
- Atrocities against Dalits on rise
- Manual Scavenging is being practised by Dalits as a form of earning livelihoods.

{What can be actually done?}

Thus these demand to relook the special measures given to the scheduled caste community to make the set up more inclusive:

- The Supreme Court has advised the government to look into the matter of creamy layer concept in Scheduled Castes.
- Further strengthening of implementation of laws against Untouchability and Atrocities.
- Community oriented approach of these measures to make sure that real change is seen on ground.

Scheduled caste communities thus require special attention so that every member could be provided with required benefits and support.

The history of Indian freedom struggle is replete with the saga of sacrifice, selflessness and bravery of women. Illustrate with examples

- Parts : 2
- Background Theme : Indian Freedom Struggle
- Focus Point : Role of Women
- Question word : Illustrate

(Introduction)

At the peak of the Indian freedom struggle, women participated in massive numbers and played vital roles in different capacities. Few examples to highlight the value of their struggle is as follows :

Saga of sacrifice -

1. Rani Lakshmibai gave her life on the battlefield during the Revolt of 1857.
2. During movements like non-cooperation, civil disobedience etc women participated by picketing liquor shops and in mass protests.
3. Sarojini Naidu faced violence and led a March in Dharasana.
4. During Surya Sen's Chittagong raid, Priti Lata waddedar, Bina Das and Kalpana Dutt held arms and killed the Britishers sacrificing their own lives.

Saga of selflessness -

1. Savitri Bai Phule opened schools for destitute women, rape victims and serve them all her life.
2. Ramabai Ranade and Saraswathi led the social reform organisation
3. Margaret cousins Mehribai Tata founded national Council for women advocating women's economic and educational rights

Saga of bravery-

1. Madam Bhikaji Cama unfurled India's flag for the first time at Paris.
2. Anasuya Sarabhai supported textile workers against her own brother.
3. Women over-subscribed the Tilak fund by selling jewellery.
4. During the Quit India movement, Aruna Asaf Ali led the congress when leaders were in jail.

Gandhiji had said India can't be free if half of India's population does not contribute to its freedom struggle. Women participated, cooperated and supported the Indian independence movement with full heart.

Stating reasons for rising incidents of forest fires across the globe, analyse the forest fires on the environment. 15 Marks

- Parts : 3
- Background Theme : Forest fires
- Focus Point : Reasons and Impact on Environment

- Question word : State reasons, Analyse

(Introduction)

Forest fires are the fires that originate in forest due to natural and anthropogenic reasons and tend to spread widely in forest. Recent Australian bushfires has deserted more than one lakh hectares of forest and deprived the livelihoods and assets of about thousands of people.

Reasons for increasing forest fire -

1. Rising temperature of the globe due to climate change. Earth's average temperature was raised by 1^0C in 2015.
2. Human intervention like -tourist & trekkers who may accidentally light the fire in the forest area. For example black forest in Germany
3. Presence of invasive species-it facilitates the spread of wildfire. For example, in Southern India, lantana Camara is dry and pine tree leaves in the Himalayas.
4. Shifting cultivation-tribes clear a portion of forest area for the cultivation of crops. It may accidentally spread to other regions.
5. Intense dry summers may also lead to forest fires. For example in California.
6. Absence of forest fire line also leads to the spread of wildfire
7. Depleting water resource can also be rated as another reason

(Analysing the impact)

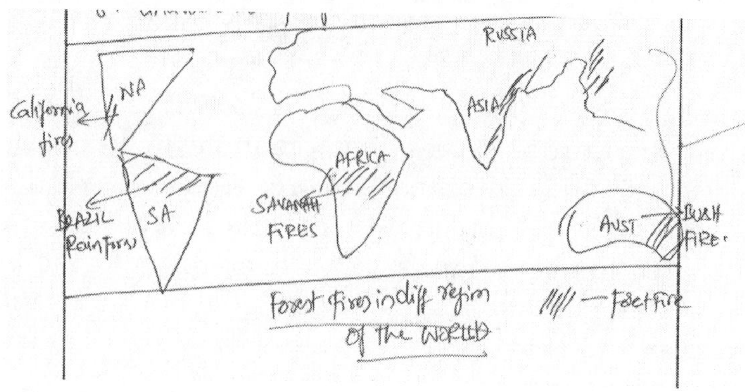

Impact of forest fires

1. Threatens ecological biodiversity and causes habitat destruction affecting the survival of species. For example, koalas in Australia
2. Severely impacts soil health altering the pH levels and causing destruction of the soil microbes.
3. Loss of lives, both human and livestock
4. Burning of wood and plants causes greenhouse gas emissions and particulate matter leading to global warming and air pollution.
5. Degradation of catchment area and water pollution negatively affecting aquatic ecosystem as well.

(Quick representation)

Measures

- **Communication** → **Through Satellite Input**
- **Forest line** → **To Prevent Spread**
- **Improving Manpower Availability**
- **Remove Invasive Species**

According to the United Nations Environment program, the forest fires will rise by 50% by the year 2100. Hence a comprehensive strategy is required to be formed at both the national and global level in order to avert the threat to the environment and human life.

GS Paper 2:

Elaborate the Doctrine of Separation of powers and NJAC in context of Indian Constitution. Do you think the Supreme Court's denial to form the National judicial appointment commission is against the doctrine of Checks and balances? Give reasons in support of your answer?

DECODING THE QUESTION:

- Parts- 1
- Background theme : Indian Constitution
- Focus point: Separation of Powers and NJAC
- Hinted Flow:

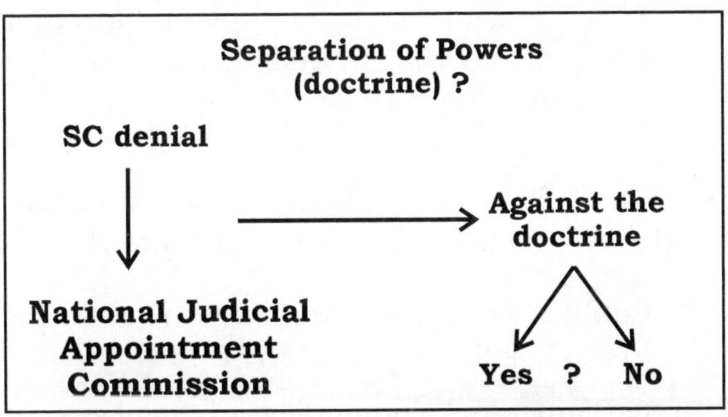

- Question words : Elaborate, Do you think; Give Reasons.

DECODING THE ANSWER

{Introduction}

Separation of powers envisages the differential distribution and delineation of power amongst the 3 organs of government - executive, legislature and judiciary. In Indian context, though strict separation is ensured in Article 51 between judiciary and executive, legislature and executive have functional overlap.

Due to parliamentary nature, the executive is drawn from the legislature itself and hence ministers are also members of parliament.

{Elaborating with Constitutional References}

Provisions of Separation in the Indian Constitution:

1) Article 121, 211, Conduct of judges can't be discussed in parliament
2) Article 122: Supreme court cannot call in question the privileges of the parliament
3) MPs are not liable for any justification for anything said or any vote given on the floor of the house in courts.

{Additional Arguments}

The system of check and Balances ensures that no one part of the system becomes excessively powerful.

1) Cabinet / Council of Ministers are accountable to the Lok Sabha (Article 75)
2) Parliamentary committees can call executives to hold them answerable for action Eg. RBI Governor etc.
3) Judicial Review (Article 13) forms the basic structure of the constitution over any legislative/executive law.

4) Article 124 and 218 of the Constitution of India lay down the procedure for impeachment of judges of the Supreme Court and High Court.

{Addressing the second part of the question by explaining NJAC and then giving reasons}

National Judicial Appointment Commission was conceived to provide a broad forum for judicial appointment that consisted of Chief Justice, 2 other Supreme Court Judges, Union Law Minister, 2 eminent persons (one from SC, ST, OBC, Minority, Woman).

SC's denial to NJAC appears breach of this doctrine as:

1) It prevents Checks and Balances in appointment of higher judiciary causing poor accountability.
2) The Collegium system is opaque and promotes the idea of 'Judges Appointing Judges'. It leads to a form of'selfrecruitment'
3) NJAC was passed by the 99th Constitutional Amendment Act of parliament and had the full public mandate but was struck down as 'Unconstitutional and void'. This undermines the power of the Legislature to make laws.
4) This leads to domination of one organ, unhealthy for separation of powers.

{Concluding with why doctrine is essential}

The idea of Separation of Power is essential for democracy and an effective state to prevent absolutism and concentration of power.

Asymmetry is an important characteristic of federalism in India, which has helped in the accommodation of diverse demands inherent in our democracy. Discuss. 15 Marks

- Parts : 2
- Background Theme : Federalism
- Focus Point : Asymmetry between States
- Question word : Discuss

(Starting from defining background)

Federalism is a form of government, where power is constitutionally divided between the union and the regional governments and each of them operate in their spheres independently.

(Why Asymmetry ?)

India adopted the unique feature of asymmetric federalism which sought to provide special powers to a few states compared to the other due to different reasons like.

a) To Avoid secessionist tendency.

b) To Maintain unity and integrity of India

c) Provide Self governance rights to the people

d) For the Protection of traditional customs and rights

e) For the Sustainable financial resource management

f) For Strategic reasons

(Provisions of Asymmetry)

Manifestation of asymmetric federalism-

1. Schedule 5,6
   a. Self governance rights to scheduled areas with sizable tribal population - Schedule five.
   b. Rights to form autonomous districts in the states of Tripura, Assam, Meghalaya and Mizoram-schedule six
   c. Panchayat Extension to scheduled areas Act.

In this way, to protect the tribal people, their customs and traditions.

2. Special category status to the states which are-
   a. Having Border and strategic location.
   b. Don't have economic viability. For example Himachal Pradesh
   c. Tribal population dominated
3. Status of union territory for accommodating areas with strategic reasons.
   a. Protection of tribal and minorities. For example, in the Lakshadweep and Andaman Nicobar Islands.
   b. National security reasons. For example those in the Ladakh region
4. Article 371 series where special boards are set up by the Governor to provide special development assistance to the backward areas. For example, article 371 A is for Nagaland. Article 371 H is for Arunachal Pradesh.

India is a diverse nation with diverse aspirations and different developmental needs. And also, India was not born in an atmosphere of hope but an atmosphere of fear, which necessitated the adoption of asymmetric federal characters. These accommodated the diverse interests and helped preserve the unity and integrity of the nation.

Given its impact on both individual resilience and the resilience of the economy. Is there a case for strong universal social protection in India. Discuss. 15 Marks

- Parts : 3
- Background Theme : Universal Social protection
- Focus Point : Its impact on individuals & economy (resilience)
- Question word : Discuss

(Define Universal social protection)

Universal social protection is the process of providing a Social Security net either through monetary or non-monetary services (ration, health care, education) to all the citizens of the country irrespective of their identities.

(To justify the line - 'Given its impact on resilience ')

Possible Impact on individual and economic resilience -

1. Fulfils the right to life and dignity to the weak and the vulnerable sections of the population as desired in Article 21 of the Constitution.
2. It would reduce out-of-pocket expenditure on health, education and other basic services. According to the Economic Survey Yr 2018-19, Out of pocket expenditure is 48.2 % of total health expenditure.
3. This inturn helps break the vicious cycle of poverty and prevents poor people from falling into extreme poverty in emergency circumstances.

4. A healthy and well educated person contributes to the social and economic well-being of the country.

5. Ease of implementation as inclusion and exclusion errors can be avoided.

6. Better human capital development leads to better use of demographic dividend. India has two/third the working population in the age of 15 to59 years.

7. Studies show that in the long term it will improve demand and savings in the economy leading to economic growth.

8. It leads to reduction of economic inequalities among the people.

(Since its a 15 marker &' Discuss', and we have established the case for it, we can explain the possible challenges ahead)

Given the widespread impact on the individual and economic resilience as explained above, the Universal Social Protection also promotes the idea of a welfare state. But there are certain challenges associated with its implementation:

1. Huge Economic burden on the state. For example, the universal basic income will cost 11% of India's GDP.

2. Better Infrastructure and quality of services is a major challenge. For example, the poor quality of education reflects poor learning outcomes and inadequate health infrastructure.

3. Just providing food grains to ensure food security is not enough. The Government also needs to provide nutritional security to fight malnutrition.

4. State providing all the services might be a moral Hazard in the long term.

(Constitution reference in Conclusion)

Social protection is a universal human right and a precondition for a world free from poverty. It can help the societies tackle the crisis situations like COVID 19 and help fulfil the idea of welfare state in the Directive Principle of State policy as mentioned in Article 38 in Indian Constitution.

GS Paper 3:

What are the problems, ailing the real estate sector of India ? Discuss various measures taken by the government to address the problems of the real estate sector.

DECODING THE QUESTION:

- Parts- 1
- Background theme : Real Estate Sector in India
- Focus point: Problems, Measures
- Hinted Flow:

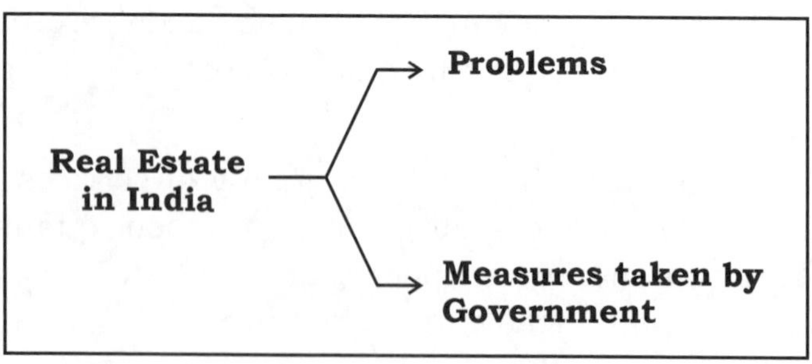

- Question words : What, Discuss

DECODING THE ANSWER

{Introduction}

Real Estate sector in India is a booming sector owing to increasing GDP, disposable incomes, rising middle class as also 'Government's goal of affordable housing for all'. Despite this its ailing with several issues:

1) Corruption and poor tax law implementation: Since property prices touch the sky, real estate builders indulge in corrupt practises with bureaucratic hands and cause trouble to the common masses.
2) Since, Real Estate does not have "industry status" acquiring loans as capital for investment becomes difficult.
3) Land is a state subject due to which inter state disparity in clauses / rules is highly prevalent.
4) Lack of clear land titles due to oral agreement or non registration hampers growth and causes revenue loss.
5) Lengthy approval process hampering foreign direct investment in this sector and multiple taxes causes hassles. (As there is No GST).
6) Involvance of Black Money.
7) Harassment by lawyers, untimely delivery of houses etc.

Measures Taken:

{Mentioning Act, Rules and Schemes}

1) Real Estate Regulatory Act 2016 which regulates transaction between buyer and promoters
2) Real Estate Regulatory Authority - at state level to look into issues and enforce it.

3) Norms for registration of all projects>= $500m^2$

4) Single window clearance for approval enhances 'Ease of doing business'.

5) Definite amount to be deposited in bank by the constructor to ensure security of funds of buyers.

6) Separate tribunals as also alternate dispute resolution mechanism

Effective implementation of law can ensure that real estate sector growth rebounds which contributes 11% GDP and enhances infrastructure in India.

Monoculture is one of the major threats to ensuring food security and sustainability of Indian agriculture. Discuss. 10 Marks

- Parts : 2
- Background Theme : Indian Agriculture
- Focus Point : Monoculture as threat
- Question word : Discuss

(Define monoculture)

Monoculture is a cropping pattern which focuses on growing a single variety of crop both in temporal and spatial arrangements. For example, wheat and rice are grown in the Punjab plains.

(How does it affect ?)

Monoculture is said to hamper food security and sustainability as -

1. It negatively affects soil health due to loss of soil fertility and nutrients. For example, alkaline soil in Punjab has reduced productivity.

2. Increased frequency of resistant diseases and pest attacks affecting the crop.
3. Focus on a single variety of crops affects nutritional security and enhances the problem of malnutrition.
4. Economic risk - monoculture is subject to market fluctuation and may affect the economic condition of farmers.
5. It negatively impacts the ecological biodiversity and the pollinators.

(Answer demands some discussion of what can be done as well since we established that it is a threat.)

Measures to overcome-

1. Agro climate zone based minimum support prices in order to promote the local crop varieties.
2. Extension services and subsidies to create awareness and benefits of multi cropping among the farmers.
3. Promotion of organic farming and zero budget natural farming by incentivising these practices.
4. Better implementation of the Crop diversification scheme.

Green revolution, lack of awareness about the consequences of mono cropping and skewed focus of Minimum support price policy of the government had in turn promoted monocropping. Multi cropping will benefit not only the farmer, but promote nutritional security and sustainability.

The Andaman and Nicobar Islands' strategic significance in the Indian Ocean region has been underplayed by India's policy of "masterly inactivity and benign neglect". Critically discuss.

- Parts : 3
- Background Theme : Andaman & Nicobar Islands and Indian Ocean Region
- Focus Point : Recognition of its strategic importance
- Question word : Critically Discuss

The Andaman and Nicobar Islands form the core pillar in the promotion of India's Indo Pacific policy because of its strategic location.

(Why is it important?)

Strategic significance of Andaman Nicobar Island—

1. Location is at the choke point that is near the Strait of Malacca.
2. Access and securing the sea line of communication and trade. For example, India's 50% of trade by volume passes by this route.
3. Net security provider in the Indian Ocean region to support countries like Vietnam, Philippines for anti-piracy patrolling and dealing with natural disasters.
4. To curb the aggressive tactics of the Chinese, for example, countering the string of pearls strategy and the OBOR projects astounded by the Asia-Africa growth corridor by India and Japan.
5. Security and defence exercises. For example KAVACH and MPX with Japan

6. Sea and Underwater patrolling.

(About the policy mentioned in question)

In Spite of the above mentioned strategic significance since long time The Andaman and Nicobar Island were ignored under the policy of Masterly inactivity and benign neglect-

1. Neglect of development at the Andaman and Nicobar Islands.
2. Slow pace of building infrastructure projects.
3. Mainly seen as a tourism destination and not as a strategic one.
4. General Isolation of the tribes in these islands.
5. Low presence of the armed forces, which leads to increased presence of China in the Indian Ocean region.

(Critical discussion showing the current efforts and policy)

But recently there has been a change in approach and acknowledgement of the Island' s significance and its strategic utilisation and a policy of 'Proactive development' is being pursued. This can be through the following steps taken,

1. High speed optical fibre connection between Chennai and Andaman Nicobar.
2. Andaman Nicobar Integrated theatre command was set up for effective use of the trilateral armed forces. Regular kavach exercise is being conducted.
3. Focus on development by the building of a ship repair facility and dry dock.

4. Building of strategic infrastructure to counter the rise of China in the Indo Pacific region.
5. Sagarmala project for port development.

(Conclusion showing broader picture)

The long existent policy of masterly inactivity and benign neglect has rightly been revisited and there has been a policy shift towards proactive government engagement in order to promote Andaman and Nicobar island as a strategic location. This will help India to be better prepared in the backdrop of the changing geopolitical scenario.

GS PAPER 4

You are an officer in charge of transfer and posting of personnel ofa particular department. This position is very difficult mainly for two reasons: (i) people closer to the power corridor try to influence you and (ii) women officers often send requests to postpone transfers orders on the pretext of family responsibilities. Consider the following situations and give your views with suitable explanations.

(a) A Cabinet Minister sends a D.O letter to you regarding posting of an official on a supposedly 'lucrative assignment' for which you have already decided about the name of a more competent officer with a good track record for honesty, integrity, probity and timely delivery. What will you do?

(b) As per the rule in your department, every officer needs to be transferred from one destination to another after three years. A woman officer comes to you with a request to provide medical treatment to her ageing and

sick in-laws who need constant clinical help. But according to her innate qualities and high level of expertise, the new destination would need only an officer like her to deliver best results and meet official targets. What will you do?

(c) The position of in charge of transfer and posting provides a very lucrative opportunity to cultivate liaison for a lifetime. One should not be 'too idealistic' to Opportunities '. and adopt a 'pragmatic approach'. Do you agree? Give reasons

{Role is that of a Civil Servant and hence, the characteristics best relevant here are highlighted at the very outset. Challenge in this job is also given}

Being a civil servant, adherence to public service values of Impartiality, Integrity, Transparency as well as efficient duty is of paramount importance. Since, this posting makes one vulnerable to pressure, careful analysis and objective decisions alone can ensure effective discharge of duty.

(a) In this scenario, the Minister is trying to make an undue influence on authority by proposing a name for appointment without any objective criteria. This can harm effective functioning at work. Hence I would appoint the person who has been already selected based on track record for the assignment. In addition, due to the considerable position of recommendatory authority, I would carefully analyse the competency of the recommended candidate for suitability on another position based on past work record, efficiency, honesty, promotion level and career choice. If the candidate is found suitable, he/

she can be appointed at a similar position but based only on objectivity and Impartiality.

{We are trying to balance the rule of transfer along with value of Sensitivity and Consideration towards staff}

(b) In this case, since the officer has genuine capabilities and appears to be an honest woman officer, I would try to choose an area which is closer to her current posting, out of goodwill and as a recognition of her dedicated work. But if no such possibility is found, then I would personally exhort her to uphold the duty and take up the charge in paramount public interest. I would also brief her about the importance of her assignment. Meanwhile, suitable arrangements can be made for the sick in laws, in the current area itself and she could be considered for a lighter assignment after this one.

(c) Every position in administration has a distinct set of demands and opportunities which require specific kinds of behaviour and thinking. Being in charge of transfer, allows one to cultivate liaison and act as a communication link between subordinates and seniors. But this liaison can also force one to sacrifice on values of impartiality and objectivity. The work of an officer in charge is not to develop liaison but to discharge duty to the best of his/her capability.

Here ignoring such opportunities might sound prima facie idealistic, but it's rather pragmatic to avoid being favoured or favouring other relations, indulging oneself in needless "deals" and "compromises". This will prevent future trouble and help one discharge duty without any question on integrity.

Strength does not come from physical capacity but from an indomitable will – Gandhi.

What does strength mean to you and how far do you agree with the given statement?

Discuss with suitable examples

- Parts : 1
- Background Theme : Strength as a quality
- Focus Point : what does Mahatma Gandhi's statement mean to you
- Question word : Discuss with examples

(What is Strength ?)

The strength in ethics is about the strength of morality and character of an individual. The background of the statement is that for a human being and society, the will power is far more important than the physical strength to achieve the desired goal.

(What does strength mean to you?)

Strength to me is about the ability to stand by my values even during adversities. For example, during college, there is a pressure by peers and few teachers to have alcohol but my strength was to say NO. Further as a believer of karma yoga, my strength is to make purposeful decisions showing empathy and actions that are beyond selfishness.

(Views on Quote given)

I strongly agree with Gandhi's statement that physical strength is only temporary and it is the will to stand strong without being defeated mentally which makes the difference. For example Kauravas in Mahabharata had much stronger army and better generals but the will of the Pandavas and right advice of Dharma by Krishna helped them win the war. Krishna Gopal Tiwari, IAS became the first blind person to be leading the district like any other collector.

Hence, it is the spirit of service and the mental ability to do your best even against adverse circumstances is what will make any individual a strong personality.

How are ethical concerns and work culture of public institutions different from those of private institutions? Examine the desirability of adoption of work culture similar to private institutions in public institutions

- Parts : 2
- Background Theme : Work culture and Ethics
- Focus Point : Comparison of Public and private institutions
- Hinted flow :

	Public	Private Institutions
Ethical concerns	–	–
Work culture		

Desirability of adoption

- Question word : How, Examine

(Introduction- what is good work culture)

A Good Work culture refers to creating a positive, safe and inspirational working environment for all. Ethical concerns and work culture of private and public institutions are compared below :

(I Part- comparison in both)

Public Institutions	Private Institutions
Public service delivery to the citizens is the major goal.	Service delivery to the customers from a profit making perspective is the goal.
There are general promotions and stability of work roles & jobs .	Performance-based incentives and promotions that encourage training and better quality of work.
Gender representation is a matter of right. For example, the Panchayati Raj institutions have fixed reservations for women.	Skewed gender ratio at managerial and decision making positions.
Funds are public in nature and the government is accountable to each and every citizen.	Financial accountability is limited only to the investors.
Public accountability on operations keeps external checks. Example - RTI, public protest etc	Policies like hire and fire are prevalent and since profit is the major motive.

Social security protection is much deeper.	Social security is not generally considered as the institution's responsibility.

(II Part - desirability)

Desirability of the adoption of private work culture in public institutions is because of the following reasons -

1. Person with good performance is promoted and incentivised to do better.
2. Better efficiency since there is a competitive environment for the available positions.
3. Less rigid hierarchy in working and reporting. Informal environments are also promoted in order to make a better working atmosphere.
4. Teamwork is promoted and greater freedom of expression.
5. Training and upgradation of skills is incentivised.

(Conclusion telling the objectives of public institutions)

But the social objective of public institutions in good governance like the values of compassion, sustainable development should not be diluted while adopting the private work culture. Also the private institutions must learn discipline and accountability mechanisms of the public sector for better corporate governance.

***

14

Essay Writing

PATTERN AND SYLLABUS OF ESSAY PAPER

The Essay Paper is one of the nine papers in the UPSC civil services mains exam. In this paper, one will have to write two essays in the span of 3 hours, each with the word count of 1000 - 1200 words.The Essay Paper is for a total of 250 marks. This Paper is divided into two parts, A and B. Each part will contain 4 essay topics. The candidate will have to choose one topic each from these two parts, and each essay will be evaluated for 125 marks.

There is no set syllabus mentioned by the UPSC for this paper. The only thing mentioned in the syllabus part is the following,

"Candidates may be required to write essays on multiple topics. They will be expected to keep closely to the subject of the essay to arrange their ideas in orderly fashion, and to write concisely. Credit will be given for effective and exact expression."

But broadly we can divide the type of topics asked into,

1. General Studies and Static topics related Essays.

2. Philosophical and quotation based Essays.

The combination of these two types of essay in both parts of the paper varies every year and hence one cannot predict and prepare only one type of an essay.

IMPORTANCE OF ESSAY PAPER

Even though this paper forms only 20% of the weightage according to the marks distribution of General Studies (250 on 1250), this paper plays a vital role in deciding your final total. There are ample examples to show us how this paper affects one's rank.

For Example - Our dear friend and batchmate Girish K had scored 434 / 1000 marks in all the General studies papers combined, which must be among the top 20 in our batch. But he ended up scoring only 105 marks in essay paper that year, which brought down his overall written total. Despite a good optional score of 312 he got a Rank of 307. Even with an average marks of around 130 he could have easily ended up within Top 100 that year and could have been alloted the Indian Administrative Service.

Another important aspect of this paper is the Uncertainty of the marking pattern. No matter even if you have scored very well in your test series papers and are very confident about your capability of writing a good essay, you might end up scoring poor marks in the Final examination if you are not careful enough while attempting the paper.

This variation was evident in Nagarjun's marks at two consecutive attempts in UPSC. In CSE 2017, he scored a good 146 in the Essay paper. He had attempted the Farmers Issue and Women Empowerment related essays. But in CSE2018 he scored a lesser mark of only 101 which in turn affected his overall rank. In the quest of scoring higher marks he chose an essay topic (Philosophical essay this time) whose interpretation was dicey over an essay topic which he was sure about. He did this because he felt that the other topic would have been more commonly chosen by the other examinees. This proved to be a mistake retrospectively. This is to say that this paper can make or break your years of effort over a small lapse of concentration or judgement. So along with your preparation for this paper one must be very vigilant while attempting this paper.

HOW TO PREPARE??

SOURCES

There is no set syllabus, materials or resources for Essay. While the essay paper is generalistic, the evaluation will be quite subjective. This is a reason for a lot of variation in the marks obtained by the same person in this paper over different years. Essay paper is not majorly a test of your knowledge, but more about your thought process and the way your points are arranged and presented in a specific concise manner.

While preparing for General Studies, you will go through a lot of static material and current articles. Basically, this is your fodder for essay paper. There is absolutely NO requirement to exclusively study some topic only for essay paper. What you read for GS is more or less sufficient background knowledge and finally it comes down to the understanding of the question and presentation of the available knowledge in the form of an essay. If you observe past 5-10 years of Essay Paper, there are certain topics which have been asked multiple times in various forms. For these topics, one can prepare brief notes in the form of compilation of static material and facts so that you have a ready reference of resources. This will be your material when it comes to essay paper and will come handy in GS papers too.

Content wise as a paper this requires the least effort among all and thereby strategizing and smartly framing your essay becomes vital in scoring good marks.

The relevant topics have been compiled for your reference.

1. Women Empowerment related issues.

2. Social Justice topics like Equality, Equity, Climate justice etc.

3. Human Development of India and World - Poverty, Health and Education .

4. International Relations specially in the context of neighbouring countries, border disputes and major global issues like Climate Change, Terrorism, Post covid world etc.

5. Farmer Welfare Issues.

6. Emerging Technologies like Artificial Intelligence, Cryptocurrency, Metaverse, Blockchain Technology, Big data etc (Disruptive technologies) and its impact, relevance on different sections of the Society and Economy both Global and Indian.

7. Traditional and Social Media with focus on News and Journalism.

8. Centre and State Relations.

9. Ethical issues, Human Values, Emotional intelligence and other important topics mentioned in GS 4 paper in the form of Quotations and sayings.

10. Multi Dimensional aspects of the Indian Economy.

One can prepare brief notes on these above-mentioned topics with Definitions, Facts, Figures, Reports, Rankings, Quotes, Examples, Anecdotes etc. An example for the same is attached below.

—/—/—

WOMEN AND INVISIBLE WORK

1) We can't have women's liberations w/o questioning the fundamental division of labour that drives patriarchy. -women primarily burdened w/ unpaid care work and confined to home / hearth, private sphere.

2) We can't break the public/private binary by women competing in a man's world, by foll. the rules set by men and in a world made for men.

3) In this process, what's problematic is not women losing feminine traits but erasure of female labour & contribution to sustaining humanity.

[Women's Unpaid Care Work: Women perform 75% of whole
India:- 10 to 12 times.]

>> It's because women cannot give up unpaid care work that their access to paid work is severely limited leading to a vicious cycle. Even if they do find a work, they are saddled w/ both paid & unpaid work.

>> Women constitute ✓ - 60% Agricultural labar force Asia Africa
Women own ✓ 20% Agricultural land
Women constitute ✓ 60% World's Chronically hungry

>> Even when women enter sports, they are forced to conform to dominant notions of feminity.

* Even when some women, break out of the private sphere and enter public sphere, unpaid work falls on lowly paid women domestic help from the most marginalised backgrounds & poor immigrant women.

* Women's Empowerment is not merely about becoming wrestlers, fighter pilots etc for real equality, its imperative that women's care work be given its due material recognition.

* It would mean a thorough rendering of gender norms, not by a few women entering the men's turf but by men entering women's turf. & taking on 'feminine' unpaid work which is what will allow women secure paid employment.

* Female Labour force participation in India
  - ✓ 2004 – 31%
  - ✓ 2011 – 24%

  India ranks 11th from bottom in Women's Labour force participation rates.

→ Along w/ Mahavir Phogats, Arunachalam ~~Mudanth~~ Muruganantham.

CRIMES AGAINST WOMEN : FACTORS & TREND ANALYSIS

Factors that tend to affect crimes against women.

1. Affluence / GDP.

1% inc in GDP ⟶ 0.42% dec in crime

If alcoholism / substance abuse are treated better, chances of crime are low.

2. Sex Ratio :

1% inc in Sex Ratio ⟶ 8% dec in crime

Skewed sex ratio undermines the affluence effect

Eg: (Delhi, Haryana)

3. Female literacy and Labour Force Participation

(−) backlash by unemployed males - retaliatory physical sexual abuse

(+) If brutality in marriage is unbearable, exit options are more viable.

4. Rural to Urban Population Ratio

1% dec in ratio ⟶ 0.4 dec in crime

Though crimes in urban areas have ↑ visibility, rural women are ↑ vulnerable.

5. Religion / Customs / Cultural Norms

1% inc share of Hindus ⟶ 1.64% inc in crime

wife beating, dowry deaths, bride burning still relevant.

6. Media Activism

1% inc in readership ⟶ 1.9% dec in crimes

greater reporting greater crime deterrance effect

ESSAY WRITING PRACTISE

The most important strategy of preparation for this paper is practising writing a sufficient number of Essays during your preparation. This is the key around which your whole essay paper preparation should be based.

When to start practising Essays ?

Essay questions are mostly generalistic in nature unlike your Optional and General Studies questions. So one can start practising essays right away from the beginning days of your preparation without waiting for any sufficient background knowledge to be acquired or portions to be completed.

Everybody would have written essays in their school days. So one knows how to write an essay and the framework of an essay. It's just that they will be hesitant to start writing.

Consider the following questions -

1) Destiny of a nation is shaped in its classrooms.

(UPSC CSE 2017)

2) Your perception of me is a reflection of you; my reaction to you is an awareness of me.

(UPSC CSE 2021).

These two essays were asked in the CSE Mains paper. Now if you look at these questions as a beginner, you do understand the meaning of the Quote. This is enough to begin with, to understand the given question. You just have to sit down and prepare a broad framework of your essay by jotting down the points which strike your mind and then start writing the Essay right away.

Remember this, The quality of the first essay of all the aspirants will be the same. It is only how one builds upon it and sustains the practice makes the difference between Toppers and Aspirants subsequently.

Time table for Essay writing practice?

Every week, you must practise writing at least one essay. This can be alternatively either related to static subject or philosophical essay. Allot a specific time every week to write on a topic and try adhering to the Word limit (I used to write every Sunday afternoon). Initially, timing can be kept flexible as developing the thought process and structure is more important.

The framing of essays, inclusion of arguments and its presentation will only get better with practice, just like GS answers. Sample questions can be found online on various websites, from some test series or one can choose previous years topics (suggested).

Kindly make sure you write at least one essay on each of the topics above mentioned to get a hold of the facts of each of those while reproducing on the paper. This will be particularly helpful in static topic related essays in the final exams. For Philosophical essays, you can choose any random quote and practice,as in these essays it's the understanding of the question and the flow of thought in support of your argument that is more important than facts.

How to improve the language and vocabulary?

Essay is a complete text in itself. It should come out as whole with different parts attached to each other in an orderly manner. Though Subheads can be given, Writing in points is definitely not an option in Essay. Hence, proper language and good vocabulary is helpful in essays.

To develop these, Reading Newspaper, Reports, Articles will be more than SUFFICIENT. There is no need for separate preparation of any sort just to improve your Language and Vocabulary.

Choose some reputed newspaper and magazine as your source of reading. Your daily News paper reading will make you come across new words and subject related terms, noting down these words with meaning would be a useful exercise to improve your vocabulary.

It is important to remember that Essay writing does not require flowery language or advanced Vocabulary. All it requires is concisely presenting the ideas in an effective manner. The more dimensions you illustrate in your essay, the more it reflects your deep understanding about the topic.

CHOOSING A TOPIC IN THE EXAM

As stated above, you are required to write a text of 1000-1200 words, this comes down to around 8-10 printed pages depending on the hand writing (12 pages are allotted on the UPSC answer sheet per essay) . Writing such a long text requires explaining multiple dimensions of the topic given. For this, you must have a fair understanding of the topic, or what is being conveyed in any quotation/ statement.

Many times, it happens that among the topics given, one of them appears to be very common which we have a fair idea about. There might be another topic, which we are not very sure about, but still to appear different, we choose the latter and end up not writing up to the mark.

So the following points can be kept in mind while choosing:-

1. Understanding the question and its requirements.
2. Awareness level about the topic.

3. Knowledge of multiple dimensions around the topic.
4. Additional Fact, Report, Quotation, Current Development about the topic.
5. Chances of showing out some positive mindset in the conclusion.

Understanding the question becomes the most vital aspect in choosing the essay topic on the day of examination. If one understands the essay question and its requirement in the answer correctly, with the available GS background knowledge they will mostly end up scoring at least average marks in that essay.

Many aspirants whohave ended up scoring less marks in the essay would have gone wrong in this aspect. This is why philosophical essays are difficult. If the interpretation of the question goes wrong, (most common among philosophical essays) then your whole essay would be wrong.

Consider the following Essay questions -

1. If development is not engendered, it is endangered. (UPSC CSE 2016).

   This particular question created a lot of noise during CSE 2016, the word engendered was differently understood by different candidates and thus creating confusion among the candidates who attempted this question (Later on UPSC gave clarification about the same). It is generally advisable to avoid selecting such confusing questions.

2. Customary morality cannot be a guide to modern life. (UPSC CSE 2018)

   This question was asked in the background of Sabarimala case proceedings in the Honourable supreme court , as this was one of the burning issues during that year. If one has paid enough attention to the case proceedings they will be aware of the topic and can come up with a better essay than their counterparts ending up with better marks.

Another mistake that many candidates make is to change the chosen topics midway while attempting the paper. This mistake should be avoided at any cost. Answer papers will have a fixed number of sheets and this will also cause you to lose a lot of precious time and create panic in your mind in the examination hall. Take your own time while selecting the question based on the above mentioned checklist and once selected dont change the question if not for an absolute necessity.

So it is to say that selection of the question becomes a vital preliminary step in scoring good marks and the candidate must be double sure while deciding upon the questions and once chosen there should be no second thoughts.

PLANNING THE ESSAY/ BRAINSTORMING

Before you actually start writing the essay, it's important to give some time to brainstorm and chalk out the arguments around which your essay will be based. Do not hurry to start the essay right away. One gets 1.5 hrs to write one essay in the exam. For writing a text of 1000-1200 words, 1 hour 15 minutes is more than sufficient. You can use 10-15 minutes in brainstorming the structure of the essay. A sample of my essay brainstorming note is attached herewith.

In this, you can write down the Points, Quotes or Arguments, Data and whatever you feel will be relevant in the essay and number them in sequence to get the right flow of the essay . This Essay skeleton will provide you with a framework while you are actually writing the essay. There may be other points which you think about in the course of writing. Add them appropriately without breaking the flow of the text.

For an essay titled - Are We witnessing the lowest point of parliamentary democracy in India? Attached following is the brainstorming rough work followed by the first page of the essay.

Are we witnessing the lowest point of Parliamentary Democracy in India?

"There is no higher a responsibility than to be a member of the sovereign body responsible for the fate of vast number of human beings"

— J.L. Nehru

The ethos with which our founding fathers adopted the Constitution of India on Nov 26, 1949 were firmly based on democratic principles. They chose the Parliamentary democracy not only as it reflected our experience by Govt of India Act 1935, but as it also suited Indian diversity. The Institution of Parliament could incorporate viewpoints of vast majority in Lok Sabha, while Rajya Sabha gave voices to the States as federal units or stakeholders. The separation of judiciary ingrained in Article 50 ensured sound practical judgements / jurisprudence. Similarly, a system of checks and balances for executive scrutiny and a constitutionally established Election Commission gave expression to our Civil and Political Rights.

UPSC provides 2 rough pages/essay, you shall use these pages for the brainstorming purpose.

CHARACTERISTICS OF A GOOD ESSAY/ HOW TO WRITE A GOOD ESSAY?

A general question we often come across is, how to write a good essay?? Though there is nothing such as Good essay, there are certain characteristics, Do's and Don'ts which are generally advised to be followed while writing an essay to present your ideas in a better manner and thus to score good marks.

1. **Word limit-**

   Adhering to the word limit will always be well rewarded. Word limits are designed to let the candidates express their view points in a complete yet concise manner. It's a good practice to know the number of words one generally writes in a page while writing test series essay papers. You can also roughly calculate the number by counting the words in the first line and multiplying it with the number of lines written in a sheet. Maintaining an average count will be sufficient, neither on the higher nor on the lower side.

2. **Flow of Text** -

   Since Essay is a long composition, the flow and coherence of ideas is very important. All the dimensions, arguments or aspects that you talk about in the essay must be put one after the other in a logical flow. If you give enough time for planning what to write, it will be better for arranging the ideas in an organised manner. This will give a proper flow to the text.

3. **Transition Sentences and Phrases** -

   Having smooth transitions in the essay text is very crucial. They help the examiner to progress from one idea to the next idea. Thus, helping to build up coherent relationships within the text. How the ideas are connected with one another, needs to be illustrated very clearly in context.

In case of Paragraphs, this can be done by giving a hint at the End of Previous Paragraph or at the start of Next Paragraph as to what particular topic/ aspect is being addressed later. Question sentences can be made or an explanatory sentence can be added like - 'Are there any Political factors involved?' Or 'We will explore the importance of data in the Health sector.' Apart from between paragraphs, Proper Connecting Words and phrases must be used within the text also.

For Example,

a. To show Agreement-Moreover, Equally, In Consequently, Firstly, addition, similarly, secondly etc

b. To show Opposition - On the contrary, In Contrast, Albeit, Although, however, Nevertheless

c. Examples and Emphasis - As an illustration, notably, in fact, For Instance, Truly, Important to realise, Significantly

d. To show result -Thereby, Accordingly, Henceforth, For this reason

e. For Summary - In the whole analysis, After All, to sum up, Altogether, ultimately

f. For Chronology - Sooner or later, Eventually, To begin with, Occasionally, As soon as

4. Subheadings and Underlining -

To provide proper flow to the text and still address various aspects, You can use subheadings to indicate the change in upcoming ideas. This will make sure that the multiple ideas in your essay are directly highlighted in the eyes of the reader. Similarly, Underlining major ideas in any paragraph or key terms will help emphasise it.

5. **Language and Vocabulary-**

   As mentioned before, flowery language or complicated vocabulary should be better avoided. UPSC Essay is not a piece of Literature, but a comprehensive account of the topic asked. The language should be simple yet effective. Grammatical Errors must be avoided as much as possible. They take attention away from the idea of the text to language. Some Keywords relevant to the topic, can be mentioned accordingly.

6. **Legibility and Neatness -**

   Handwriting need not be calligraphic, but should be legible enough. The Reader should be able to read out what's written without putting in much effort. Scribbling, Over- Writing or Cancellation of words / Paragraphs should be avoided as far as possible. Basic neatness in the paper makes it adequately presentable.

The best examples of a Good Essay will be editorials and various magazine articles which you read during the course of your preparation. These articles/editorials are basically written on a particular topic, the author will try to convey his/her viewpoint to the reader through an essay. While reading these, pick up those articles which convince you strongly towards the author's ideology / observations and observe carefully how they have conveyed it in the form of an essay and later try to inculcate the learnings in your essay writing practice. This exercise will help the aspirants immensely in essay writing.

STRUCTURING THE ESSAY

After brainstorming about what all to include, you must structure the essay. Usually an essay is structured in the form of Introduction, Body Paragraphs and then Conclusion. Let's look at them one by one, what all to include and what to avoid in different parts.

INTRODUCTION

Introduction is the starter of an Essay whose purpose is to convey to the reader what will be covered in the text or body to follow. In the Exam, How you write an introduction shows whether or not you have understood the topic and its scope. The first one or two sentences are the 'Hook' where you can grab the attention of the reader and make the essay appear interesting to read. Here, Clear Concise statements must be used and long-complex statements are to be avoided.

1. When writing an introduction, you can use a 'general to specific' structure. That is, introduce the problem or topic of the essay in a general sense to provide context, and then narrow it down to one's particular position and line of argument.

   Example : For an Essay Titled- "Self- Reliance in Energy Sector"

   India is the third largest energy producing and consuming country in the world. The energy consumption pattern in India is changing with the better standard of living and high propensity to consume. Overall energy use has doubled since 2000 due to macroeconomic factors like expanding economy, urbanisation, industrialisation and population.

So to catch up with the increasing demand of energy, there is a need to make arrangements for a secure and sustainable form of energy.

2. One can use an anecdote or a story format to write an introduction and provide context to the Essay subject.

   Example : For an Essay titled "Data is the New Oil of 21st Century but it may smoke out Privacy"

   Mahesh is a software engineer educated in the USA and an entrepreneur. His start up has been hitting headlines and conversation in the film industry. He has developed a software which captures the 'Expression of person'using their own Mobile Front camera while they watch a preview movie clip. Using facial recognition technology, this information helps movie producers correct their scenes for best experience! No wonder, he has been getting calls from Fox Studios, Pixar, and many more. Sounds Great? Truly! But think again. What if the facial markers and video clips of his clients are leaked? What if the data is manipulated and pictures are morphed? This brings us to the fact that Data has really become the new Oil or Resource in the 21st century, however it also poses new challenges and threats.

3. Using a Quotation or Couplet can convey the idea in a brief yet effective manner. After the quote, the central idea can be elaborated further.

   Example : For an Essay titled, "Role of MicroFinance and Microcredit in transforming Rural India"

   "Give a man a fish, he'll eat for a day, Give a woman, micro credit, she, her husband, her children and her extended family will eat for a lifetime."

   - Paul David Hweson

Example : For an Essay titled, "The highest result of Education is Tolerance"

"It's the mark of an educated mind to entertain a thought without accepting it"

- Aristotle

4. Using relevant data points and examples as evidence to support can also be used as our opening statements.

   Example : For an Essay titled, "Child Labour - A Necessary Evil or Plain Evil?"

   According to the United Nations Report, there are 30 Million Child labourers in India in the age group of 5-18 years. This striking figure presents a gloomy picture about the 'State of Childhood' in India. Being an agriculturally dominant country, it is natural that more than 50% of child labour is concentrated in the farm sector. Besides this children work in hazardous places like firecracker making, bidi rolling, zari work, carpet weaving, bangle making etc. In urban areas, roadside dhabas and other hotels employ children largely. Families with both working parents employ young girls for the household chores and for taking care of little children at home.

5. Using Question words to connect the topic is another way in which the idea is conveyed in a conversational style.

   Example: For an essay titled, "Normal Human activity is Worse for nature than the greatest Nuclear Accident in History"

   The Indian Philosophical thought lays emphasis on 5 elements of Nature that are said to compose a human body. The water, the Air, the Fire, The Sky and the Soil. These elements are the basic foundation of our life on Earth. Nature is the best gift of mankind which allows us to grow, adapt, survive and develop. But do we care about the Nature that Nurtures us each day? Have we tried to use it sustainably and conserve it in pristine form? Probably Not.

6. Sometimes the Essay consists of certain keywords. These can be elaborated on appropriately in the initial part of the essay. In the following title, terms like Social Justice can be elaborated as that is the central theme of the essay.

   Example : There Can Be No Social Justice Without Economic Prosperity But Economic Prosperity Without Social Justice Is Meaningless

Ending the Introduction :

It's helpful to end the introduction by signposting what will be covered in each part. Here you can provide a clear sense of direction so that a structure is created in the reader's head. This can be done by telling what all dimension the essay will be covering sequentially. Thus in one paragraph, the reader can understand the flow of your text.

Similarly, one link paragraph can be created that recognises the other side of the topic and creates a background for the forecoming text.

Example : For an Essay titled "Language should not be a barrier, but a facilitator"

Language allows you to not only communicate your feelings after a careful articulation of thoughts but language is also what gives us our identity and cultural mark. Presumably this is the reason why language is also used often politically to segregate us and create barriers among humanity.

Every essay has a central theme around which the arguments are based. This central theme or focus must be conveyed at the outset in the introduction. On an average, it can be around 10% of the Essay, which comes to 100 - 120 words.

BODY PARAGRAPHS

After introducing the Central theme of the Essay, we then move forward to convey our arguments in different dimensions one after the other.

These are covered in the Body Paragraphs of the essay. It is here that the topic is elaborated, illustrated and explained in detail.

HOW TO WRITE?

1. The number, length and order of your paragraphs depends on what you're writing and how you're trying to convey. This is where the Flow of the essay comes into picture. The arguments should be presented in a coherent manner and should be relevant to the Central idea of the Essay.
2. Each body paragraph must start with one key idea or claim which will be the Topic Sentence. It will make clear what dimension is being addressed in that paragraph. Next you can elaborate this idea further.
3. Then, the idea must be supported by Relevant examples and evidence in the form of statistics, case studies, government initiatives, quotations, documentary evidence etc.
4. Finally, a Link should be provided as to how this argument is relevant to the central idea. Transition sentences or phrases must also be used to explain what to expect further in the essay.

Example: For an essay titled,"Child Labour - A Necessary Evil or Plain Evil?"

At this juncture we must find out if we have taken any steps to tackle child labour. *(Topic sentence)* The Child Labour law in India was recently amended to prohibit all kinds of work for children aged 5 - 14 years and hazardous work also. But exceptions for media, own family business and entertainment was made which is a grey area in itself that can be exploited badly. Besides, the new Anti Trafficking legislation establishes a stringent framework to nab the perpetrators and rehabilitate the victims. Also, many NGOs and private institutions like Bachpan Bachao Andolan, Child Rights and You (CRY) work towards alleviating the condition. (Providing examples of Law, Policies, NGOs etc) But these efforts might not be enough. For a problem that is rooted in our socio-economic milieu, punitive or temporary provision cannot be a long- term solution. (Linking the upcoming idea of how the laws are not enough, but social change is a must)

Subheadings can be used in an essay to show what exactly the coming paragraphs are about. In an essay, note that a subheading should comprise at least 2-3 paragraphs. Do not put sub heads like in GS answer.

Example : For an essay titled, "The Changing Identities of Cities in 21st Century" following subheadings can be used:

Structural Changes in the city

Paras about : Economic Aspects

: Technological and Innovation based changes

: Cultural Changes

: Recreational Aspects

The Negative Changes in the city

Paras about : Rising Socio-Economic Inequalities

: Crime and Law & Order issues

: Changes in family structure and Individualism

: Environmental Damages

WHAT TO WRITE?

The body paragraphs are meant to open up different dimensions of the topic and provide a respective viewpoint on them. This can be done in multiple ways. Some examples are listed below and you can mix and match based on the nature of the topic.

1. Temporal : For those topics that are linear in nature or can be represented on a timeline, the Essay can be started from a Historical perspective i.e the Past, then addressing the Present Situation or condition and finally, writing how it is expected to be in the Future.

   Example : For an essay titled, "Importance of Indian Ocean Region for India and India's influence over it"

   The Essay can open up how historically the Indian Ocean Region has been important for the country by giving examples of historical trade, exchange of goods, exports, travel of culture during Ancient times, Cholas, British times etc. Then the current opportunities and importance can be elaborated and finally the prospects can be highlighted.

2. Issues/Problems --Causes Solutions Challenges -- Opportunities : If an essay is talking about some social problem or national/international issue then flow can be designed by opening up different aspects of the problem, then writing about their causes or reasons, offering solutions. If need be, challenges in

implementing the solutions can be highlighted. The opportunities can be highlighted as well.

Example - For Essay titled, "Neglect of Primary Health Care and Education in India are reasons for its backwardness "

The topic is a blunt comment on the reason for India's backwardness. In this, the problems of Healthcare and education can be elaborated with examples, data and impact it has had. But the essay should not be completely based on it. Outlining the challenges being faced in the sectors, you can suggest some Solutions and also give examples of best practises or opportunities.

3. Various aspects like Social, Economic, Political, Administrative, Legal, Cultural, Technological can be talked about in an essay which has such scope. This is especially possible when impact or reasons for some fact are supposed to be elaborated. Here to remember the various fields of impact or reasons you can just skim through the mains syllabus in your mind like in Paper 1 - Historical, Cultural, Social, Gender related, Geographical etc.

4. If it's a debatable issue, both the aspects must be talked about. In any case, the essay should not come out as only Descriptive- i.e. elaborating only on the words mentioned in the topic, but should appear Analytical - i.e. writing about the other side of the coin as well. It's not necessary to express your personal opinion but whatever you argue, you must substantiate with relevant data and examples.

5. In an essay, we can start writing on the given statement by supporting the quotation with examples and arguments. This can be done in the 70% of the essay. But in the last 20-30% of the essay, one can

provide an antithesis of the statement as well.

Example for an essay titled, "The curse of Geography"

One can start the essay by explaining how the geographical factor has caused harm and has been like a curse for people, states, economy, societies and nations. Then, as an antithesis, you can talk about how geography can be a boon and how we can turn the curse into a boon. This way we are deeply analysing the topic on various dimensions.

Whichever way you choose to open up the essay, the flow should be maintained. In a bid to include multiple aspects, losing the flow is not recommended. An essay is not as much a test of knowledge as that of your comprehension and writing.

CONCLUSION

The purpose of a conclusion is to draw together the main ideas discussed in the body of the essay. Your conclusion should give a sense of closure and completion to your argument.Whatever your essay is about, the conclusion should aim to emphasise the significance of your argument.

In introduction we move from general to the specific structure but in conclusion we do the opposite i.e. specific to general.

1. To begin your conclusion, signal that the essay is coming to an end by returning to your core argument.
2. End the conclusion by giving a broader view rather than limiting the scope of the topic. Let the argument be futuristic and optimistic also it may have practical recommendations.
3. Try to end with a strong and decisive sentence so that it gives a closure to your write up.
4. A Quote, Poem,Linking original anecdote if used in

introduction, Government Slogans etc shall be used if possible in the conclusion to add that extra flavour.

What shouldn't go in the conclusion?

1. Don't include a new argument. Any argument or analysis that is essential to supporting your thesis statement should only appear in the main body of the essay.
2. The conclusion might include minor pieces of new information-for example, a sentence or two, discussing broader implications or a quotation that nicely summarises your central point.
3. We should not bring in any new sources or ideas that need further explanation to understand.
4. Avoid simply summarising each paragraph or repeating each point in order.
5. Don't use "concluding phrases" like
   - "In conclusion..."
   - "To sum up ... "
6. Avoid using apologetic phrases that sound uncertain or confused, these undermine our argument. For example
   - "This is just one approach among many."
   - "There are good arguments on both sides of this issue."
   - "There is no clear answer to this problem."
7. Even if your essay has explored different viewpoints, your own position should be clearly emphasised in the conclusion.

Sample Essay for Understanding structure

Digital minimalism-the path towards solving social media paradox.

We all were born free but are we really?

Data and big tech around our life ;

NFTs have become the new 'art of life'.

They say, you are not alone as you have million followers and friends, but where are they when the digital game ends?

Social media could be the new cool way but an 'Apple' a day No more keeps the doctor away.!

Consider a scenario -a joint Marwari family in Gujarat Is having a family dinner together on one table but elders are discussing stock prices, females are looking at new fashion websites and children are talking on Instagram.

Now consider a scenario - Parsi urban parents in Mumbai are having dinner with a laptop on table with their young daughter, a student from Australia and a doctor in England, their son giving details of his day. Both families are connected marwadi physically and the Parsis digitally but the question is are they really connected?

> Note the usage of Anecdote or story format in the Introduction to provide a context to the paradoxes of social media.

Can social media platforms fill in the physical and emotional gaps created due to distance? Or do they increase as social media world takes over the real world?

In this essay, we aim to understand these paradoxes and contradictions of social media. We further analyse whether digital minimalism as an idea, can be a successful tool to solve this paradox or not?

Ending the introduction by signposting what can be expected in the essay or the flow of thought.

Social media - a box full of paradoxes

Social media led to a 'revolution' in connectedness, Mark Zuckerberg, exclaims, connectivity is a basic human right. We all remember coming back from school and logging into orkut profiles or Yahoo emails IDs to discuss, debate and express our day to our same school friends who we met three hours before but before those three hours we also talk to our mothers and siblings who gave us our grounding of home.

In today's world, this balance of life has taken a shift. We end up having digital conversations with family and friends, but not real conversations? The conversations with tears could be felt, laughter could be heard, touch could be experienced?

In a Netflix series, black mirror, they give an idea of how the future would look like. Like food, people would connect on the basis of ratings given to them. You would be swiping left or a ride based on profile, giving rise to 'new untouchability'.

Well, we have taken a few steps towards women empowerment through Metoo movements, but the Bois locker room controversy, (Delhi school girls graphic images pornified) explain the hollowness of empowerment.

Digital applications or channels like 'cult fit' are promoting good health but long hours on screen are giving rise to new eye, back and mental health problems. environmental consciousness through trends like Sadhguru save soil movement or Greta Thumberg 's climate change protests are on rise but the e-waste and trends like consumerism and environmental exploitation et cetera disgrace the efforts. Politically people have come together to fight the governments like the yellow nest movement or the Hong Kong democracy movement using Twitter as a tool for social change, but Cambridge analytical skills and the rise of digital surveillance. For example Pegasus spyware express an alternate picture

Further rise of social media success stories like Baba Ka Dhaba story in Delhi or Laxmi acid attack survivor through Chhapaak movie bring positive narratives but objectification and trolling of celebrities lead to dehumanising deaths through social media trials like Sushant SinghRajput case. The more connected we are becoming the more isolated we feel. Can an alternate model of digital minimalism be a solution?. Let's explore

In this first part of essay, through examples from online series, day to day happenings, the paradoxes of social media were highlighted. Note the range of examples used. The last line seeks to address the second part of the essay which is about digital minimalism.

Digital Minimalism: a way out

Digital minimalism in simple terms can be traced to the philosophy of minimalism-having as much as you need and not As per your wants. it would encompass having a limited digital life and an unlimited real existence-after all we have made digital gadgets. Digital gadgets must not define our existence. But with more than 3 billion internet users can we really step back now?

Note how the concept of Digital minimalism is being defined in simpler terms.

The social dilemma highlights how every moment of our life we are nudged to be socially active by apps like Facebook, Instagram et cetera. The giants make profit but at our cost. Every day economics could be delinked with the internet instead of 10 minute deliveries, we must look at positives of 10 minute walking to a grocery store. Of course marginalised Social sections like elderly, disabled must be given opportunities to access digital services but able to should be nudged to move away from digital world.

The political festivals called elections and religious festivals like darshanas are not about formalities and rituals. They reflect agencies of hope and open values like democracy and spiritualism. Hence we must lay emphasis on physical yatra and not digital Yatra.

An ideological, Social movements like detox weeks must be promoted to develop real social connectedness. The idea of love and marriage can be complimented by platforms like Tinder but at the end meet up and real stories must be promoted.

> How the balance of minimalism can be attained is given through practical examples.

Digital minimalism can best solve the challenge of entertainment. In this new world, binge watching movies and TV series cannot become the sole medium. watching Sachin win the World Cup of which the tunes of Vande Mataram in 2011 is unparalleled. Highlights and recordings do not do justice to the moments, the realities and the experiences.

It will not be easy but as Gandhi ji said, "we must be the change we wish to see". A family making no phone rules at the dinner table, a company promoting team bonding exercises, a nation rewarding ideas which are not digitally dividing, for example, Har Ghar Tiranga Abhiyan and a globe, promoting conversations and likes will be a happy and prosperous world. Gautam Buddha when asked about problems of life advised to go for a middle path. We must also look out at balancing the circles of digitalisation through self-awareness of the problem.

See how the penultimate paragraph comprises philosophical references to Gandhiji and Gautam Buddha in order to justify the stance of the writer. This shows rootedness of ideas in culture and philosophy.

We as a world have come out of challenges like Covid-19 pandemic and world wars. When united, we could also make a significant move towards meaningful connectivity. The world is changing and adapting to change the essence of human life. Our aim must be Sarva Loka Sukhino Bhavantu,(let the entire world be peaceful and prosperous).

Futuristic and Optimistic concluding remarks.

NOTE ON PHILOSOPHICAL ESSAY

In CSE 2020 and 2021, most of the essay options provided to choose from in the paper were either quotations or philosophical statements. Such types of essays are considered difficult by most aspirants and given an option, they try to avoid attempting them. This trend of the past few papers is more likely to be repeated in the coming years. Therefore, one must learn and practise writing philosophical essays also.

1. What to read : No separate source is required to be read for writing such essays. Reading habit of Non-fiction books might help to think in such essays in a rational manner but it's not necessary. You can rely on General studies preparation i.e. Newspaper articles, magazines, Books etc. The important thing is to use these examples to link the arguments to the topic given.

2. Selection of Topic: One and only criteria is whether or not you have understood the meaning / context of the statement? This is because in these types of essays, you will not have ready content like GS topics. You will have to create or come up with the arguments. With this, you may face a dilemma between the choice of a couple topics. Here, you must consider the supporting examples, quotes, facts, different dimensions you can explore in that topic etc. Then, based on these factors you must select your question.

3. How to Approach:

   a. Introduction : Particularly in a Philosophical essay, it is always better to elaborate the holistic meaning of the topic in the introduction itself. The motive of the introduction is to show the examiner that you have understood the topic.

Example for an essay titled, "What is research but a blind date with knowledge"

In this essay, one can start by giving an idea of the concept of blind date that is an encounter with an unknown person. This way you can explain the context of the quotation and give a background to your discussion on knowledge and research. Then we can explain how we start with a theory in research, but the actual outcome is unknown. It is only after using scientific methods of data collection and interpretation that we get to the real outcome.

b. Transition Paragraph between Introduction and Body helps in maintaining the flow. This should give an idea to the examiner about what to expect in the upcoming write up.

Example : For an Essay titled "The process of self discovery is now technologically outsourced"

In this essay, we shall discuss the meaning, various dimensions and significance of self discovery. Also, we will look into the implications of not discovering ourselves. Then, the conventional means of self- discovery will be explored. Later, we will provide examples of the technological outsourcing of the process of self discovery and its implications. In the end, we will see to what extent has it been outsourced and what other means still exist for self discovery.

c. In the Body part of such philosophical essays, one ideally cannot mention dimensions like Social, Political, Economic etc. For brainstorming you can use these dimensions to think of contextual examples. But one should not explicitly mention them topic wise.

d. How to Interpret : Since you can't open up the essay, in a usual manner, you must work on interpreting the given statement in multiple ways. This we shall discuss with an example. For an essay titled, "We can't let fear of falling let us from Flying", we can think on the following lines.

- What is meant by fear of falling? (2-3 paragraphs)

- What are the causes of fear of falling ? (2-3 paragraphs)

- Implications or Consequences of having the fear of falling - this is the actual demand of the Statement given and hence you must spend at least 40-50% of space and time on this dimension.

- What are the methods to overcome the fear of falling? (3-4 paragraphs)- As this aspect will bring about an optimistic perspective in the essay.

- Before concluding, one can talk about the antithesis of the statement i.e. Why fear is necessary at times. (2-3 paragraphs)

- [Such interpretation might not be possible for all the topics given, but if there is a scope, you should discuss on those lines.]

- For each dimension, you can give certain examples, references from books or movies or personal experience also to substantiate your argument.
- In these parts, you can also use sub-headings to make it clear to the examiner about your multiple interpretations of the statement.

We need to reiterate the key words given in the statement so that your writeup remains relevant and specific to the topic given. This shows how you can bring out multiple interpretations by reading the statement back and forth and questioning the statement.

This is just a brief idea about how to approach a philosophical essay. There is no perfect or ideal way to write such essays, but you will ONLY get better with practice. So, it is advised to practice as many philosophical essays as possible. We have given two philosophical essays written by Top two scorers of CSE 2018 in the essay paper for your reference in the annexure.

***

15

Choosing The Optional Paper

Choosing one's optional in UPSC is one of the most crucial choice in our journey. The total marks of 500(250+250) can make or break your final score. Hence, much thought and effort should be put in the same. Often times, we get confused over the choice of the subject.

There are a wide range of subjects which UPSC offers for optional. But which is the best for me? Humanities or Engineering? Pub Ad or Political Science? I faced the same dilemma and thankfully chose the right subject for myself in the first place.In this article, I'll approach some of the common questions I faced and how I handled it. On reading, you might pick up some useful things.

So, I did my graduation in Chemical Engineering. But as I had found out, it was not there as an optional for CSE, it was for Forest Service. Then next preferred based on professional qualification was Chemistry. I also realised Core chemistry is way too different. So, then I knew I would have to choose from a humanities background. I would say, it's good if you are able to choose a subject you have partly studied in graduation. As you have a basic idea about it and have given exams on the same. But if that's not possible, you can still do good.

<u>When to choose?</u> Should it be the first thing I do, when I start preparation? No, for the first 3-4 months, read General Studies and understand the subjects involved. A basic NCERT reading of history, geography, economics, sociology and political science will help you out to know what interests you and what doesn't. Give it time, don't jump the gun.

<u>What are the factors put under consideration?</u>

1. INTEREST-

How much a subject interests you is the most important factor for choosing an optional. Ultimately you will have to study the subject till Bachelor's if it's a technical subject and till Master's level for Humanities' subject. This will require devoting long hours to thick books and lots of answer writing.

2. GRADUATION SUBJECT or OVERLAP WITH GS-

If you are studying somewhat decently in your graduation, then choosing that subject will be fine, but if not so, then see the overlap of the subject with the General Studies. How much the subject can help you out with Essay or any GS paper with respect to the content? This will help you out at a later stage when you start consolidating your answers.

3. GUIDANCE and MATERIAL AVAILABLE-

One must also see what kind of guidance is available for understanding the subject if required. The approach of UPSC and answer writing is different from any other college exam. So, it is better if we have some source of guidance in any form- teacher, mentor, senior, books specific to UPSC approach etc. And also the availability of a quality test series also needs to be considered as a factor.

4. COST- BENEFIT ANALYSIS -

Also consider the time required to be invested in preparation for the optional subject. There are few optionals which have huge syllabus and are highly technical and volatile, for example optionals like Medical science. Scoring high marks is very difficult in these optionals. So you should consider if the optional preparation between Prelims and Mains will take away considerable time from your GS preparation or not while choosing the optional.

What are the factors you shouldn't really consider?

1. POPULARITY -

Please do not go by which subject is popular amongst aspirants and which is being chosen the most. If the above factors are important, then popularity will distort it and you might end up choosing a subject which does not interest you at all.

2. HIGH SCORING-

In my personal opinion, if you have interest and guidance, a good score will follow. And there is no guarantee that you will perform the same way as others are doing in the same optional subjects. And remember the fact that the UPSC scoring pattern is highly unpredictable. So this factor should be particularly avoided in your decision making.

3. PEER PRESSURE -

Many times aspirants end up choosing a particular optional based on just the advice of some senior aspirant or under the guise of group preparation with friends. This should be avoided as every individual's interests and capabilities are different.

How to narrow down on a subject if there is confusion?

This happens as more than one subject might fulfil all required parameters. In this scenario, what I did was, I chose to read the 2-3 subjects' basic books like NCERT, Prime Reference book etc for 1 WEEK EACH. This gave me an idea about the basic concepts in that subject. In this process, also go through the Previous Year's

Question Papers of the respective subjects. This will help you to understand the scope and demand of UPSC in that respect. After one week of reading each, you will be able to narrow down on 1 subject whose concepts and scope interests you the most and seems doable.

How to start with a subject in which you are a complete novice? I chose Sociology, despite doing Chemical Engineering and studying Science in 12th. My exposure to 'Sociology' as a subject was nil. But the following approach helped me to master at least the UPSC portion of the subject.

1. At the outset, I got the syllabus and past 5 years papers printed. I studied them and tried to understand basic things.

2. I studied base NCERTs of 11th and 12th to get a fair idea of subject matter.

3. Then, I made my own list of important books required for the subject. This was based on certain blogs, videos, lectures etc.

4. Since, I could not go to a professional UPSC sociology class, I used to spend some hours a day with a teacher who had some basic idea about the subject. This was the only source in my city. So, it was more of discussion, follow ups and thinking with him.

5. I saw that the DYNAMIC portion was also equally important in my subject. If that is so in yours, put this filter in your mind when you study the newspapers. This helps us to sift through articles that can be useful in our subject.

6. I referred to some online notes, but relied heavily on my own notes. They had the best of all worlds and

helped me to frame good answers.

7. In the due course, I kept referring to previous year's papers. This helps to align one's trajectory with the UPSC demand. Do not try to 'master' the subject as a whole or become an expert. Just master the UPSC portion required. That is all.
8. Adequate answer writing, framing of pattern of approaching an answer can be really helpful.
9. In most optional subjects, some themes and concepts are repeatedly asked across many years. So, while studying, put more effort into understanding those repeating concepts. This will help secure some marks in the exam.
10. Joining a test series after mains or around December the previous year, helped me out to gauge my level of preparation and make course corrections.

To summarise, the optional should be chosen very rationally considering all the factors with subject interest being the primary criteria. This is because at the end of the day, the ratio of the successful candidates in all the optionals to the number attempted will be more or less the same with few exceptions of technical subjects. Optional marks are very crucial, so choose wisely the one in which you can maximise your individual marks.

***

16

Compulsory Language Paper

In UPSC Mains, apart from the above mentioned papers, there are 2 Compulsory Language Papers as well. The scores of these papers do not add up to the final score of Mains, but they are qualifying in nature. It is compulsory to qualify these papers which means that if you do not qualify in these 2 language papers by getting the bare minimum marks, your other papers will not even be evaluated.

One paper is the Compulsory English Language Paper and the other one is to be chosen by the Examinee among the scheduled languages . Many students choose Hindi or regional languages like Marathi, Gujarati, Kannada, Tamil etc.

According to the syllabus,

The aim of the paper is to test the candidate's ability to read and understand serious discursive prose, and to express his ideas clearly and correctly in the English/ Indian language concerned.

Since it's qualifying in nature, one is not generally required to do some separate preparation for this paper. You only need to score 75 out of 300 Marks in both the papers.

But, this does not mean you completely ignore it and be overconfident. One can Solve past 3 years papers' to understand the pattern and see if there are any areas that you will need to brush up.

As for the English Language Paper, the pattern of questions would be broadly as follows:-

1. Short Essay :

Word limit is 600 words and it comprises 100 marks. There are 4 options available out of which 1 has to be chosen. This is a shorter version of the Essay which you will write as a separate paper. So you would have already prepared for this part thoroughly.

Examples of Essay Topics in this sections are:

a. Journalism has been rendered into Sensationalism

b. Education as a means to serve Humanity

c. Not Rural, Not Urban, India needs Rurban Growth

d. The Crying need for embracing Minimalism

2. Comprehension :

The Reading Comprehension is like an Unseen Passage which is of 75 marks. It is a common question which we would have faced in our Schools or Colleges. One has to read the passage and then answer the questions which are based on the comprehension. One can pick up lines from the passage and supplement it based on your own understanding.

3. Precis Writing:

Precis is basically a short piece of a writing that gives only the main facts or ideas about something. For Precis, consisting of 75 marks, you are given a long passage and are asked to reduce it into 1/ 3 rd as a precis. In this, you can use your own words to reduce the size of the piece and provide a summary of the passage given.

4. Usage, Vocabulary and Grammar:

Remaining 50 marks are asked from English Usage, Grammar like Indirect - Direct Speech, Active-Passive Voice etc. But this portion is less and one need not put in large efforts in this area.

Once you solve past 3 year papers, you'll get a basic idea of how the questions are asked and the paper is mostly asked on similar lines every year.

Note : For the candidates who aren't from an English medium background, one need not worry much as the paper is generally on the easier side and with basic English knowledge one can easily understand the questions and come up with a suitable answer. If you still feel underconfident about it, you may attempt previous year papers and see the answer keys in detail. One can then work on specific topics where ever required.

As for the Indian Language Paper, you must take the language which you would have chosen for study till at least 8th or 10th Standard in school. For Example, I am fluent in spoken Marathi, but chose Hindi as my language as that is what I've studied in written form till my 12th Standard.

For Illustrating the pattern, I have taken the Example of Hindi Language, but the pattern is similar for other languages as well.

1. निबंध/ Essay :

This is again for 100 marks and has 4 options available out of which one needs to be chosen. Fluency in spoken form of this language will be helpful in writing.

2. गद्यांश /Comprehension:

This is for 60 marks and questions are provided at the end which need to be answered based on your reading of the passage.

3. अनुच्छेद का सारांश/ Precis :

A passage is provided and a precis is to be written in 1/3 rd part for 60 marks. You can summarise the important points in the passage in your own words.

4. गद्यांश का अंग्रेजी में अनुवाद/Translation of Passage to English:

For 20 marks, a passage is provided to be translated to English. In this one must try to use as close / exact words as possible from either language.

5. गद्यांश का हिंदी में अनुवाद/Translation of Passage to Hindi:

For 20 Marks, a passage will be provided in English and that will have to be translated in the Indian Language chosen.

6. व्याकरण और शब्दावली/ Grammar and Vocabulary:

Another 40 marks are awarded for Grammar and Word usage in which matriculation level language usage is asked.

Reading vernacular language newspapers or a few articles and practising writing of at least 5 to 6 pages before sitting in the exam is recommended. This is because many of us wouldn't have read or written in these languages for a long time and one shouldn't fail in this paper due to negligence.

I know of an officer who in his earlier attempt happened to attempt only half of the paper due to slow speed of writing and was confident of clearing the paper but to his surprise he had failed in the language paper. This resulted in wastage of one long year of preparation, and we don't want this to happen with any of the candidates. So kindly do at least a very basic preparation of Vernacular languages.

***

17

Mains 2021 Questions Analysis

GS I

Q2. Trace the rise and growth of socio-religious movements with special reference to Young Bengal and Brahma Samaj. (150 Words)

- Parts - 1
- Background theme: Socio-religious movements
- Focus point : Rise and Growth, specially Young Bengal and Brahmo Samaj
- Hinted Flow:

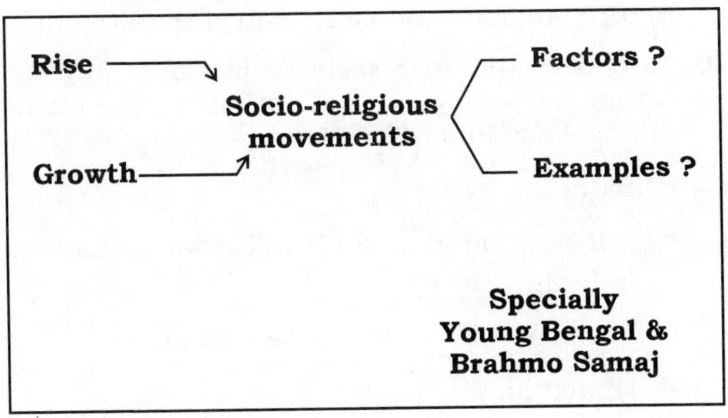

- Question words : Trace

The Historical, linear development of these Social and Religious movements needs to be explained briefly only as it's a 10 marker.

Q 9. Examine the uniqueness of tribal knowledge system when compared with mainstream knowledge and cultural systems. (150 words)

- Parts - 1
- Background theme : Knowledge and system Cultural
- Focus point : Tribal Knowledge systems

- Hinted Flow:

Aspects ? Uniqueness?	Knowledge and cultural systems	
	Tribal	**Mainstream**

- Question words : Examine

Certain aspects like Art, Skill, Medicine, Food, Conservation etc can be compared and shown how the tribal systems are unique in their proximity to nature and mode of passing on of the system.

Q20. How does Indian Society maintain continuity in traditional social values ? Enumerate the changes taking place in it. (250 words)

- Parts-2
- Background theme : Traditional social values in Indian Society
- Focus point : Continuity and Changes
- Hinted Flow:

I) Continuity in Traditional Social Values

- **Family ?**
- **Religion ?**
- **Culture ?**
- **Caste ?**

II) Changes ⟶ List out

- Question words: How Enumerate

GS II

Q 6. 'Besides being a moral imperative of a welfare state, primary health structure is a necessary precondition for sustainable development'. Analyse (150 words)

- Parts: a Statement, a Question word
- Background theme : Sustainable development
- Focus point : Importance of Primary Health Structure
- Hinted Flow:

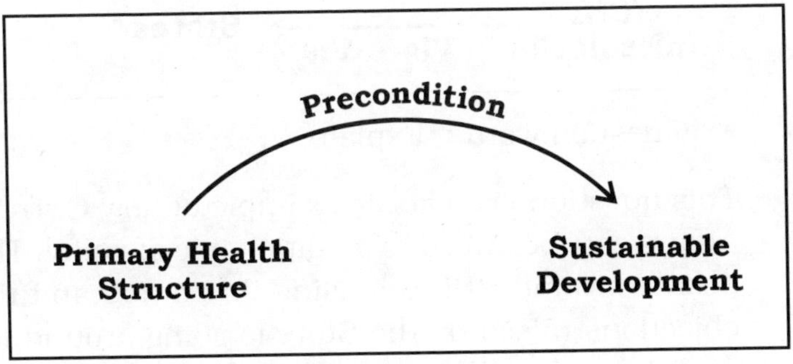

- Question word : Analyse

Note some key words like Moral Imperative, Welfare State etc. which can be elaborated. Basically the importance of Primary Health structure needs to be highlighted while connecting it to the concept of Sustainable Development. The SDG Goals of 2030 can be connected here.

Q11. The jurisdiction of the Central Bureau of Investigation regarding lodging an FIR, and conducting a probe within a particular state is being questioned by various states. However the power of States to withhold consent to CBI is not absolute. Explain with special reference to the Federal character of India. (250 words)

- Parts: 2 Statements, a Question sentence
- Background theme : Centre - State Relations in India
- Focus point: CBI jurisdiction and State Tussle
- Hinted Flow:

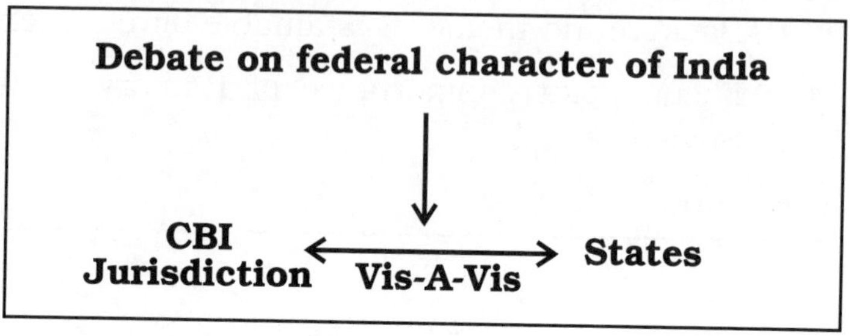

- Question word : Explain

This question is a classic example of how Current Affairs can be linked to a static topic of polity. The debate around CBI exercising its powers and the objections raised by the State is going around for a while now as the states withdrew their 'General consent' to CBI. Hence giving reference to Court judgements one can explain the nature of agency of CBI and how the relation has evolved.

Q12. Though the Human Rights Commissions have contributed immensely to the protection of human rights in India, yet they have failed to assert themselves against the mighty and powerful. Analysing their structural and practical limitations, suggest remedial measures.(250 Words/15 Marks)

- Parts: 1Statement, a Question sentence
- Background theme : Human Rights Commission
- Focus point: Limitations and Measures
- Hinted Flow:

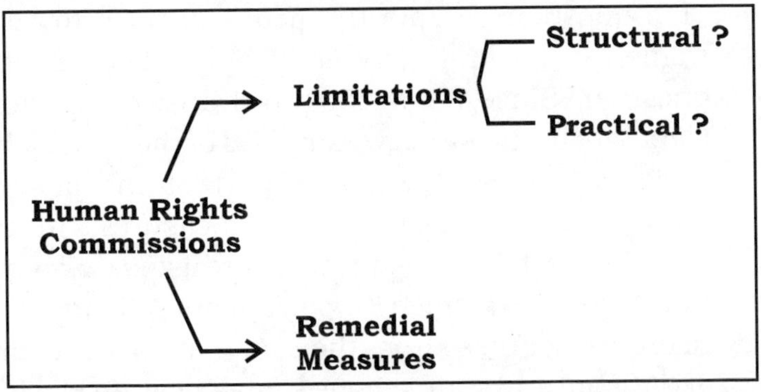

- Question word: Analyse, Suggest

Q17. Though women in post independent India have excelled in various fields, the social attitude towards women and feminist movement has been patriarchal. Apart from Women Education and Women Empowerment Schemes, what interventions can help change the milieu? (250 words)

- Parts : 1 Statement, a Question sentence
- Background theme : Social Attitude towards Women
- Focus point: Interventions required
- Hinted Flow:

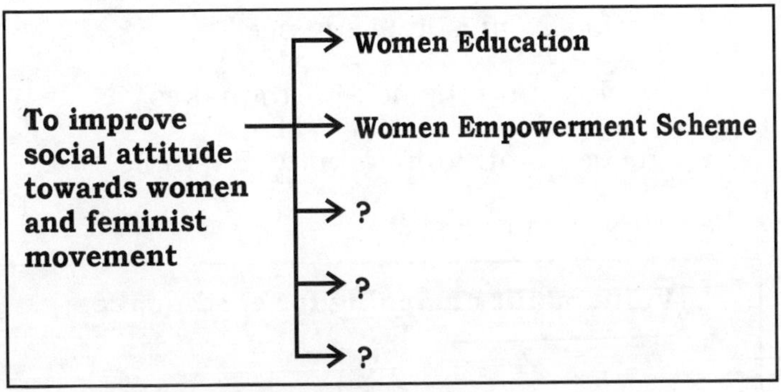

- Question word : What

This question accepts the poor attitudes towards women in its first statement, but that is not the question. Since it's a 250 word answer, you can elaborate by giving a few examples of the patriarchal social attitudes. The major part of the answer, however, is to suggest some measures. In the question part, two existing ways are listed i.e Women Education and Women Empowerment schemes. Few references of these from the contemporary scenario of National and state schemes must begiven like Beti bachao Beti Padhao, Ladli lakshmi Yojana from MP, Sukanya Samriddhi Yojana, UJJWALA, One Stop Centre, Working Women Hostels, Bhagyalakshmi Scheme of Karnataka etc.

But, you must suggest other ways for improving attitudes apart from the ones mentioned. This will finally fetch marks for the answer.

GS III

Q8. Discuss about the vulnerability of India to earthquake related hazards. Give examples including the salient features of Major disasters caused by earthquakes in different parts of India, during the last three decades. (150 Words/15 Marks)

- Parts : 2 Question sentence
- Background theme : Earthquakes
- Focus point: Vulnerability, Examples
- Hinted Flow :

Vulnerability mapping for earthquakes **+** **Examples and features of incidents**

- Question word: Discuss, Give Examples

In this question, the Earthquake (zonal) vulnerability mapping can be shown. Not only this Geographical data, but the examples of past incidents also need to be explained. For this, a sound illustration of past examples needs to be done too.

Q12. Investment in Infrastructure is essential for more rapid and inclusive economic growth. Discuss in the light of India's experience. (150words)

- Parts: 1Statement, 1 Question
- Background theme : Indian Economy
- Focus point : Infrastructure, Inclusive and Rapid Growth
- Hinted Flow :

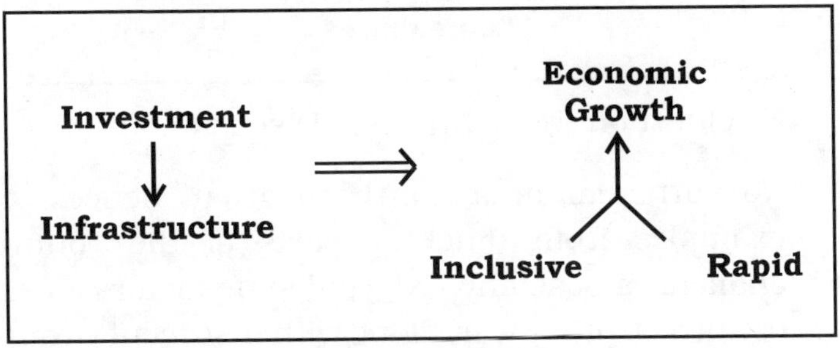

- Question word : Discuss

The idea of Inclusive growth is asked in one way or the other. Infrastructure and investments and discussed in detail in the Economic Survey. These ideas need to be discussed in detail in this question. Examples can be given of how Investments in Infrastructure like - Power, Energy, Digital, Transportation, Sewage, Social- Health,

Education can lead to rapid and Inclusive growth. Examples of some cities and towns can be given.

Q19. Analyse the Multidimensional challenges posed by external state and non- state actors, to the internal security of India. Also discuss measures required to be taken to combat these threats. (250 words)

- Parts : 2 Question statement
- Background theme :Internal Security of India
- Focus point : Challenges by Non- state and external state actors, Measures to combat
- Hinted Flow :

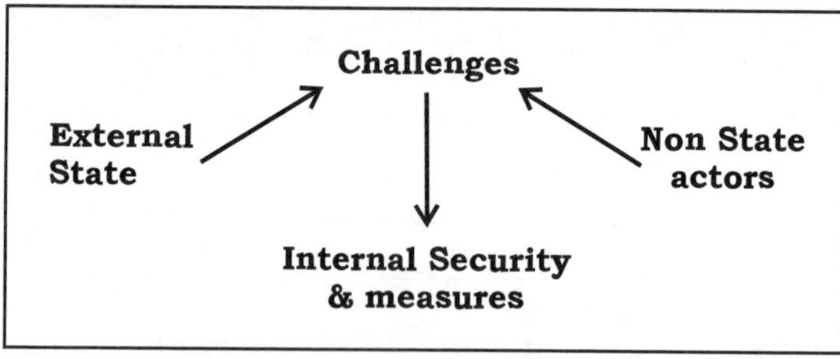

- Question word: Analyse, Discuss

No particular area has been given, hence, with examples from different parts of the country, challenges posed by External state factors (enemy countries, proxy war) along with Insurgent Groups, Terrorist Organisations etc can be given. Measures can be discussed in the other part of the question words.

GSIV

Q3(c). Life doesn't make any sense without interdependence. We need each other and the sooner we learn that it is better for us all.' -Erik Erikson (150 words)

The key word in this question is 'Interdependence'. One has to elaborate on its importance in the answer. While it can be written in multiple ways, one way is to illustrate the importance of interdependence in various walks of life like Personal - Family Relations, Work - between colleagues, highlighting teamwork, Neighbourhood as mentioned in Bible also, Community level like how cooperation during COVID helped one and all. Such ways of illustrations can be used to interpret any quotation given

Q5(a). Refugees should not be turned back to the country where they would face human rights violation or persecution. Examine the statement with reference to the ethical dimension being violated by the nation claiming to be democratic with open society.

(150 words)

- Parts : 1 Statement 1 Question statement
- Background theme : Refugee Crisis in the World
- Focus point: Turning back refugees/ Refusing to Accept Refugees
- Question word : Examine

This question is a subtle sarcasm for countries that claim to be democratic and open and still discriminate and refuse entry, while pushing refugees back to countries where they would face persecution. Like Myanmar Rohingyas, Refugees from Afghanistan and Syria. The Ethical dimension of - Humanitarianism, Responsibility as a democratic society, Concept of Global Citizen, Impartiality, Accountability, 'Practising what They

Preach'- all these aspects can be covered in this answer.

Q6(a). An Independent and empowered Social Audit Mechanism is an absolute must in every sphere of public service including judiciary to ensure performance, accountability and ethical conduct. Elaborate (150 words)

- Parts : 1 Question statement
- Background theme : Social Audit Mechanism
- Focus point: Public service, specially judiciary
- Question word : Elaborate

Social Audit mechanism is required for maintaining accountability in public service. Its importance can be highlighted in the first part of the question. But major focus has to be given on the Judiciary elaborating on it as it appears to be less transparent in terms of Public scrutiny in terms of Appointment, Working etc. Explaining how Social Audit is helpful in enhancing performance can be shown as well through examples.

***

18

Mains 2022 Questions Analysis

GS 1

Q9. How is the growth of Tier 2 cities related to the rise of a new middle class with an emphasis on the culture of consumption? (Answer in 150 words) 10

- Parts : 1
- Background Theme : Urbanisation
- Focus Point : New middle class
- Hinted flow

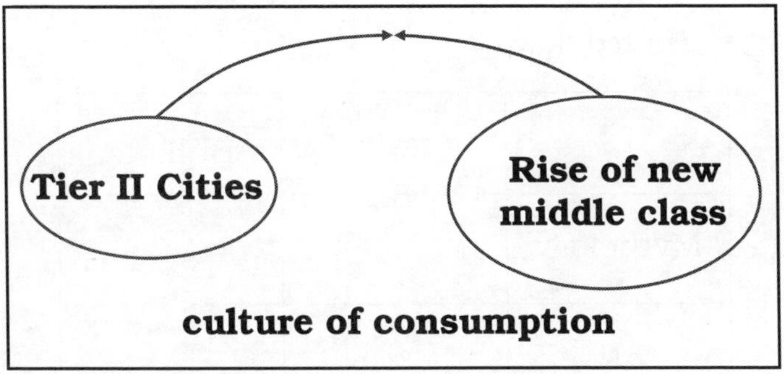

- Question word : How

In this question, one is supposed to explain the relation between rising urbanisation i.e. growth and expansion of tier 2 cities like Agra, Chandigarh, Indore, Patna, Ranchi, Vijayawada with the rising new middle class population. The context of- 'culture of consumption' is to be emphasised. Due to the rise of materialistic culture, the new middle class is associated with greater consumption of branded apparel, restaurants, automobiles, electronics etc. This attitude to show off one's belongings fuelled with the rise of social media is promoting the culture of consumption. Many global brands are now targeting these cities for marketing. The youth who have started earning decently especially in the IT Boom and industrial business are driving this new middle class population which is both aspirational and ambitious. The increase in disposable income is directly linked with the demand for goods and services. Examples of cities and their characteristic features can also be given.

Q13. Discuss the significance of the lion and bull figures in Indian mythology, art and architecture.

(Answer in 250 words) 15

- Parts : 1
- Background Theme : Indian culture
- Focus Point : lion and bull figures
- Hinted flow :

	Lion	Bull
Mythology		
Art		
Architecture		

- Question word : Discuss

Since, this question is a 15 marker, introduction can throw light on the prevalence of animal figurines in Indian cultural forms. In the main body, each bull and lion can be discussed in 3 aspects of Mythology, art and architecture. In such surprise questions, one can be creative and put in as many relevant examples as one can remember. In mythology, the lion is the vehicle of the Goddess Durga and the Narsimha avatar is a God's form itself. It signifies power and strength and also tries to instil fear in Rakshasa i.e. evil. The lion has been immortalised in architecture in the form of the Lion Capital of the Ashokan pillar which is now the national emblem symbolising Pride.

Similar analysis needs to be done for the bull with historical and contemporary examples and cultural events like that of Jallikattu.

Q 20. Elucidate the relationship between globalisation and new technology in a world of scarce resources, with special reference to India. (Answer in 250 words) 15

- Parts : 1
- Background Theme : Globalisation and scarce resources
- Focus Point : New technology
- Question word : Elucidate

Globalisation is a common theme in GS 1 and its multiple interpretations can be asked in the exam. The context given in the question is that of scarce resources and how the interconnectedness is related with use and production of new technology in reference to India. As the keyword is elucidate, examples can be quoted from different fields like pharmacy, satellite, electronics, transportation, IT etc. Many times these resources are harnessed in a sustainable manner being a part of the global value chain. Conversely, the recent discovery of lithium in J&K which can be used for electric vehicles and clean energy technologies can also be mentioned. With growing interlinkages across countries, resource sharing and exchanges of new technology for better living are the way forward.

GS 2

Q1."The most significant achievement of modern law in India is the constitutionalization of environmental problems by the Supreme Court." Discuss this statement with the help of relevant case laws.

- Parts : 1
- Background Theme : Judicial decisions
- Focus Point : Environmental jurisprudence
- Question word : Discuss

In the introduction, the phrase - constitutionalization of environmental problems - can be explained as to what is the likely understanding. Judiciary has elaborated the right to clean environment as part of Article 32, 226 and even Article 21. As the keyword is Discuss, both the pros and cons can be highlighted in regard to the way the Supreme Court has handled the environmental problems. Relevant case laws need to be written along with arguments to justify one's stand as it is explicitly mentioned in the question.

Q12. Discuss the essential conditions for exercise of the legislative powers by the Governor. Discuss the legality of re-promulgation of ordinances by the Governor without placing them before the Legislature.

(Answer in 250 words)

- Parts : 2
- Background Theme : Powers of the Governor
- Focus Point : Legislative powers
- Question word : Discuss

The question is relevant with regard to recent happenings in the National Capital region and other states. Such core conceptual questions in polity can be asked and hence a thorough understanding of the constitutional posts and legislative powers of President and the Governor is essential. Legislative power of the governor as in Article 213, can be elaborated and a pointwise description can be given. The legality of these ordinances have been commented upon by the Supreme Court in several judgments which can also be quoted here.

Q20. 'Clean energy is the order of the day.' Describe briefly India's changing policy towards climate change in various international fora in the context of geopolitics.

- Parts : 1
- Background Theme : India's climate change policy
- Focus Point : geopolitical context
- Question word : Describe

The Energy topic is mentioned in the syllabus in GS - 3, but given that this question is asked in GS 2 and the context of geopolitics is clearly mentioned, it is clear that the Clean energy utilisation is to be described in a *slightly different perspective.* India is a developing nation and is highly dependent on other nations for crude oil import. This causes pressure of being caught up in regional politics, cartel practises and affects India's Energy security. This is the reason, India has been positively taking part in various international forums for climate change agreements like Paris Agreement, COP27, G20 to name a few. Setting ambitious targets and also achieving them in order to harness the renewable energy present in the country can be a gamechanger for India from a geopolitical perspective lending independence and autonomy in crucial sectors.

GS 3

Q11. "Economic growth in the recent past has been led by an increase in labour productivity." Explain this statement. Suggest the growth pattern that will lead to creation of more jobs without compromising labour productivity. (Answer in 250 words) 15

- Parts : 2
- Background Theme : Economic growth and employment
- Focus Point : Jobs and labour productivity
- Question word : Explain, Suggest

Labour productivity can be defined at the outset in the answer. The question comprises two parts, first is to explain the statement. The economic growth and its analysis needs to be done in the background of productivity and involvement of labour. In recent times due to rising levels of urbanisation, education, skill training and technology enhancement, labour productivity has increased. And has led to growth in production of goods and services. This is especially true in case of digital transformation and IT services.

The second part of the answer demands point wise suggestions as to how economic growth can be made more labour intensive. Agri-processing industries, textiles, MSME, leather etc can produce employment. Logistic industry and electronic manufacturing units can also be promoted which will engage productive labour. In such core economy questions, Economic Survey data can be quoted and graphs/ charts can be used as well.

Q12. Do you think India will meet 50 percent of its energy needs from renewable energy by 2030 ? Justify your answer. How will the shift of subsidies from fossil fuels to renewables help achieve the above objective ? Explain. (Answer in 250 words) 15

- Parts : 2
- Background Theme : Energy Source and energy security
- Focus Point : Renewable energy shift
- Question word : Justify, Explain

Note that the question comprises both the Question sentences (2) and Question keywords (2). The phrase 'Do you think' is given and hence one must justify the stand taken through appropriate facts and data points. The current scenario in several states, their commitments can be analysed and presented. Challenges with regard to achieving this target can be given as well. The current energy ratio and usage should also be mentioned.

The second part of the question is to explain the impact of subsidies. Current subsidy distribution and probable effect with shift can be explained.

Q15. Launched on 25th December, 2021, James Webb Space Telescope has been much in the news since then. What are its unique features which make it superior to its predecessor Space Telescopes ? What are the key goals of this mission ? What potential benefits does it hold for the human race? (Answer in 250 words) 15

- Parts : 3
- Background Theme : Space Sciences
- Focus Point : James Webb Telescope

- Hinted Flow :

James Webb Telescope
↓
→ Unique features
→ key goals of mission
→ Potential benefits

- Question word : What

The GS 3 Paper questions usually consist of different parts, each of which carry some marks. One must read the question carefully and answer the parts objectively. In this question, James Webb telescope project and its three elements are asked as mentioned in hinted flow. Addressing each part with crisp points is important. Since its a 15 marker there is scope to talk about importance of such space science inventions and projects that are beneficial to mankind and give a futuristic perspective.

GS 4

Q1. (b) Apart from intellectual competency and moral qualities, empathy and compassion are some of the other vital attributes that facilitate the civil servants to be more competent in tackling the crucial issues or taking critical decisions. Explain with suitable illustrations. (Answer in 150 words) 10

- Parts : 1
- Background Theme : Competence of civil servant
- Focus Point : Role of empathy and compassion
- Hinted flow :

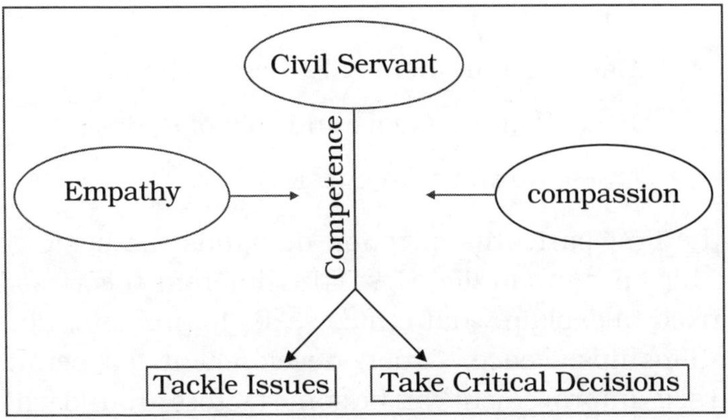

- Question word : Explain with illustrations

The question recognises the importance of intellectual competence and moral qualities, but the demand of the question is to highlight the importance of empathy and compassion. Since it's a 10 marker, the points should be limited to explaining how empathy and compassion helps a civil servant to decide effectively whether it is in terms of policy making or that of policy implementation. Examples must be given for both these values from news or imagined scenarios. They can range from land acquisition projects, disaster management, displacement issues etc are scenarios where being compassionate is of utmost importance. In routine work, relaxation of certain rules to benefit the spirit of law and vulnerable sections can also be mentioned.

Q2.(b) It is believed that adherence to ethics in human actions would ensure the smooth functioning of an organisation/system. If so, what does ethics seek to promote in human life? How do ethical values assist in the resolution of conflicts faced by him in his day-to-day functioning? (Answer in 150 words) 10

- Parts : 2
- Background Theme : Ethics in Human Action.
- Focus Point : Goals and role of ethics
- Question word : What, How

In the first part, this question demands the basic goal of ethics in human life. Here, the different theories can be used to explain what ethics seeks to promote. Better relationships, Peace, Order, development, cooperation and self- improvement can be some factors around which points can be written. For the resolution of conflicts, some examples can be given about situations of ethical dilemma where some of the other ethical virtues guides us to take correct decision.

***

19

Annexures

- General Doubts Of Answer Writing
- Booklist and Resources for CSE
- Quotations
- Economic Survey 2022-2023
- Sample Essays
- Sample Answers

General Doubts Of Answer Writing

1. Should we focus on Question directives like Examine, Critically Analyse etc while answering?

It is always advisable to give attention to the directives provided in the question. That gives you an idea of how the flow of thoughts should be aligned in your answer. Similarly, each part of the question should also be given the required weightage.

2. Is it necessary to write the subheadings? How to write them?

Yes, it is necessary where it is applicable. Subheadings make your answers more structured and make it easy for the examiner to understand the various dimensions you have included in your answer. This is especially true for questions which have multiple parts.

When there are various parts of the question, you can directly write the keywords from the question but when the answer includes multiple dimensions, then it is advisable to use those dimensions as subheadings.

3. Should we focus more on our handwriting? Are more marks allotted for good handwriting?

Legible and clear handwriting helps the examiner to comprehend your answer easily and this gives you an extra edge. There is nothing mentioned as such with regard to marks for handwriting and so you need not worry. But if one feels that their handwriting needs to be improved, then it's worth spending some time on how to write clearly while maintaining the speed of writing in the exam.

4. Which is more important: presentation or content?

Content is the most important thing of the answer but how you present the available content in a comprehensible and innovative manner will definitely be rewarded.

5. What is the importance of word limit and writing within the margin?

These have to be followed strictly. Not overshooting the word limit also helps you give adequate time to each answer so that you can complete attempting all questions. Similarly, writing within the provided space is very crucial. Chances are that you may even be penalized for not following them.

6. Which is a better format to write - point wise or in paragraphs?

Both can be used and It depends on the nature of the question. If the question demands you to enumerate or to list down certain things it's better to go for point format, if it requires you to elaborate a certain viewpoint, you can use paragraphs. Answers can be a combination of the two and there is no strict prescription regarding the same.

7. Should we prepare for writing introductions and conclusions in an answer?

The topics are so vast that you cannot prepare individually but you can have a couple of ideas on how to frame them. And your basic GS knowledge will give you the content for the same.

8. Does the pen we write with matter?

It doesn't matter much as long as you're able to write clearly. Use a pen you are comfortable in writing 60 pages. You must decide and practise with the same pen in your mock tests. (I had used Pilot V7) Avoid using different color pens in the exam. Same pen can be used for underlining the important points.

9. Is answer writing practice necessary? And is it necessary to get the copies evaluated?

Yes it is an ABSOLUTE NECESSITY to do answer writing practice. Copies must be evaluated either from some good test series or from seniors / qualified persons who have first hand experience in mains answer writing. With time, you should be able to evaluate and improvise your answer writing skills. (I extensively used to write answers and had joined test series as well.)

10. Is peer evaluation necessary?

It is not necessary to get your answer peer evaluated, rather it should be avoided. This is because everybody's competing for the same exam and there are high chances of you being misled by other interested candidates. And they might not even be aware and aptly equipped to guide you. Hence, taking feedback from qualified persons and teachers is recommended. (I did not have any group as I didn't prepare from any major preparation hub.)

11. Should we do daily answer writing practice ?

Yes, it will help. At least 2 answers everyday with an essay on Sundays will be a better strategy to prepare for the Mains Examination. But one should start writing after having a basic knowledge about the subject, at least covering the NCERTs. (After I read once through the syllabus, I used to write on Current Affairs at least 2-3 questions daily.)

12. What are the factors we should consider while choosing a test series for doing answer writing practice?

Following factors can be kept in mind while choosing a test series.

- Quality of questions
- The Schedule which suits your preparation
- Reputation of the test series
- The kind of Feedback and Evaluation

13. Ethics case study writing:

a. Do we need to write stakeholders for every case study,if yes, how is it to be written?

It's not necessary to write stakeholders for all the case studies. You can do them for a couple of them as required. Just mentioning the stakeholders wont help you, rather you need to do the role analysis of each stakeholder and need to write the importance of each one of them in the context of the case given.

b. Is it necessary to identify ethical issues / ethical dilemmas for every case study?

i. Yes its important to identify the ethical issues, key terms or dilemmas involved in the case studies. To make your case studies more diverse you can instead write each one of the following in 6 case studies:

- Stakeholders and their role analysis
- Ethical issues involved

- Ethical dilemmas involved
- Facts of the case
- Observations that can be made from the case
- Ethical values need to be upheld by you / officer / person involved
- What is the difference between options before you and the course of action?

ii. Options before you refers to the various possibilities you need to explore and for each of the possibility you have to analyze the merits and demerits

iii. If the question asks you to provide the course of action, you need to give the sequence of steps you will follow to come to a solution.

c. How to utilize ethical theories while writing case study?

i. Use ethical theories while you are giving ethical justifications to the arguments or the options you are exploring. Viz you can analyse with the help of 'means vs ends' debate or can use the theory of 'golden mean' by Aristotle or the 'social contract theory' of Rousseau when justifying the role of state. Ethical theories from texts like Ramayana, Mahabharata can also be used.

d. Can we use examples in case studies?

i. Yes you can provide real life examples while justifying your arguments. This will show your ability to relate the asked concept with the real life incidents.

14. Is there negative marking in Mains?

There is no clear guideline as to negative marking in Mains. But recently, there have been scorecards where penal marking was done. These may be for :

a. Breaching Word limit

b. Writing outside margins

c. Writing irrelevant answers.

15. How to write perfect answers for all the 20 questions?

In a UPSC Mains Exam Paper, even a topper does not know proper answers to all the questions. There will be 6-8 questions which you know and can write comfortably. 8-10 questions will be those, which you will have only partial knowledge of. Finally, there will be 1-2 questions which you have very minimal knowledge of. Someone cannot write perfect answers for all questions and must not worry about it.

16. How to complete the paper?

Many people tend to give more time to the questions they know and this way they miss out on attempting all the questions. The extra point you will score by giving more than allotted time to any answer will always be lesser than the marks which you lost by not attempting the question. This should not be done. While writing the answers, focus should be on the time available for each question, rather than writing the perfect answer. So you must write the best possible answer in the allotted time. Completing a paper is quintessential. (This does not include the questions which you have NO IDEA ABOUT.)

17. Should we attempt the questions which we have no idea about?

The chances of you guessing the expected line of thought in an answer are very less. It is advisable not to write irrelevant arguments or do guesswork in a Mains answer. This might lead to negative marking and will surely waste your time.

18. Is it essential to start attempting the paper from the start? i.e. from 10 markers? What should be the ideal sequence?

There is no ideal sequence as such. Some people feel that writing very good initial answers will create a better impression on the examiner and which will reflect in the marks given for the later questions, but this is not true. every answer is evaluated for what is written in those 2-3 pages. so you can choose your own sequence of answering the questions but you should follow proper time management. (I used to start from the first question and give 7 and 11 minutes for 10 and 15 markers respectively.)

19. Essay:

a. Can we write a good essay based on general studies preparations?

Yes. General studies preparation is the mainstay of your preparation for essays with regard to the content. In addition you need to do writing practice while taking valuable feedback on your essays.

b. What is the ideal size of a paragraph?

4-5 sentences per paragraph are sufficient. You must Write short, crisp and simple sentences and avoid complex sentences

c. **How many pages should we write?**

14 pages will be provided to you. Generally you have to at least write 12 pages. And this again depends on your handwriting and presentation.

d. **What is meant by thesis statement and is it necessary to write it?**

Thesis statement is a linking paragraph between the introduction and the actual body of the essay. It gives an idea about what to expect from the following writeup. It is advisable to write it so that the examiner will have the idea as to on what dimensions your essay will be.

e. **Can we write antithesis to the statement given?**

Yes, such a writeup will broaden the scope of essay and makes it further analytical

f. **Can we use subheadings ?**

Yes, use subheadings to write different dimensions. These subheadings will help the examiner to clearly understand what exactly you are writing and elaborating

g. **Can we use diagrams , points, maps and flowcharts?**

Advisably No. Essay requires analytical writing and it can be best done by writing in paragraphs

h. **How frequently should I do essay writing practice**

Weekly two essays

20. Should we do answer writing practice for compulsory language papers? How long should we prepare for them?

No need of doing answer writing practice for these extensively. Preparing through past year papers will be enough.

21. In UPSC Mains, what is better for Vernacular medium students, writing Mains in English or in the regional Language?

The medium of giving examinations, whether English or other languages, should depend on your comfort and hold on the language. Nowadays study materials, current affairs, test series, notes and other resources especially on the internet are readily available in English compared to other languages. And hence,preparation becomes easy in the English language. But if one is comfortable writing in any other Indian languages, that can be taken as the medium as well. UPSC does not differentiate between any candidates based on the Language medium of examination. The Content and presentation hold the key. There are many students who have scored well writing in vernacular languages. Hence, you should confidently choose a medium where you can think properly and write appropriate answers.

***

Booklist And Resources For CSE

Based on the General Studies Syllabus of UPSC CSE, it is advisable that your Base Books be NCERTs from 6th - 12th Class of Social Science Subjects. i.e. History, Geography, Civics, Economics. Political Science and Sociology can be done from 11-12th Class. NCERTs will build your foundation and give you direction for the preparation. Some basic processes, facts and themes are directly picked up from NCERTs in the Exam and hence a thorough reading is a must at the very outset. After this, I referred to different Books as Standard and Reference Books. Standard Books need to be read cover to cover as they cover most syllabus appropriately. But the Reference can be used for selected topics which are given elaborately in that book. I've listed them below Subject Wise.

1. HISTORY

A. <u>ANCIENT AND MEDIEVAL HISTORY :</u>

Tamil Nadu Text books are detailed accounts of History.

a. Ancient History : Tamil Nadu Text Book 11th Standard

b. Medieval History : Tamil Nadu Text Book 11th Standard

Reference- Ancient and Medieval India by Poonam Dalal Dahiya

B. MODERN HISTORY:

A brief History of Modern India By Rajiv Ahir Spectrum Publication

Reference - India's Struggle for Independence by Bipin Chandra

C. CULTURE:

Indian Art and Culture by Nitin Singhania

Reference -

CCRT Website: http:/ /www.ccrtindia.gov.in/

2. GEOGRAPHY

Certificate Physical and Human Geography by GC Leong

Reference Websites :

a. PMFIAS: https:/ /www.pmfias.com/geography/

The Geography and Environment part notes available on this website are well explained.

b. Rajtanil Mam's Lectures : On Mrunal Channel on Youtube

c. Amit SenGupta's Lectures: On you tube Channel of same name in which NCERT Chapters are explained well in simplified manner.

3. INDIAN SOCIETY

NCERT- Class XI and XII

Reference:

a. Economic and Political Weekly Magazine - selective reading of few articles based on Caste,

Reservation, Women's issues etc can enhance your understanding.

4. POLITY

Indian Polity by M. Laxmikanth

Reference:

a. Introduction to the Constitution of India by DD Basu

b. Landmark Judgments (covering More Than 50 Leading Cases OfIndia Book by Universal's)

c. Vikaspedia: https:/ /vikaspedia.in/

Government owned website which has an official brief of policies and schemes. Comes handy for Polity reference.

d. PRSLegislative Research: https:/ /prsindia.org/

Good quality Material like Summary of Bills, Policies, Acts, Parliamentary Committee Reports are really helpful in writing Answers.

5. INTERNATIONAL RELATIONS

Reference Website :

a. The Manohar Parrikar Institute for Defence Studies and Analyses (MP-IDSA) https:/ /www.idsa.in/

The articles on International Relations are good quality, non- partisan and provide a balanced perspective on any issue.

6. ECONOMY

Indian Economy by Ramesh Singh

Reference Websites:

a. ARTHAPEDIA:

http://arthapedia.in/index.php / Home_Page

The website is maintained by Indian Economic Service Officers and is a ready reference for terminologies in Economics. Any new concepts are also covered here in brief which will help you understand concepts.

b. LIVEMINT: https:/ /www.livemint.com/

News Website covering articles specially related to Economics. One can subscribe or visit the website now and then torefer articles.

c. WORLD ECONOMIC FORUM :

https:/ /www.weforum.org/

Certain Issues of Global Importance are covered well in this website. For eg issues related to Unemployment,Energy Usage, Climate Change, Impact of technology etc.

7. INTERNAL SECURITY

Challenges to Internal Security of India by Ashok Kumar Vipul Anekant

8. ETHICS

a. The LEXICON for Ethics Integrity and Aptitude by The Chronicle

b. Case Studies in Ethics, Integrity and Aptitude by R Rajagopalan

Reference Websites :

a. SKILL YOU NEED:

https://www.skillsyouneed.com/

Many topics like Honesty, Emotional Intelligence, Personal and Professional work are explained in a very simplified manner

b. Organisation for Economic Co-operation and Development (OECD): https://www.oecd.org

The official publications and reports on Corruption, Public Integrity on this website have explained concepts in a concise manner with a global perspective.

9. WORLD HISTORY

a. Selective Readings from Mastering Modern World History by Norman Lowe

b. Vision IAS notes

10. DISASTER MANAGEMENT

2nd ARC - 3rd Report Crisis Management

11. ENVIRONMENT

a. Shankar IAS book

b. Down to Earth magazine

12. CURRENT AFFAIRS

1. PIB Website :

   https://www.pib.gov.in/indexd.aspx

   You can subscribe to the feed and read selectively. A brief account of any topic is given in which the version of the government can be understood from here.

2. NEWS ON AIR: https:/ /newsonair.gov.in/

   This Radio channel can be listened to through an app or website. The Spotlight News Analysis programme is a good conversational program that highlights the various aspects of any issue.

3. RSTV:

   https: / / rajyasabha.nic.in/ rsnew /webcast/ rstvliv e.html

   Can be viewed on Youtube or otherwise. Programmes like Big Picture and India's World are good forums for effective discussion.

4. NITI AAYOG: https://www.niti.gov.in/

   Initiatives, Publications and Rankings from Niti Aayog are very crucial in having data points for the answers. Reports provide deeper knowledge about subjects of economy, development and others.

5. OBSERVER RESEARCH FOUNDATION

   https:/ /www.orfonline.org/

   This website provides detailed articles on multiple subjects. Their analysis is good and points can be used in the answer directly.

***

Quotations For Essay

1. Women Empowerment related issues

By Mahatma Gandhiji :

- Women are more fit than men to explore and take bolder action in non-violence.
- Woman is the companion of man, gifted with equal mental capacity.
- If by strength is meant moral power, then woman is immeasurably man's superior.
- If nonviolence is the law of our being, the future is with women.

A woman with a voice is, by definition, a strong woman." -*Melinda Gates*

"There is no limit to what we, as women, can accomplish." -*Michelle Obama*

"Human rights are women's rights and women's rights are human rights, once and for all." - *Hillary Clinton*

"Women have discovered that they cannot rely on men's chivalry to give them justice." -*Helen Keller*

"A gender-equal society would be one where the word 'gender' does not exist: where everyone can be themselves"

"Achieving gender equality requires the engagement of women and men, girls and boys. It is everyone's responsibility" - *Ban Ki-Moon*

"I measure the progress of a community by the degree of progress which women have achieved" - *B. R. Ambedkar*

"Women are the largest untapped reservoir of talent in the world" - *HILLARY CLINTON*

"You educate a man, you educate a man. You educate a woman, you educate a generation" - *BRIGHAM YOUNG*

"Gender equality is more than a goal in itself. It is a precondition for meeting the challenge of reducing poverty, promoting sustainable development and building good governance" - *Kofi-Annan*

"To educate girls is to reduce poverty" - *KOFI ANNAN*

"Empower a woman - Empower a community" - *KOFI ANNAN*

"When women do better economies do better"- *CHRISTINA LAGARDE*

"There is no chance of the welfare of the world unless the condition of women is improved. It is not possible for a bird to fly on one wing" - *SWAMI VIVEKANAND*

"We cannot all succeed when half of us are held back" - *MALALA YOUSAFZAI*

2. <u>Social Justice:</u>

By Martin Luther King Jr.

"Of all the forms of inequality, injustice in health care is the most shocking and inhumane." -

"The moral arc of the universe is long, but it bends towards justice."

"True peace is not merely the absence of tension; it is the presence of justice."

"Oppressed people cannot remain oppressed forever. The yearning for freedom eventually manifests itself."

"It is not beyond our power to create a world in which all children have access to a good education." - *Nelson Mandela.*

"When education and resources are available to all without a price tag, there will be no limit to the human potential." *-Jacque Fresco.*

3. Human Development- Poverty, Health and Education

   a. Education:

      "True education must correspond to the surrounding circumstances or it is not healthy growth." *-Mahatma Gandhi*

      "What is really needed to make democracy function is not knowledge of facts, but right education." *-Mahatma Gandhi*

      "You must be the change you wish to see in the world." *-Mahatma Gandhi*

      "You must not lose faith in humanity. Humanity is an ocean; if a few drops of the ocean are dirty, the ocean does not become dirty." -Mahatma Gandhi

      To be successful in life what you need is education. *-Jawaharlal Nehru*

      "Literacy is a bridge from misery to hope" - *KOFI ANNAN*

      "One child, one teacher, one book and one pen can change the world" -MALALA YOUSAFZAI

      "We want the education by which character is formed, strength of mind is increased, the intellect is expanded, and by which one can stand on one's own feet" - *SWAMI VIVEKANAND*

Education is the most powerful weapon you can use to change the world. *-Nelson Mandela*

It is the mark of an educated mind to be able to entertain a thoughtwithout accepting it.*-Aristotle*

To educate a person in mind and not in morals is to educate a menace to society. *-Theodore Roosevelt*

b. Poverty:

There are people in the world so hungry that God cannot appear to them except in the form of bread. *-Mahatma Gandhi*

A nation's greatness is measured by how it treats its weakest members. *-Mahatma Gandhi*

"Poverty is like a punishment for a crime you didn't commit." *-ELIKHAMAROV*

There's enough on this planet for everyone's needs but not for everyone's greed. -Mahatma Gandhi

To a man with an empty stomach food is God -Mahatma Gandhi

Poverty is the greatest violence. *-Mahatma Gandhi*

c. Health:

"The cheerful mind perseveres, and the strong mind hews its way through a thousand difficulties." *- Swami Vivekananda*

"It is health that is the real wealth, and not pieces of gold and silver." *-Mahatma Gandhi*

The doctor of the future will give no medicine, but will instruct his patients in care of the human frame, in diet, and in the cause and prevention of disease." - *Thomas Edison*

Healthy citizens are the greatest asset any country can have." - *Winston Churchill*

To keep the body in good health is a duty... otherwise we shall not be able to keep the mind strong and clear." - *Buddha*

4. Farmer Related Quotes

Agriculture is our wisest pursuit, because it will in the end contribute most to real wealth, good morals, and happiness." -*ThomasJefferson*

"No race can prosper until it learns there is as much dignity in tilling a field as in writing a poem." -*BookerT. Washington*

"If agriculture fails, everything else will fail" - *M S SWAMINATHAN*

5. Human Values:

"In order to lead a meaningful life, you need to cherish others, pay attention to human values and try to cultivate inner peace." - *Dalai Lama*

"Education is discovering your full potential and flourishing that potential for the benefit of humanity." -*Amit Ray, World Peace: The Voice of a Mountain Bird*

If money helps a man to do good to others, it is of some value; but if not, it is simply a mass of evil, and the sooner it is gotten rid of, the better. - *Swami Vivekananda*

"Happiness is when what you think, what you say, and what you do are in a harmony" - *MAHATMA GANDHI*

"Be truthful, gentle and fearless" -MAHATMA GANDHI

"Heart is a very good fertiliser; anything we plant love, fear, hate, hope, revenge, jealousy-surely grows and bears fruit. We have to decide what to harvest" -*SWAMI VIVEKANAND*

Emotional Intelligence:

* "There is no separation of mind and emotions; emotions, thinking, and learning are all linked." - *Eric Jensen*

* "Use pain as a stepping stone, not a campground." -*Alan Cohen*

* "We are dangerous when we are not conscious of our responsibility for how we behave, think, and feel." -*Marshall B. Rosenberg*

* "What really matters for success, character, happiness and life long achievements is a definite set of emotional skills - your EQ - not just purely cognitive abilities that are measured by conventional IQ tests." -*Daniel Goleman*

* "Whatever begins in anger, ends in shame." -*Benjamin Franklin*

* "Where we have strong emotions, we're liable to fool ourselves." - *Carl Sagan*

* "In a very real sense we have two minds, one that thinks and one that feels" - *Daniel Goleman*

* "emotional self-awareness is the building block of the next fundamental emotional intelligence: being able to shake off a bad mood" - *Daniel Goleman*

"We may have different religions, different languages, different colored skin, but we all belong to one human race" - KOFI ANNAN

6. Environment And Climate Change

"What we are doing to the forests of the world is but a mirror reflection of what we are doing to ourselves and to one another" *-MAHATMA GANDHI*

"Climate change is simply, the greatest collective challenge we face as a human family" *- BAN KI MOON*

"Sustainable development and climate change are two sides of the same coin" *- BAN KI MOON*

"Climate change does not respect borders; it does not respect who you are- rich and poor, small and big. Therefore, this is what we call global challenges, which require global solidarity" *-BAN KI MOON*

7. Sustainable Development

"Sustainable development is the pathway to the future we want for all. It offers a framework to generate economic growth, achieve social justice, exercise environmental stewardship and strengthen governance" *- BAN KI MOON*

8. Youth

"Any society that does not succeed in tapping into the energy and creativity of its youth will be left behind" *-KOFI ANNAN*

"Young people should be at the forefront of global change and innovation. Empowered, they can be key agents for development and peace" -KOFI ANNAN

9. Inclusive Development

"You cannot have peace without security, and you cannot have security without inclusive development" -KOFI ANNAN

10. <u>Children</u>

"Children are like buds in a garden and should be carefully and lovingly nurtured, as they are the future of the Nation and the citizens of tomorrow" - Pt. JAWAHAR LAL NEHRU

11. <u>Science and Technology</u>

"I fear the day when technology will suppress human interaction and the world will have a generation of idiots" -*ALBERT EINSTEIN*

'"The great thing about social media was how it gave a voice to voiceless people." - *JON RONSON*

"The Internet is becoming the town square for the Global village of tomorrow" - *BILL GATES*

Issue	Quote
Free Speech	• I do not agree with what you have to say, but I'll defend to the death your right to say it. - Voltaire
Caste	• The caste system is opposed to the Religion of the Vedanta. Caste is a social custom, and all our great preachers have tried to break it down. - Swami Vivekananda
Corruption	• Righteousness is the foundation stone of peace and good governance. -Confucius • Nearly all men can stand adversity, but if you want to test a man's character, give him power. • Abraham Lincoln

Peace	• When the power of love overcomes the love of power, the world will know peace. - William Gladstone • Peace and Justice are two sides of the same coin. - Eisenhower
Democracy	• The tyranny of a prince in an oligarchy is not so much dangerous to the public welfare as the apathy of a citizen in a democracy. - Montesquieu • I understand democracy as something that gives the weak the same chance as the strong. - Mahatma Gandhi • The price good men pay for indifference to public affairs is to be ruled by evil men. - Plato
Science v/s Religion	• All thinking men are atheists. -Ernest Hemingway • Our scientific power has outrun our spiritual power. We have guided missiles and misguided men. - Martin Luther King • Science without religion is lame, and Religion without Science is blind. - Einstein

***

Economic Survey (2022-23)

30 points summary for Mains

1. India to witness GDP growth of 6.0 per cent to 6.8 per cent in 2023-24, depending on the trajectory of economic and political developments globally.

   (projected)

2. Credit growth to the micro, small, and medium enterprises (MSME) sector has been remarkably high, over 30.5 per cent, on average during Jan-Nov 2022 supported by the extended Emergency Credit Linked Guarantee Scheme (ECLGS) of the Union government.

3. Private consumption as a percentage of GDP stood at 58.4 percent in Q2 of FY23, the highest among the second quarters of all the years since 2013-14.

4. Reasons for optimistic GDP growth expectations –

   a. Rebound of private consumption has given a boost to production activity.

   b. Higher Capital Expenditure (Capex)

   c. Near-universal vaccination coverage enabling people to spend on contact-based services, such as restaurants, hotels, shopping malls, and cinemas.

   d. Return of migrant workers to cities to work in construction sites leading to a significant decline in housing market inventory

   e. Strengthening of the balance sheets of the Corporates

f. Well-capitalised public sector banks ready to increase the credit supply and the credit growth to the Micro, Small, and Medium Enterprises (MSME) sector.

5. Despite the three shocks of COVID-19, Russian-Ukraine conflict and Rate hikes by countries like US to contain inflation, leading to appreciation of US Dollar and the widening of the Current Account Deficits (CAD) in net importing economies like India, agencies worldwide continue to project India as the fastest-growing major economy at 6.5-7.0 per cent in FY23.

6. According to Survey, India's economic growth in FY23 has been principally led by private consumption and capital formation and they have helped generate employment in the country.

7. The Capital Expenditure (Capex) of the central government, which increased by 63.4 per cent in the first eight months of FY23, was another growth driver of the Indian economy in the current year.

8. The Survey brings to the fore an interesting fact that in general, global economic shocks in the past were severe but spaced out in time, but this changed in the third decade of this millennium, as at least three shocks have hit the global economy since 2020.

The Survey notes with optimism that the Indian economy appears to have moved on after its encounter with the pandemic, staging a full recovery in FY22 ahead of many nations and positioning itself to ascend to the pre-pandemic growth path in FY23.

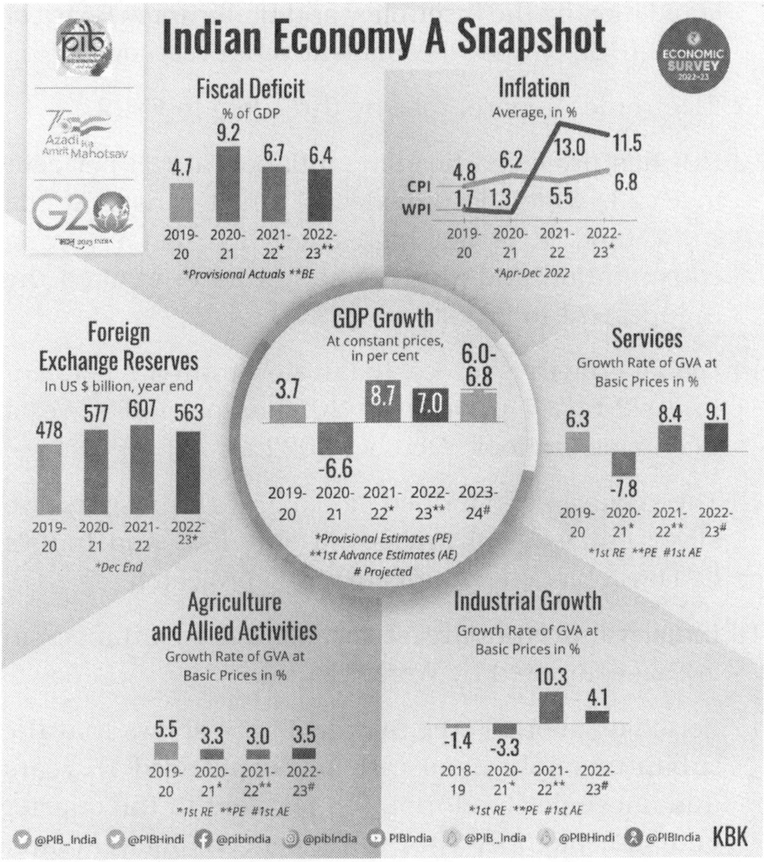

9. The growth estimate for FY23 is higher than for almost all major economies and even slightly above the average growth of the Indian economy in the decade leading up to the pandemic.

10. IMF estimates India to be one of the top two fast-growing significant economies in 2022.

11. The finances of the public sector banks have seen a significant turnaround, with profits being booked at regular intervals and their Non-Performing Assets (NPAs) being fast-tracked for quicker resolution/

liquidation by the Insolvency and Bankruptcy Board of India (IBBI). Gross NPA Ratio at seven year low of 5%.

12. Electronics exports rose by three fold in FY22.

13. RBI has projected headline inflation at 6.8 per cent in FY23, which is outside its target range. At the same time, it is not high enough to deter private consumption and also not so low as to weaken the inducement to invest.

14. Global growth is forecasted to slow from 3.2 per cent in 2022 to 2.7 per cent in 2023 as per IMF's World Economic Outlook, October 2022.

15. The scenario of subdued global growth presents two silver linings – oil prices will stay low, and India's CAD will be better than currently projected.

16. India will be the largest recipient of remittances in 2022 (estimated by World Bank).

17. Periodic Labour Force Survey (PLFS) shows that the urban unemployment rate for people aged 15 years and above declined from 9.8 per cent in the quarter ending September 2021 to 7.2 per cent one year later (quarter ending September 2022).

18. CIBIL report (ECLGS Insights, August 2022) showed that the Emergency Credit Line Guarantee Scheme has supported MSMEs in facing the COVID shock, with 83 per cent of the borrowers that availed of the ECLGS being micro-enterprises. Among these micro units, more than half had an overall exposure of less than Rs10 lakh.

19. The GST paid by MSMEs after declining in FY21 has been rising since and now has crossed the pre-pandemic level of FY20.

20. Mahatma Gandhi National Rural Employment Guarantee Act (MGNREGA) scheme has been rapidly creating more assets in respect of "Works on individual's land" than in any other category, helping in improving livelihood of the rural households.

21. According to the Economic survey, 'Indian economy in FY23 has nearly "recouped" what was lost, "renewed" what had paused, and "re-energised" what had slowed during the pandemic and since the conflict in Europe.'

22. The Survey narrates about six challenges faced by the Global Economy.

    a. COVID-19 related disruptions in economies.

    b. Russian-Ukraine conflict and its adverse impact along with disruption in supply chain, mainly of food, fuel and fertilizers.

    c. Central Banks across economies led by the Federal Reserve responding with synchronised policy rate hikes to curb inflation.

    d. The fourth challenge emerged as faced with the prospects of global stagflation, nations feeling compelled to protect their respective economic space, thus slowing cross-border trade affecting overall growth.

    e. The fifth challenge was festering as China experienced a considerable slowdown induced by its policies.

    f. The sixth medium-term challenge to growth was seen in the scarring from the pandemic brought in by the loss of education and income-earning opportunities.

23. Growth Magnets (2023-2030)-

    i. Sound & healthy financial system,

    ii. Digitalisation reforms,

    iii. Gain from global supply chain diversification.

24. Under tax composition, GST is at first followed by Personal Income tax & Corporate tax, excise duty then customs.

25. Maximum carbon stock in forest - 1st place Arunachal Pradesh followed by MP.

26. Per hectare forest Carbon stock storage - 1st place J & K followed by HP then Sikkim.

27. The Indian agriculture sector is growing at an average annual growth rate of 4.6%. India emerged as a net exporter of agricultural products.

28. Industry sector contributing to 30% share in total GVA.

29. According to the World Investment Report 2022 by UNCTAD, India is the 7th largest recipient of FDI.

30. India is the Largest recipient of Remittances & 6th largest Forex reserve holder.

***

Sample Essay O1

Philosophical Essay By Nivedita B

Number of Years does not Determine Age

"He slept beneath the moon.
He basked beneath the sun.
He lived a life of going to do,
And died with nothing done."

-James Albery

A life well lived is ultimately what we all possibly aim for. But what determines the ultimate accomplishment differs for each one of us. To each her own. Do we say that the centenarian neighbour, who lived a hundred years and more, lived her life well And thus, aged well? If we did, what did we base out judgement upon? The family she had, the love she shared or the compassion she extended. Clearly, the number of years was not what we based it upon alone.

Coming to the aspect where a thirteen old came up with an innovative solution to save a millions from starving, do we say that the number of years determined his mental age? We may not. Thus here lies the question whether number of years determines the age.

While on a technical or a literal basis, or plain chronological number of years may determine the age, but in every other sense be it philosophical, behavioral, scientific and so forth, number of years does not determine age.

To begin this discussion, we will first try to define or understand what age or aging essentially means. Further a number of areas are touched upon to understand what determines the 'Age' factor. We will further discuss the relationship between our understanding of age and the impact it has on society and well-being. Thus, we make an attempt to understand what matters and what does not.

Of Ageing and Living

Before we delve upon the determinates of age, we need to understand what age means to us. By the definition that science gave us, in a physiological sense, age could be the level of development of the body, the number of divisions our cells have gone under and the capabilities we have thus grown into. But in a broader sense age is the term we use when someone has a life of purpose and impact. For instance, we can say that Ruth Bader Ginsberg lived well, and aged well.

Not just for an individual but be it an organization, an empire or even a civilization, we tend to remember the ones which had a lasting impact that the ones which just existed for longer. Thus, we could say that Amul has aged well over the years.

Further as discussed, Mental age is quite different from Chronological age or just the number of years. It is the abilities, intelligence and the tendency to adapt oneself best to the environment that determines the age. This very idea led Simon and Binet to come up with the concept of Intelligence quotient. Thus reiterating that number of years does not determine age.

If not years, then what determines Age?

Let us now dwell upon the same.

Life into years:

As James Albery's epitaph read, days and nights are spent by us but where did the life happen? They say that, it is not the years into the life that matters, but the life into years. That is to say, what we need to use to determine age is the life that happened in the years that onespent.

We want to live a life with a purpose. As Viktor Frankl suggests in his book 'Mans search for meaning' we look into the reason why we live even in the worst possible circumstances. Thus the purpose we kept in mind could determine the age. For instance consider the case of Sister Nivedita born as Margaret Elizabeth Noble who left a life of comfort in Ireland, only to follow this purpose and the vision that Swami Vivekananda led her into.

While she died at the young age of 43, it is not the number of years that determines the 'age of impact' it had on the women in our country, our science (Indian Institute of Science) or on the very idea of the nation that we know of.

Coming to the idea of survival of the fittest by Charles Darwin it is clear to us that fitness is what determines the age which eventually shows up as the number of years. Thus, it can be said that age determines the number of years we get to live.

For instance consider the Lancet study on the Disease Burden and Disability Adjusted life years (DALY). What good a life of many years but only to survive the days and nights and thus, kept pushing ourselves.

While it is debatable the idea that how we age determines years of life instead, is true to an extent. Further consider the case of civilizations and empires. The number of years of civilization may not determine the age but the impact it had on people, and society. Harappa and Mesopotamia survived for long. Indeed, but were washed away with the flow of time. But the Mauryan Empire and even Mughal Empires are remembered for the battles they encountered, the monuments they built and the message they delivered. We could say that the empires aged with an impact. This also reminds us of French Revolutions and its ebbs and flow over time. It is true that the ideals it created with the impact of liberty and freedom are far more last living than the number of years it is accounted for historically.

Finally coming to the organizations that we see today, the old set up of Microsoft search engine seemed like a dwarf in front of the young google. Considering the case of ISRO and AIR INDIA, both have aged over time in different ways and the impact it has created. Thus, we cannot say that the number of years determines the age but the expertise it has developed is what determines the age.

Age and Society:

Through a series of instances, we have come to understand that the determinants of age are vast and not limited to sheer number of years alone. We also need to understand the impact that the aging has on society and well-being around us. We need to thrive and not just grow says Kate Raworth even in an ecological sense.

Instead of focusing our lives on just the number of years, our minds should focus on a life well lived with a purpose, on aging well ultimately. Our Policies and laws need to accommodate this aspect of life into years, the happiness and well being of each life, as giving due importance to sustainability.

Carl Jung suggests that there is a collective unconscious that we as a society share. Each of our actions has an impact on the overall well being of, not just our generation, but many others to come. For we cannot assign the number of years to our society. It is continuous and infinite and ages every moment into eternity.

What matters and what does not?

As we said society is an ever living dynamic entity and we each have a role to play. We all have one thing we must do as Rumi would put it. However, there are some of us who could still say age is just a number at the end of the day. Maybe it is true for the cynics of the lokayatas who believe in living in the moment and forgetting the rest. Even then, it is not the number of years that determines the age but how well they enjoyed the days, the nights and the years thus lived.

Thus, what matters is that we live to the fullest that we can. When we look back, as Albery would have, it could bring us wisdom and peace if we liked it with a purpose, to accomplish our tasks in the limited time that we have. For that would help us say that we aged well regardless of the number of years that went by.

***

Nivedita B, IRTS has scored the second highest marks in Essay - 148 during the year CSE 2018.

SAMPLE ESSAY 02

Essay: Importance of the Indian Ocean Region for India and India's Influence over it.

The geographical location of our country India is unique in itself. On one hand, we are connected to the vast Asian mainland in the North through the Giant snowy Himalayas. On the other hand, our landmass in the south tapers and extends in the vast Indian Ocean.

Historically our peninsular situation has allowed us to forge links with the civilizations beyond. The archaeological remains indicate extensive trade of Indus valley people with the Mesopotamian civilization. The use of the Arabian Sea for trade exchanges has kept our doors open to inputs in culture, cuisine, and language.

In the mediaeval period also, the trade routes acted like threads of connection that bound us to the world. The maritime silk route promoted extensive trade with China. One must not forget that during the 10-11th centuries, Imperial Cholas of Tanjore established their supremacy over SriLankan Island of Sri Vijaya and also Malaya.

Fast forward to the 17th Century, one finds that it was our ocean linkages that brought the European powers to our doorstep. This connection opened up a door for colonial rule, Modernization and also democracy.

Given this background, it would not be wrong to say that the Indian Ocean Region has single handedly driven Indian Civilization to what it is today. This depicts its importance historically.

"History need not remain the same, But geography will certainly.."

Even in contemporary times, the Indian ocean region has played a crucial role in our country. The economic significance can be judged by the fact that more than 80%of our trade and commerce is from the ocean. We import crude oil for energy security, electronic products for digital growth and other needful resources like gold, plasters etc. Our exports are also driven by this route to reach different places worldwide.

India recently became the second biggest exporter of fish and shrimp etc, signalling the livelihood prominence. Coastal states like Andhra, Tamil Nadu, Kerala harness the productivity of Bay of Bengal and Arabian Sea for food security and employment opportunities.

Indian Ocean regions play an Indispensable role politically also. Our strategic position also. Our strategic position right in the middle provides surveillance capability. For Regional security of our neighbours like Bangladesh, Srilanka, Seychelles etc. Our presence is reassuring. India's growing stature has encouraged nations like US, UK, France etc to forge enduring this with us to keep the trade routes safe and open for all.

Beyond this strategic perspective, the Indian Ocean Region plays a deterministic role in our agrarian economy. The differential temperature and pressure systems that drive Indian Monsoon, provide rainfall to our tropical lands. It's the life breath of our nation, relief from summers and source of food security for all. Even today due to lack of irrigation it's the 'Pressure cells' in the Indian Ocean on which our farmers depend. Our biodiversity and Environmental richness is also driven by this factor. It is notable that the Indian Ocean has played a crucial role in the Socio-Cultural sphere also. It was the ocean via which our rich cultural traditions of Buddhism and Indian philosophy made way to southEast Asia, Japan, China etc. This is a prominent pillar of Indian soft power today. The islands in water bodies like Lakshadweep and Andaman Nicobar host a truly indigenous population of tribals like garawas, Onges etc. They reflect our rich anthropological heritage.

In the contemporary scenario of Climate Change, our ocean links offer energy security. Geothermal and Tidal energy are non-conventional sources. Along with offshore wind and solar power, it can feed our energy hunger. Even the desalination technology can help alleviate the impending water crisis.

The above narrative has provided a bird's eye view of how the Indian Ocean region is really important for us. But in today's transactional world, our seriousness towards its importance would only be judged by our influence over the Indian Ocean region. The first aspect in this judgement is to evaluate our Strengths. From the past four years, the importance of the Indian ocean in our policy and defence domain has been growing. The modernisation of the Indian Navy, with nuclear powered submarines, aircraft carriers and support of satellite information, radars is underway.

India has been depending on its co-operation through joint navy drills, security doctrine and prompt assistance, during disasters. The Indian contingent has managed to deal with piracy in Somalia also. Our continued engagement with ASEAN nations has projected India as a Net Regional Security provider. The trust in Indian presence steps from our non-aggressive stance and belief in rules based order. This is in contrast to the Chinese attitude in the South China Sea. The reformation of Quad-grouping among Japan, US, Australia and India reaffirms our primary and stake holding in the Indian Ocean region.

But our influence is also unfortunately outlined by our weaknesses, Poor coordination among coast Guard and lapse of Vigil had caused deadly Mumbai terrorist attack via sea. Even today, command control for Integrated action is in the pipeline and plans for the Blue water Navy have not seen the light of day.

Countries like Sri Lanka, Maldives in the Indian Ocean region have shown affinity to China's huge investments and free trade agreements. To go on the geographical and the environmental front our influence has not been able to add to our capacity to respond to massive disasters. The Tsunami, Earthquakes, floods etc. pose a serious threat not only for human life and property but also to our image as a regional leader.

The loosening grip of our influence is visible in the deepening presence of China here. They bluntly assert that the 'Indian Ocean 'is not "India's Ocean". This growing threat to our security can undermine our strategic imperative. It may also lead to the destabilisation of regional peace and order. India must make amends soon to prevent the Indian Ocean region from becoming an area of contestation among world powers.

But our prime geographical location and historical engagement can help maintain our primacy and influence. The SAGAR-Security and Growth for all doctrine of foreign policy depicts our philosophy very well. The coming of Asian Century and rapid economic growth present us with ample opportunities. Like the Asia-Africa growth corridor supported by Japan can bolster our maritime linkages with the African continent. Advancements in space technology can help predict the changing weather and impending calamities. Our role in helping small developing islands tide over the humanitarian concerns of poverty and climate change can also enhance our goodwill and influence.

Moving forward India must play a pioneering role in the overall development of the Indian ocean region. Based on our values of peace and co-existence the resources in the oceans can be harnessed for mutual benefits. India must set the blueprint for a rule based order based on 'Vasudhaiva Kutumbakam'. Our larger concern for nature and ocean must drive our commitment for a sustainable future.

***

SAMPLE ESSAY 03

Philosophical Essay By Vikram Grewal

The Love of Power and the Love of Liberty are in Eternal Antagonism

The greatest 20th Century Spanish author Gabriel Garcia Marquez explores the conflict of power and liberty in his novels. Through his trademark style of 'Magical Realism' Marquez delineates the concept of 'Solitude of Power' in his celebrated novel. 'The Autumn of the Patriach' that tells the story of a powerful dictator in a village in Bolivia who ends up chaining himself by the use of excess of power.

There are several other works that pose questions over the eternal antagonism between the love for power and the love for liberty. Both these desires run against each other in several forms. For example in George Orwell's 'Animal Farm' the passion for liberty in Animals drives them to overthrow the seat of power of the owner of the farm. A strange sequence of events renders them powerful but ultimately lacking any liberty.

Power may be defined as 'control over resources or ideology'." You either tell them what to do or tell them what to think". A Classic excerpt from the Orwellian Dystopian novel'1984'. This notion of power is in direct contrast to liberty.

The Stalinist regions in USSR derived its strength from Lenin's principles of communism along with the hopes and desires of the proletariat that had brought about the Russian Revolution in 1917. However, Joseph Stalin's 'love for power' had reached a stage where the liberties of the subjects of the state were exceedingly curbed. Thus the love for power and liberty were natural rivals.

The above case is at the level of the state. We must also consider the 'eternal antagonism' on the levels of the individual and the society subsequently. The individual's yearn for power may occur as a desire for respect and authority in the family or friend circle. This however may cause him to behave in a certain way. This desire for power would drive his mannerisms, thus restricting his inmate or natural perspective and ultimately restricting his liberty of thought and action.

At level of Society, a community may conceive its position in the social matrix in a certain way. The typical example of the caste system- the Varna -ashramadharma in the context of the Indian Society exhibits a constant battle between the powerful Brahman and the powerless Shudra. These 'drama' roles have translated into Social stereotypes that thrive even today. These erode the liberty of the 'have nots' as opposed to the power and privilege of the 'haves' thus perpetrating the 'eternal antagonism'.

Beyond the levels of individual society and the state, the conflict between the love of power and the love of liberty is prevalent at the level of humanity. As John Locke one of the greatest thinkers of the age of greatest thinkers of the age of enlightenment remarks - a persistent battle between inalienable rights and their suppression by totalitarian forces within or outside is the story of humanity.

Similarly the theory of 'Class Conflict' by Karl Marx is built on the foundations of the antagonism between power and liberty. The renowned paper "On Liberty' by John Stuart Mills puts forward the potential of power to do "maximum good' to 'maximum people' thus propagating the 'Utilitarian' definition of power.

The Utilitarian notion that stems from Jereny Bentham and Occupies a respectable position in the Colonial ideology that aided the British in ruling the Indian Subcontinent is refuted by Mahatma Gandhi. Gandhiji focuses on the primacy of the soul and the continuous fight between power and liberty within itself. He emphasizes the value of truth that would help in resolving the fight. The power of truth, heremarks, is what liberates the soul.

Gandhiji's perspective is amongst the first to collaborate power with liberty. This collaboration is consolidated further by the constitution of India. The Preamble categorically mentions the promotion of 'Liberty' along with equality justice and fraternity. It also mentions the source of power of the document which is 'We the People'. Therefore it marries the power of the people by ensuring their liberty.

The Political notion of power has pervaded the human imagination since the liberty of the citizen came to be at stake during the French Revolution. This revolution has been the fountainhead of ideas all across the world. However, even this event failed to resolve the crisis between power and liberty. As we notice, the love for power of France's Napoleon was overarching and oppressing the love for liberty of the French post 1794 after the Jacabins tried to do the same.

We have come a long way since 1789's revolution. So much so that we realize that power is not always 'Politically' rivalled by liberty. Swami Vivekanand gave a call to delve in social service as each individual was powerful enough to liberate his own suffering as well as the suffering of the society. Acharya Vinoba Bhave of Sarvodaya Samaj too believed in a similar concept of power. According to him, power did not lie in potential to do good but the intention to do good.

The great debate of the post-enlightenment world is the debate between the opposing ideologies of "Capitalism and Socialism". These ideologies differ massively when we look at their orientations- while the former is 'Power- Oriented' the letter is 'Liberty- Oriented' but with limitations. Liberalism and Conservatism are also oriented differently to power and liberty. However, the former is a clear supporter of liberty in the antagonism it faces eternally from the corridors of power.

Despite the acknowledgment of the eternal antagonism between love of power and love of liberty. We must realize that their relationship is also complementary. Power checks liberty and liberty checks power. A concept that is the basis of separation of powers between Judiciary, Executive, and Legislative- all three have power and liberties that are in turn checked by each other's jurisdiction.

The power- liberty relationship is in fact supplementary as well. Consider GWF Hegel's theory of 'dialectics' a balance between thesis and its anti thesis is not antagonistic but supplementary in order to establish balance in the system- a synthesis. Therefore, according to Hegel, Power and Liberty form a synthesis.

We must also consider the view of Kautilya here as it is imperative to see the eternal antagonism of power and liberty in the context of Ancient India that was marked by Monarchial Mindset. The 'Arthashastra' in one of its volumes, puts down the time-table/ routine of a King that he must follow daily. A simple look at this brings us to notice- how even after having exponential power the King's liberty is bound by the virtue of serving his subjects.

Another interesting observation in the context of power and liberty is the suffragette movement. This movement was aimed at gaining the women the right to vote. In other words, the 'liberty' to exercise their vote would add 'Power' to their political rights.

Hence, we have seen how liberty begets power and how in some cases power results in increased liberty. However, the eventual assimilation is something that is intangible and might be exceeding abstract from the materialistic approach of looking at it. This brings us to two antagonistic views that demarcated the World War Era as a direct challenge between "power's love' and 'Liberty's Love'.

Adolf Hitler in 'Mein Kampf' writes how power needs to be taken away from a certain section of people and given to the 'higher' race that deserve it. This idea stemmed from 'eugenics' - a philosophy completely rejected by Roosevelt, his American counterpart. The Allied powers and Axis powers were both hinged at acquiring 'power' - whatever be the means but this clearly withered the liberty of their populations through war practices such as compulsory recruitment, increased industrial output and mandatory national duty rendering. Thus, they imposed shackles on their own liberty to acquire power - an illustration of the eternal antagonism.

Liberty and Power as we have seen are in confrontation with each other since time immemorial. However this constant duel must continue as it is a source of an abstract discourse that can lead to enlightenment by knowing more about human virtues. The Upanishads also state that the knowledge of the self (atma) is the knowledge of the universe (Brahman).

***

Vikram Grewal, IFS has scored the highest marks in Essay - 161 during the year CSE 2018.

SAMPLE ESSAY 04

If any machine is misused, the moral evil is in the man who misuses it, not in the machine

"Our scientific power has outrun our spiritual power. We have guided missiles and misguided men."

-Martin Luther King Jr

Scenario one- Year was 2014. Floods in Chennai had created havoc in the lives of many. Public thought of using the internet to address the calamity. Regular updates were provided, whereabouts of rescue team, call for relief, material etc. Through the right use of the machine , the incident was largely prevented from becoming a disaster.

Scenario two- Whereas in 2012, Bengaluru, the Silicon Valley of the nation gave birth to Frankenstein's monster. The Internet was used to spread the lies of rumours and violence, against the people of Northeast. This created confusion and fear amongst the migrant population resulting in their mass exodus to their home states.

In both the scenarios, the internet was used to produce different outcomes. So, where did the mistake lie? What is it about the machine or us humans? Through this essay we will try to address this very question.

Use of machines across history

The development of modern machines started post the advent of compasses, steam machines etc. People like Vasco-Da-Gama used this compass to find new continents and increase the connectivity of the world. However, the same machine formed the basis of colonialism and imperialism. Increased expeditions led to increased territorial control by the major powers of the time. So who was at fault here? The machine or the humans who used it. Clearly the answer is humans.

After that, machines like the press, railways came up. Freedom fighters like Mahatma Gandhi, LalaLajpat Rai used them to spread the ideas of justice, liberty, independence and arouse nationalist feelings among the masses.

However, colonial powers used the same machines to discriminate among the people and cause further exploitation.

Thus, history is a testimony to the fact that it is the (wo)man who decided on the proper use or misuse of the machine. Therefore, the model responsibility of its outcome falls on the humans. If it is misused, the moral evil indeed lies in the human being.

Machines in the contemporary world-

In the health sector, humans have made tremendous progress. We have designed machines which can perform surgery with much accuracy, detect the abnormalities and diseases, beforehand and provide chemotherapy for diseases like cancer. The machines have also ensured greater access, availability and affordability of drugs through mass production of generic drugs.

However, the same machines when misused have cost certain issues. For example, sex determination through ultrasound machines leads to identification of sex of the foetus and has been misused for female foeticide. The advent of bio - designer babies where selective genes can be used for the development of desired characteristics in a human baby has high potential of misuse. This is because of the ignored ethical and moral values that are a part of the human conscience. And hence the burden of its misuse must fall on the man.

In the agriculture sector, machines are enabling farmers and thus improving food security of the population in general. For Eg- Use of machines has led to greater productivity, faster transportation and better connectivity. This has increased their incomes and profits. Effective Irrigation has also been possible because of such machines.

However, the overuse and misuse of such machines is hampering the sustainability of agriculture. Use of fertilisers has caused soil degradation. Water pump exploitation has resulted in agriculture becoming a major use of groundwater (89%) and resulting in water stress. Machines are not at fault here, but the man who has used them.

Similarly, the genius pursuit of the theory of relativity led to the development of nuclear technologies. It was perceived as a solution to the energy problems the world is going to face. But the moral evil in the man found a way to misuse it. It was soon misused to produce nuclear bombs and hence threatened the survival of entire humankind. It has given birth to irresponsible nuclear powers like North Korea, Pakistan etc.

Space sector is another domain where morality has been ignored. Space - a global common was meant to be used for peaceful purposes. For example, the International space station for coordinated research activities, Bhuvan portal for the Geo tagging of MGNREGA Assets etc., but mankind has started the weaponization of space. Thus, the issue is not with the rocket's or spaceships (machines), but with the man who operates it.

The advent of the Information and Technology sector has boosted the service sector of the economy fuelled by globalisation. But the same cyberspace is being misused for several activities. For instance, religious indoctrination through cyber training has been reported to be behind many terrorist activities across the world. Similarly, child pornography, cyber fraud and cyber warfare cause child sexual exploitation, cheating and harm to national security respectively.

To better understand the use and misuse of machines, ask a mother who is able to talk and see her child daily, who is studying abroad through devices like phone or computer. But also ask the pain of a mother whose child was killed in violence due to fake rumours on the same internet.

"The real problem is not whether machines think, but whether men do".

Machines themselves are not good or bad. It is we, humans who make them so. The decision lies with us. Therefore, if any of the machines are misused, it is not the fault of the machine. Machines are inhuman. It cannot differentiate between what is morally right or wrong. But, it is we who are solely responsible for it.

Towards a brighter future :

So, now the question here is , how do we decide if a machine is being misused or not?

Gandhiji's talisman comes as a rescue here. As said by the Mahatma, if we keep the interests of the poorest or most vulnerable person in our actions, the end result will bring justice for all. And also, it is when we take the path of a golden mean between the two extremes of non-use and misuse, that we will find a proper use for machines.

It is the responsibility of the society as a whole to imbibe morality in the usage of machines. Certain international initiatives taken like the Outer space Treaty to prevent space weaponization, Nuclear weapons ban Treaty etc brings in light the code of ethics that countries should follow. It is high time for mankind to universally adopt these. At a local level, a primer of ethical values and social virtues should be given to children as a part of curriculum to understand the human values of justice, fairness, love, truth and non-violence. Such righteousness in the heart while using and developing the machines will ultimately result in world peace and order.

As APJ Abdul Kalam said,

"where there is righteousness in the heart, there is beauty in character.

Where there is beauty in character, there is harmony in home.

Where there is harmony in home, there is order in the nation.

Where there is order in the nation. There is peace in the world.

***

Sample Answers

GS 1

Why do the geostrophic winds and westerly jet streams behave unusually? To what extent do they affect the weather around us. Explain with examples from India and elsewhere.

Geostrophic winds are <u>upper trophospheric winds</u> moving in relation to global permanent wind systems.

Jet streams are the <u>fast moving geostrophic winds.</u> Unusual behaviour of Geostrophic winds of jet streams

<u>Causes:</u>

- Changing surface temperatures, affecting the upper trophospheric wind circulation.
- Climate Change has played a major role in unusual behaviour of recent past like erratic monsoons, break in polar vortex etc.
- Pollution of atmosphere thus affecting the solar insolation and changing the net heat budget of the earth.

<u>Effect of Jetstream and Geostrophic winds</u>

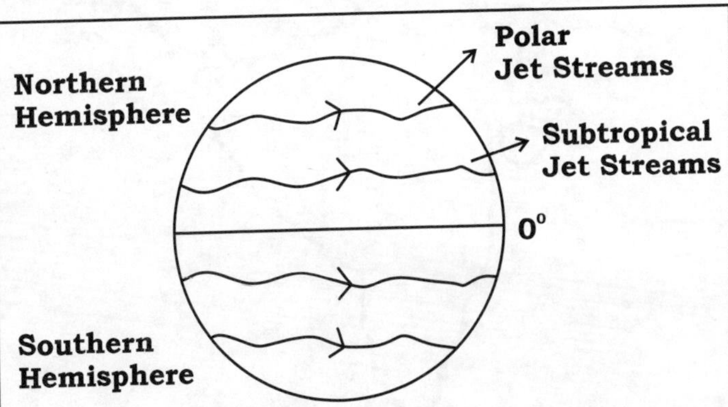

Fig:- Model of Circumpolar Jet Stream

Break in the Polar Vortex

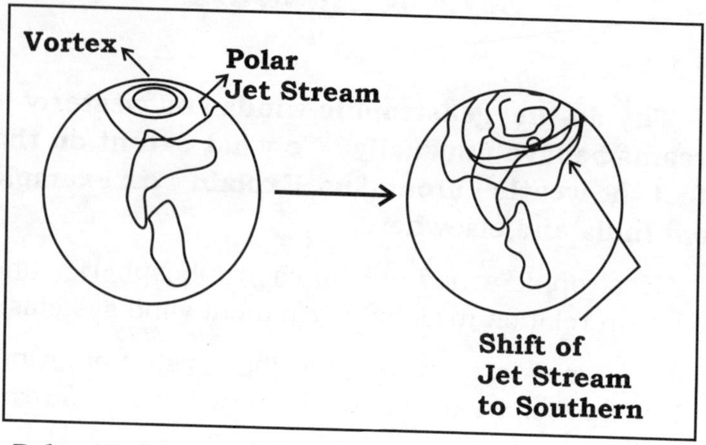

- Polar Vortex which is confined to poles, has been causing Polar Vortex events
- Cold weather in areas like Canada, USA, Europe etc.

In India:

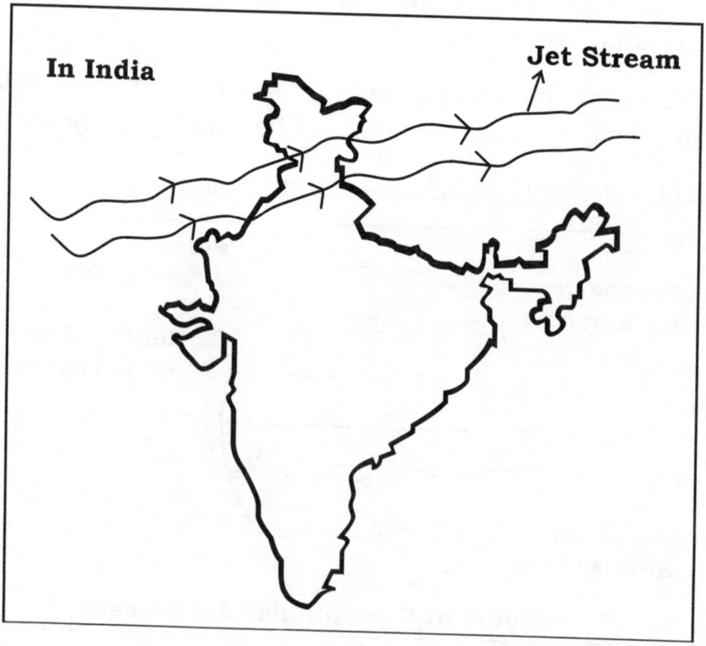

During Winter

- Jet Streams are responsible for coming of Western disturbances towards India.
- Shifting of Western Jet Streams towards North of Himalayas is the reason for sudden onset of Monsoons, failure of it leads to erratic Monsoons.

Thus, Jetstreams and Geostrophic winds have their effects on the weather system of India and Countries of the World.

Globalisation is synonymous to westernisation. Comment. Do you think that globalisation has also led to spread of Indian ideas, traditions and culture in the western world?

Globalisation refers to the interconnectedness between a country and the rest of the world. It involves seamless movement of capital, people, labour, goods and services. It eventually transforms the culture of the participating nations. For example, the K- Pop culture from South Korea is now a teenage phenomenon across the world. Spread of yoga in other countries as yoga is becoming popular and is being adopted as a lifestyle.

Westernisation refers to the spread and inculcation of the ideas, beliefs and cultures of the western world. For example the fast food like burger, pizza etc which has now spread to even our villages.

As mentioned above, both these concepts are different in various ways.

Globalisation	Westernisation
Refers to the interconnectedness of the whole world	It is restricted to the spread of ideas from the western world
Intermix of western and eastern values is seen. For example, the coexistence of spiritualism and materialism in many parts of the country	Only Western values dominate. For example, bias towards capitalistic society and dominance of individualism

Yes, globalisation has spread Indian ideas -

1. Spiritualism-western spiritual philosophy is influenced by the theory of Karma through various movements like ISKCON, Art of living etc.

2. Yoga-United Nations declared 21st June as International Day of Yoga, seeing the influence of this ancient technique in both India and the world.

3. The spread of food culture. For example,Shahi Paneer is ranked 5th most liked traditional dish all over the world.

4. Bollywood is a principal medium of the spread of Indian ideologies, ideas and culture through the portrayals of different characters and settings. Indian songs, especially, are very popular that depict the costumes, methods of celebrations, festivals, etc. in an ideal manner. Eg - Naatu Naatu won Oscars.

5. The Non resident Indians and Persons of Indian origin who are now working in the West not only

showcase their hard working and honest work ethic but also Indian festivals and way of life.

Globalisation has allowed the Indian cultural traditions and values to be spread overseas. At the same time. India is also influenced by the western values of Individualism, liberalism, materialism and way of lifestyle giving a true meaning to the world Global.

The ineffectiveness of the league of nations to check the Japanese aggression against China was first serious blow to its reputation as an agency for providing security. Discuss.

The League of Nations was formed during World War I to keep the collective security of nations at its core in 1920.

Its Failure to check the Japanese aggression can be seen through the following -

1. 1931-Japan invaded Manchuria.
2. 1935-Japan, under the dictator, Tojo expanded its base in the Pacific, for example, the Samoa islands, Fuji, etc
3. 1937-full fledged war against China and attempt to annex. When league objected, Japan left the League of Nations in 1933.
4. Annexation of Sakhalin, Kuril Island.
5. Annex Indochina-Vietnam, Cambodia, Southeast Asia, up to India that is Manipur.
6. Attack on Pearl Harbor in the United States, 1942.

Other Reasons for the failure of league of Nations—

1. Non representative i.e only 42 nations are present in which no representation from colonies was given.
2. Aggressor nations like Germany and Japan undermined their authority against which they did little in response.
3. Absence of giant powers like the United States of America, USSR, Germany.
4. Policy of appeasement by Britain and France towards Hitler.
5. Global economic crisis of 1929-no country in position to resist the aggressors.

Even though, League of Nations was able to prevent the attack of Bulgaria by Greece. And handled the refugee crisis in Palestine, it failed to attain security objectives for world peace paving the way for the formation of the United Nations.

GS 2

For India RCEP looks like a double-edged sword. Comment and explicate India's stand on RCEP.

Regional comprehensive economic partnership is a trade agreement between 10 Countries of ASEAN and its 6 FREE Trade Agreement partners.

RCEP - Double edged sword -For India

Benefits	Concerns
Market for Indian Exports- IT, Services, Textile etc.	Fear of growing our Trade deficit
Attract Investments both into India and also Indian Investor can invest abroad	Dumping of Chinese goods

More Integration of South and South east Asia	Affects the domestic producers.
Furthering of our Act-East Policy	Strict IPR regime
	Competition from Vietnam and others for our textile industry

India's stand on RCEP:

- India wants - differential trade agreement
- It does not want to provide blanket- free flow to Chinese goods.
- It wants IPR regime out of the pact.
- More protection to safeguard the Indian Agricultural market.

RCEP is a boon to the South Asian Economy but at the same time careful negotiations are the need of the hour to protect domestic business interests.

Discuss the right to the internet as a fundamental right with suitable examples

In Anuradha Bhasin vs Union of India case, Supreme court held that the Right to the internet can be construed as a fundamental right under article 19. This is because the Internet has become an integral part of human life and a basic necessity for communication and freedom of expression.

Internet as a fundamental right-

1. It is a part of the right to information as it is important for access to knowledge and resources.

2. The Internet is essential to realise the right to education in today's time. For example, online classes, information and news are available, especially this could be seen in the context of COVID-19 pandemic.

3. Right to communication and sharing of ideas. Example - Government uses twitter and facebook to inform citizens of the different schemes.

4. Right to social welfare measures. For example, direct benefit transfers, tracking status of the PDS.

5. Right to privacy as explained in the KS Puttaswamy case of the Supreme Court.

6. Most of the service sector jobs today include the usage of internet and digital media. Hence it has become essential for labour and work like in Swiggy, Ola, IT Companies etc.

Issues involved in declaring internet a part of the fundamental right basket -

1. No specific data protection law is in place in the country. It is a hindrance to realise this fundamental right.

2. E- divide -there is a huge possibility of a rural urban divide or a rich and poor divide. For example, only 23% of the government school children had access to online classes during the pandemic.

3. Cyber security issues-to enjoy the right to the internet as a fundamental right data protection law on the lines of GDPR of the order is the need of the hour.

4. Poor digital literacy among the masses.

5. It is an issue to tackle when internet is used to spread fake news, hate, for cyberbullying etc

To realise the right to the internet as a fundamental right for all the citizens it is essential to invest in infrastructure, accessibility and security of the cyber ecosystem.

Cleansing elections is the best way to promote ethics in public life, reduce corruption and governance standards. Discuss the efficacy of RPA 1951 in this regard.

India being the largest democracy, the Elections form the core of the democratic system. Rightly called as the festival of democracy due to the scale of the machinery involved, the process isn't devoid of corrupt practices.

Ethical concerns in the elections—

1. Politicians with criminal backgrounds contest elections in large numbers. For example in the 17th Lok Sabha, 31% of the legislators have criminal cases registered against them.

2. Opaque nature of political funding. For example, the recent electoral bond scheme is controversial as it eases political funding from anonymous sources.

3. Vote bank politics based on religion, caste, language, etc

4. Defections before and after elections.

5. Money, Liquor as well as muscle power used to garner votes.

RPA, 1951 has certain provisions to check illegal, unethical and corrupt practises as follows :

1. Section 123 of RPA defines corrupt practices -

Disqualification of MP, MLA if they fail to declare assets, fail to give election expenditures and seek vote on communal, caste and racial sentiments, promote hatred & enmity declared as corrupt practice. As reiterated by the Supreme Court in the Abhiram Singh vs CD Commachen case.

2. Model code of conduct is the guideline of behaviour for the candidate and parties to provide a level playing field for conducting fair elections
3. Robust election machinery. For example, expenditure officers, polling officers to oversee the free and fair conduct of elections.
4. Ban on exit polls being published when voting is going on in some areas.
5. Provides Disqualification of members when convicted for any offence for more than two years and having interest in govt contracts, involving moral turpitude etc
6. Assets and antecedents of the candidate to be disclosed on the website.

But the effectiveness of the law has been hampered due to the following -

1. Electoral bonds have not been able to bring in the required transparency in political funding
2. More than 50 % of elected representatives in the Last Lok Sabha have criminal records.
3. The extent of money power playing a role in elections has not reduced. ECI had recently given a statement that controlling the flow of money in elections has been a challenge in Karnataka Elections 2023.

4. Post elections many candidates have spoken publicly about how money, caste, religion and language have been influencing the elections and hardly any action has been taken against it.

Though cleansing the election is the cornerstone for an ethical democracy, other general measures also need to be taken to improve the overall governance standard in public life.

GS 3

The simultaneous exploration of moon and sun is a watermark of IRSO's missions. Enumerate the significance and objective of Aditya Mission. Is sun's nuclear fusion process artificially imitable for extracting civil nuclear energy? Give your Opinion

Indian Space Research Organisation [ISRO) is known for its innovative, cost effective and ambitious mission.

Two such missions are Aditya and Chandrayan I & II. Simultaneous exploration of Sun & Moon is a watermark because

- This helps us to understand the availability of Resource and their utilization for the good of mankind
- Puts India in the higher echelons of the Global Space Map.
- Gives the required edge for the future exploration. Eg: NISARetc.

Significance of Aditya Mission:

- First Mission by ISRO to explore the Sun and its atmosphere especially the Photosphere
- One among the very few countries to explore the sun.

- Helps in moving forward with ITER experiment by European Union, where India is a part.

Objective of Aditya Mission:

- Study Sun's Atmosphere
- Study Nature of Solar Winds
- Sun's spots in the photosphere - helps us to understand the interiors of the sun.

Sun's Nuclear Fusion & Artificial imitability - Energy Security

- International Thermonuclear Experimental Reactor on the border of Switzerland is being carried out to study this.
- Nuclear Fusion and its civil nuclear potential is very much important because no need of investing more on inputs.
- Very less waste generation
- No Nuclear radiation etc.

Challenges to such experiment is to control the huge energy and also the thermal conditions in the reactor.

Success of the above experiment will be a big breakthrough for the Civil Nuclear program and lead to Sustained energy security.

What are the important features of the PM Gati Shakti master plan? How far do you think it will reduce the infrastructural inefficiency and increase productivity and greater economic activity ?

answer in 150 words.

PM Gati Shakti - National Master plan for multi modal connectivity is the instrument to realise the infrastructural and connectivity needs of the Indian economy.

Its features are as below-

1. Single digital platform across ministries featuring Bharatmala, Sagarmala, electronic park, industrial park etc
2. Transparency in operation. For example an inter ministerial task force headed by the PM Monitors it
3. Integration and coordination between 16 line ministries
4. It will leverage technology extensively including spatial planning tools from ISRO
5. In line with national infrastructure pipeline, that is today's 11 lakh crore rupees
6. Private sector engagement and government to be the facilitator.

The major goal of the master plan is to bring in efficiency in infrastructure works to give required boost to the equitable economic activity as follows :

Reduce infrastructural inefficiencies	**Increase productivity**	**Greater economic activity**
Coordination among ministries	Save time and cost	By generating employment increases consumption expenditure

Avoid duplication and address regional imbalances	Holistic approach. For example, Road construction takes sewage while constructing	Attract investment
Increase resource efficiency and reduces logistics cost	Promote transparency and avoid corruption	Faster economic growth

Way forward

1. Strong regulatory oversight. For example, bodies like Parliamentary committees, etc.
2. Leverage artificial intelligence and technology
3. Innovative economic model to engage private players.

Gati Shakti, master plan is a model that, if implemented effectively can help India realise the dream of a 5 trillion dollar economy

Methane emissions contributed nearly half of the present temperature increase in global warming. Is it possible for India to control methane emission and achieve its NDC commitment without compromising development? Examine

250 words

Methane is the second largest contributor to global warming and is one of the targets for reduction in India's NDC.

Major methane emission sources are agriculture, animal

rearing, wetlands and marshes, industries, Petroleum and natural gas, coal mining, smoking, vehicle exhaust etc.

Contribution of Methane to global warming-

1. High greenhouse potential that is more than 25 times that of CO2.

2. Long period of persistence in the atmosphere.

3. No effective methods to sequester so mitigation is the only way.

Mitigation efforts by India under NDC commitments are planned such that the emissions are reduced without affecting the developmental needs of our nation -

1. Significant commitments at COP 26 Glasgow convention.

- 50 % of energy requirement from renewable energy by 2030.

- To limit carbon emission intensity to 45% per capita by 2030.

- Achieve net 0 emissions by 2070.

- Reach 500GWNon-fossil energy capacity by 2030.

2. Monitoring efforts - Methane is part of national air quality index by CPCB

3. To decrease vehicle exhaust-

- Fame-II scheme to encourage electrification of public and shared transportation

- Ethanol blending program of 2018 whose target is 20% by 2022

- Transition from BS4 to BS 7

4. Thermal power plants -

- To be phased out gradually
- Flue gas desulphurisation
- Fly ash utilisation policy

5. Agriculture

- Prevention of stubble burning and incentivisation of farm mechanisation.
- Scientific cattle rearing.
- Gobar Dhan scheme to produce energy from waste.

However, India faces certain challenges in mitigation efforts,

1. Poor EV market penetration, safety concerns and high cost.
2. Dependence on coal for 56% of the total energy needs.
3. High cattle population which are stray.
4. High net sown area of water intensive crops like rice, sugar cane etc.

The way forward

1. Re consider joining the global methane pledge for better commitments towards global warming.
2. Promotion of green public transit system intensively.
3. Increase renewable capacity on mission mode.

Balancing economic development in achieving NDC is

the need of the hour to achieve SDG 7 and SDG 12 for Climate sensitive development.

GS4

What does the following quotations mean to you in the present context?

a. The worst sinner has a future even as the greatest Saint has had a past. No one is so good or bad as he imagines.- Sarvepalli Radhakrishnan (10 marks)

b. The Rights of every man are diminished when the rights of one man are threatened - John F Kennedy (150 Words, 10 Marks)

A. The worst sinner has a future even as the greatest Saint has had a past. No one is so good or bad as he imagines. Sarvepalli Radhakrishnan

It is said that 'Hate the sin, not the sinner'. No human being is perfect in himself and defects are a part of being human.

When Angulimala confronted Buddha, he was a wicked person. After the event of interaction, he became a saint and an adherent of non-violence.

Even Mahatma Gandhiji had certain habits which he had denounced later as said by himself in his autobiography, 'My Experiments with Truth'.

Ashoka the Great, had committed several wars, only after the War of Kalinga when realisation of death and destruction struck him, he denounced everything.

Thus nobody's fate is set in stone and it is the duty of every person to forgive the sinner and give him an opportunity to become a saint. Rather than Retributive justice, Reformative justice should take precedence.

B. The Rights of every man are diminished when the rights of one man are threatened - *John F Kennedy*

It is said that poverty anywhere leads to poverty every where.

If the individual rights are encroached upon and we don't speak against them showing indifference to them, one day our rights may also be diminished.

Eg: If we don't speak against the sexual violence of a girl at Kathua, then such incident may also occur in other places in our society and then no one will be there to speak on our behalf. The pro democratic movement in Hongkong has to alarm all of us to prevent dictatorial regimes all around the world.

The environmental degradation of intentional forest fires in Amazon Forests have to alarm us to prevent our own forest from fire and to protect our mother earth.

Thus, showing indifference and acting in a manner of moral disengagement won't help mankind in the long run.

You are a CEO and founder of an Ed tech company. You are under tremendous pressure from the investors in your company to increase the profitability of the company and undertake

downsizing. After making a few bad acquisitions, the company's finances have taken a huge hit in the last couple of years. The downsizing is suggested with the hope that the company's profitability would rise as it often does when mass layoffs or downsizing decisions are carried out. Moreover, the investors hinted that such measures would attract further investment from them, which has come as a ray of hope considering the ongoing volatile market conditions slowing down in big ticket findings. Given the situation, rumours of unscrupulous firing have started doing the rounds among employees. It has increased apprehensiveness and reduced cohesiveness among them. You have informed the investors that the cost cutting exercise can affect the output as well as reputation of the company in the long run. However, they are adamant to pursue the same.

1. **Identify the stakeholders and ethical issues involved in the case.**
2. **You and the HR team have identified some options and are deliberating to put them across to the investors for consideration. Discuss the merits and demerits of each of these**

- **Identifying key high performers and offering them suitable position before implementing the lay off decision.**
- **Putting the terminated employees on retainer to work part-time**
- **executing the layoff order in the same spirit as it was asked by the investors and letting them deal with the long-term consequences**

Without restricting yourself to be above options, discuss the course of action you will take and provide adequate reasons for the same.

Downsizing and cost-cutting is often seen as a way to increase profits which violates the principles of corporate governance that are fairness, trust and focus on the stakeholder welfare being given priority.

a. Stakeholders in the case-

- myself, CEO and founder
- Employees of the company
- Investors I.e. the past investors and future investors
- Shareholders of the company
- Consumers receiving the service
- Corporate fraternity
- Government which regulates the companies

Ethical issues in the case

- Rights of the employees and the livelihood are at stake
- Violation of the corporate governance principles like rights and responsibilities towards employees and fairness towards all
- Consumer service quality may get affected due to termination and layoffs
- Government's mandate to provide social security, opportunities and wages which will also be violated.

- Negative influence on the company's work culture.
- Company Profit vs Employee livelihood

<u>Merits and demerits of options-</u>

<u>Identify and keep high performing employees by offering them suitable position before implementing the layoff</u>

<u>Merits</u>- it will help retain best employee and remove the low performers

- it will send a message that work is rewarded
- Investment will come into the company as promised.

<u>Demerits</u>- it will cause inequality and rift between the workers

- Consumers service quality may be affected
- Companies image will be affected in the long-term

<u>Putting the terminated employees on retainer to work part time</u>

<u>Merits</u> - Company will be able to provide services to the consumers.

- Adequate opportunity will be given to join other companies.
- Maintains income security temporarily of the employee who has provided service to the institution.

<u>Demerits-</u> It may still deter investors as there will be major scope for cost-cutting.

- Affects job security.
- Employees who have been terminated may not

give their best towards work.

Executing the layoff order in the same spirit as it was asked by the investors and letting them deal with the long-term consequence

Merits- increase in investment as more investors will be attracted further helping the company to compete in the big ticket business environment.

- Increase profits due to cost cutting.
- Clarity for the employees compared to part time job.

Demerits- Employees rights are violated.

- Quality of service will be affected.
- Long-term loss to the company in terms of perception as a stable workplace.
- The Company will have to let go of trained human resources.
- Might not attract efficient employees in the future.

Course of action-

As CEO I would not go completely according to the demand of the investors but do a proper analysis keeping the company's interest as the centrepoint of decision making.

1. Objective evaluation of the impact of the employees across all departments. This should help in finding out the inefficient employees and whose role has become redundant. (Being gender sensitive about maternity leaves and child care leaves)
2. Send notice of termination according to the

government laws and labour laws rules.

3. Provide adequate compensation and time to shift to other company
4. Not to go with layoff immediately
5. Reports on the consequences of layoffs should be prepared because the service quality should not be compromised. If done, the profitability will decrease in the long-term and may affect the company's image and perception in the market.

The contribution of the employee should be evaluated and an adequate opportunity should be given to the laid of employees to ensure that their livelihood is protected. Also this makes sure that the company's image as providing a good work culture and environment is preserved for attracting better talent and profit in the future.

Case Study

Shiva is the only son of Venkat and Geetha. They are stuck with poverty. In past, their family was ancestrally rich and prestigious which due to a business loss fell into status to the present condition. Venkat and Geetha work hard to raise Shiva and educate him in a high-profile school and college. From Childhood, Shiva was brought up by his parents by instructing the need of money and the status it gives in society. They instilled a desire in his heart and he at any cost wanted to escalate his family's financial status as par with its past eminence. In total, family's prestige was the non negotiable value inculcated in him by his family. Shiva is preparing for Civil Services Examination oflndia.

(a) Are Indian families right in inculcating the Value

'family prestige' so deep in children?

(b) To what extent families are responsible for various misconduct by serving officers (250 words, 20 Marks)

Right seeds, give the right tree"

The case study shows the importance of Family and Parents in the process of Socialisation of the Child. The values inculcated in the formative years of Childhood, will be with us for life time. This also shows the importance given by few parents to unbridled materialism rather than for integrated humanism.

(a) Family Prestige is something that the Indian Society favours more than anything. It is assumed to be correct that a child has the responsibility to uphold the respect of his family once he grows up.

It is natural to expect such a thing in Indian society that thrives on collectivism and social interdependence.

But inculcating the values of gaining money at any cost and thus upholding family prestige cannot be accepted at all.This makes them indulge in activities like corruption, consumerism, nepotism etc.

(b) Families are responsible in making a good citizen and all the more a good civil servant.

- Increasing corruption among Civil Services is due to such in built importance to money and the values of selfishness.
- The Bureaucratic Apathy can also be traced back to the upbringing of the Children in undemocratic parenting.

- Lack of resilience towards, the failures and disappointment by officers and thus increasing suicides is also a result of very fragile emotional investment during upbringing of child.
- Frequent quarrels between the husband and wife, may cause mental trauma to the child and once becoming an officer he may become intolerant towards the views of his subordinates or common public Leading to rude behavior.
- Increasing incidents of sexual violence against women by higher level officers as it came to notice during #Metoo movement can be traced back to the upbringing of the officers without proper gender sensitization.

In addition to Family, the peer group, schools, societal conduct, work culture etc also play a role in the socialization and value inculcation of the child but family is the first school of value education.

***

Mains 2024 Questions Analysis

GS I

Q20. Critically analyse the proposition that there is a high correlation between India's cultural diversities and socio-economic marginalities. (Answer in 250 words)

India is a multi-religious, multi-linguistic and multi-ethnic society. But these diversity indicators are often associated with socio-economic marginalities as well.

Correlations Between Diversity and Socio-economic Marginalities:

- Tribal people constitute 8.6% of the total population and are socially and economically marginalised.

  According to the Xa Xa Committee report, they have the highest poverty and the lowest literacy rate and access to basic facilities like health, education and other essential needs.

- Caste: Scheduled Castes face discrimination and untouchability, which affects their standard of living.

  E.g. 97% of manual scavengers are from scheduled castes.

- Religious Marginalization: According to the Sachar Committee Report, Muslims have a higher poverty rate, less representation and lag in education when compared to other religious communities.

- Ethnic Diversity: The northeastern region of our country is comparatively underdeveloped due to geographical inaccessibility as well as ethnic conflicts.

- Women in India face patriarchal attitude which affects their access to education and employment opportunities.

  E.g. According to the Economic Survey 2023–2024 Female LFPR is just 37%.

Though a few groups face marginality, it is not directly linked to cultural diversity. There are others factors also, which are associated with marginality.

The Marginality Indicators Do Not Always Overlap with the Cultural Diversity Categories as Seen:

1. Religious groups like Parsis, Jains and Sikhs have high income and literacy rates.
2. Reservations for SCs, STs, and OBCs have increased their representation in the legislature and their employment opportunities.
3. The cultural diversity in the states like Rajasthan, North East and so on are used to harness the potential of tourism to create economic opportunities.

Similarly, other factors are also responsible for marginalities other than cultural diversity like the lack of adequate infrastructure related to health, education, drinking water and so on.

Way Forward:

1. Affirmative action taken to secure the rights of SCs, STs, and OBCs in the form of reservation can help reduce the gap.
2. Government schemes and initiatives like Ayushman Bharat, RTE, Midday Meal Scheme, and MGNREGA can help alleviate the socio-economic distress in marginalised communities.

3. Community development models recognising the unique needs of the community can help foster better outcomes.

Targeted intervention to alleviate the socio-economic marginalities is required so as to overcome the extensive gap of development and bring the population into mainstream.

GS II

Q14. Explain the reasons for the growth of Public Interest Litigation in India. As a result of it, has the Indian Supreme Court emerged as the world's most powerful judiciary? (Answer in 250 words)

Public Interest Litigation (PIL) is a legal action initiated in court for the enforcement of public interest and the fundamental rights (FRs) for those who cannot approach courts.

Reasons for the Growth of PIL:

1. Relaxations of "Locus standii": This has enabled people acting in good faith on behalf of others to register a case in court.
2. Judicial Activism: Judges are taking up an active part in protecting the FRs of citizens.

   E.g. Navtej Singh Johar case for sec 377 and LGBTQ
3. Presence of legislative and executive vacuum encourages the court to establish guidelines as seen in case of Vishaka Guidelines for the prevention of sexual harassment at workplace after which a law was formulated in 2013.

4. Rise of public consciousness about general public interest like environment and poverty

   E.g. MC Mehta Case in which absolute liability of industries was established in multiple environmental cases.

Indian Supreme Court as the World's Most Powerful Judiciary:

1. Judicial Innovation: "Basic structure doctrine" to uphold the constitutional values and morality was seen in the Keshavananda Bharti Case.
2. Judicial interpretation of Act 21 is changed from "Procedure established by law" to "Due process of law"

   E.g. Menaka Gandhi Case
3. Protecting independence and prevention of interference by the executive

   E.g. 4th Judges Case on NJAC where the judicial appointments were established as a judicial prerogative only
4. Increase in Judicial legislation like Vishaka Guidelines, Guidelines on Mob Violence, and so on.

Limitations:

1. The Supreme Court is limited by the constitution and constitutional morality.
2. Display of Judicial Restraints like same-sex marriage rights case in which SC noted that

this question is beyond the purview of the court in the absence of statutory provision.

Though the PIL has increased the power of the Supreme Court, making it one of the most powerful courts of the world, judicial restraint is equally important to maintain the balance of power and prevent concerns of overreach.

GS III

Q15. The world is facing an acute shortage of clean and safe freshwater. What are the alternative technologies which can solve this crisis? Briefly discuss any three such technologies citing their key merits and demerits. (Answer in 250 words)

According to WHO, more than 2 billion people lack access to safe drinking water and by 2050, more than 50% of global population will live in water-stressed regions. Increased population, industrialisation, urbanisation and climate change have increased the pressure on water demand and affected the supply.

Technologies that Can Address This Crisis:

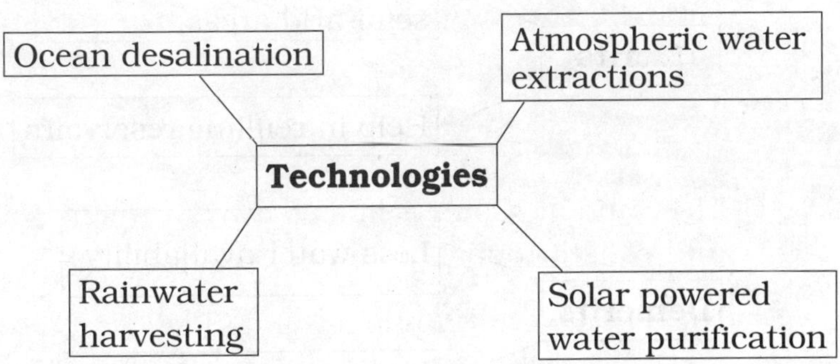

3 Technologies:

1. Ocean desalination: Converting seawater into drinking water by using Reverse Osmosis and thermal distillation

   E.g. Desalination ports found in Chennai (India) and Israel

   - **Merits**
     - Large scale potential
     - Year-round availability
   - **Demerits**
     - Increased cost of technology and maintenance
     - Increase in water discharge

2. Atmospheric water extraction: Collection of atmospheric moisture and then condensing it to water

   - **Merits**
     - Can be used in arid and semi-arid areas
     - Help in refilling reservoirs
   - **Demerits**
     - Less water availability
     - Inefficient dry climatic conditions

3. Solar powered water purifications: Use of solar heat to separate fresh water from seawater

- **Merits**
  - Low cost; easy to operate
  - Long term availability
- **Demerits**
  - Weather dependent and slow process

Tackling the water crisis requires an integrated approach of utilising innovative technologies wherever required as well as generating public awareness and action around efficient water usage.

GS IV

Q4a. "The concept of Just and Unjust is contextual. What was just a year back, may turn out to be unjust in today's context. Changing context should be constantly under scrutiny to prevent miscarriage of justice." Examine the above statement with suitable examples. (Answer in 150 words)

The concept of just and unjust changes according to space and time. It depends on socio-cultural norms, legal values, concepts of justice and so on.

Changing Concept of Just and Unjust:

1. <u>Sec 377 and legal rights of LGBTQ community</u>: It was illegal to have a same sex relationship before, but it has been decriminalised granting freedom and dignity to same sex relationships.

2. Sati was considered just during ancient and medieval times, but it was a clear violation of human rights and was thus declared illegal in the later part of the 19th century.

Changing Context Should Be Under Scrutiny to Prevent Miscarriage of Justice:

1. Data sharing and transparency on social media platforms like Facebook and WhatsApp was considered a norm a while ago, but with the increased utility and generation of data, concerns of privacy and misutilisation of data also need to be considered.
2. Artificial Intelligence is being used in newer ways replacing human voice, facial features and language. This also needs to be seen that it does not violate basic human rights.

Hence, it is required that the laws and values are changed based on changing social values, liberalism and modernism. They need to focus on basic human rights. These changes will ensure that justice changes according to the evolving needs of society and the miscarriage of justice is avoided.

Q12. Dr. Srinivasan is a senior scientist working for a reputed biotechnology company known for its cutting-edge research in pharmaceuticals. Dr. Srinivasan is heading a research team working on a new drug aimed at treating a rapidly spreading variant of a new viral infectious disease. The disease has been rapidly spreading across the world and the cases reported in the country are increasing. There is huge pressure on Dr. Srinivasan's team to expedite the trials for the drug as there is significant market for it, and the company wants to get the first-mover advantage in the market. During a team meeting, some senior team members suggest some shortcut for expediting the clinical trials for the drug and for getting the requisite approvals. These include manipulating data to exclude some negative outcomes and selectively reporting positive results, foregoing the process of informed consent and using compounds already patented by a rival company, rather than developing one's own component. Dr. Srinivasan is not comfortable taking such shortcuts, at the same time he realises meeting the targets is impossible without using these means.

(a) What would you do in such a situation?

(b) Examine your options and consequences in the light of the ethical questions involved.

(c) How can data ethics and drug ethics save humanity at large in such a scenario?

(Answer in 250 words)

The above case highlights the dilemma faced by Dr. Srinivasan, i.e., whether to focus on company's profit/interest or to focus on the right process to develop the drug.

The Steps Which Would Be Taken by Me Are:

1. Follow the right and standard procedure while developing the drug.
2. Consultation and dialogue with Company's management with respect to:
   - Shortcut and its implication
   - Company's standard/brand
   - Public interest

3. Request for more resources and time to expedite the process while following the legal framework.

4. Reporting to the concerned authorities regarding the development of the new drug and take some relaxations in the standard process and timeline to quicken the process of drug development in the interest of public good at large.

Options Available and Their Consequences:

1. <u>Take a shortcut to develop the drug.</u>

   Consequence: Faster release of the drug; higher chances of the loss of life or negative impact on health and the loss of brand image.

2. <u>Resign as Head of Research</u>

   Consequence: Escape from the dilemma, but it displays cowardice attitude and inability to take the right decision. Also, does not rule out the possibility of the negative impact on the health of general public.

3. <u>Request for additional time to follow the right process</u>

   Consequence: It is the right thing to do both as a researcher and also as a human. But it might affect the revenue, profit or brand image of the company, which might lead to the loss of job.

Data Ethics and Drug Ethics Saving Humanity:

1. Data ethics
   - It promotes transparency.
   - It will help citizens take an informed decision with respect to the new drug.
   - It will increase public trust.
   - It will lead to the faster approval of drug from the regulatory body.
   - It will increase the long-term safety, efficiency, and efficacy of the drug.
2. Drug ethics
   - Public interest and patients' needs should be given the highest priority.
     - It will improve the safety of drugs.
     - It will reduce the side effects on patients.
   - It will help in maintaining the standards with respect to drug development.

If Dr. Srinivasan follows data and drug ethics, then it will lead to protecting patients' needs and safety and also balance the interest of the company.